Global Consumer Behavior

Global Consumer Behavior

Edited by
Chantal Ammi

First Published in Great Britain and the United States in 2007 by ISTE Ltd

ISTE Ltd
6 Fitzroy Square
London W1T 5DX
UK

ISTE USA
4308 Patrice Road
Newport Beach, CA 92663
USA

www.iste.co.uk

Library of Congress Cataloging-in-Publication Data

Global consumer behavior/edited by Chantal Ammi.
    p. cm.
 Includes bibliographical references and index.
 ISBN 978-1-905209-63-7
 1. Consumer behavior. 2. Consumer behavior--Cross-cultural studies. 3. Consumers--Social aspects. 4. Internet marketing. I. Ammi, Chantal.
 HF5415.32.G548 2007
 658.8'342--dc22
                                                                            2007003376

British Library Cataloguing-in-Publication Data
A CIP record for this book is available from the British Library
ISBN 13: 978-1-905209-63-7

Printed and bound in Great Britain by Antony Rowe Ltd, Chippenham, Wiltshire.

Table of Contents

Chapter 6. The Cultural Impact on Changes in Consumption: Lithuania and Bulgaria
Jadvyga CIBURIENE and Anastasiya MARCHEVA

Chapter 7. Country of Origin: Perceptions and Attitudes of Portuguese Consumers.
Ana LISBOA

Chapter 10. Globalization and Consumer Behavior: A Case Study of Cell Phone Owners in India
Velan NIRMALA and U. DEVASENADHIPATHI

Chapter 11. Factors Affecting Technology Adoption in India: A Consumer-Based View.
Atanu ADHIKARI and A.K. RAO

Chapter 12. Chinese Culture and Chinese Consumer Behavior
Lei TANG

Introduction

Globalization is leading industry worldwide, especially the new technology sector. Globalization – the unification of goods, services, capital and labor into a single global market, based on free trade, comparative advantages and economies of scale – has created a really radical force for economic development. It speeds and expands the strengths but also the weaknesses of the market system: its inefficiency, instability and inequality.

Globalization has promoted the emergence of a new type of consumer and has had effects on industry in terms of culture, economics, marketing and social issues at every scale from local to global. We can see a proliferation of global brands and an alleged homogenization of cultures in driving regions: "Europeanization", "Westernization" or "Americanization".

Moreover, many researchers who worked on technology said that technology is a universal, uniform and consistent factor which crosses national and cultural boundaries. For them there are no cultural boundaries limiting the application of technology. Once a technology is developed, it immediately becomes available everywhere in the world with the same efficiency.

However, the reality is not so obvious and local resistances are still present and sometimes are even growing.

Despite this tendency of uniformity between all the countries with similar products, services, advertisements, etc., the cultural factor has still an important rule to play. We can see strong differences according to behaviors, modalities of commercialization, the type of products and packaging, contents of advertisements, price fixing, even the diffusion of technology. Each country, each nationality and sometimes each ethno culture or tribe has its own characteristics. To ignore this diversity would be a major risk and to integrate it in a bad or incomplete manner would create significant dysfunctions.

This book aims to analyze the importance of culture in globalization in different cases: in different countries, across different types of products or brands, according to the sector of activity, or according to the level of development.

This book is divided into two parts:

– the first part is focused on specific themes according to the degree of globalization;

– the second part is oriented to the applications at a national level in different countries, each with a different level of development;

In the first part, which is composed of four chapters, the authors aim to show the consequences of, or the reasons for, globalization across a sector of activity, the life cycle, the multiculturalism or the rule of the social identity.

Chapter 1 analyzes the sector of e-tourism and the importance of culture in this activity. Even if globalization is leading this market, each supplier, each consumer is unique and offers must integrate cultural factors.

Chapter 2 analyzes global advertisements and notes that, despite the global marketing messages for each phase of the product life cycle, it is still crucial to adapt messages for the local markets in order to target those local markets.

Chapter 3 analyzes the importance of multiculturalism inside the global market and the necessity for firms to integrate these specificities. Two cases are developed: countries with multicultural, religious, linguistic or ethnic local diversities such as India, China, Canada, Belgium and Switzerland and countries with a large flux of immigration, such as France and the USA.

Chapter 4 analyzes the influence of social aspects on behaviors and its application in different ways.

In the second part, composed of nine chapters, the authors show the importance of the local specificities across many different cases in various countries: the act of purchasing, the brands, the use of the Internet, the behavior of mobile phone users, etc.

Chapter 5 analyzes the role of gender in the purchase of goods or services and its application in a Muslim country such as Tunisia. "Is this rule the same everywhere?" and "are the cultural aspects important?" are two of the many questions asked by the author.

Chapter 6 analyzes the emergence of globalization in two Eastern European countries, Bulgaria and Lithuania. The authors notice that the consequences and the impact on the economy, behavior, or social life are not exactly the same in each country and they try to explain the origins of this divergence.

Chapter 7 analyzes the importance of the country of origin (the image of the country or origin that the item portrays) on the act of purchasing across the Portuguese market. The role of the cultural characteristics is detailed.

Chapter 8 analyzes globalization and the ubiquitous nature of the Internet which facilitates e-commerce activities across nations. Even global tastes have been homogenized; we notice online consumer segments with different purchase motivations for each local environment.

Chapter 9 analyzes the new Indian consumer. The emergence of the Indian economy has created a large local market with its own characteristics: social, religious, ethnic, regional, etc.

Chapter 10 analyzes the specificities of the local aspects on the consumer behavior for a high-tech product, such as a mobile phone, with a comparison between different countries and India.

Chapter 11 analyzes the role of factors affecting the adoption of technology in general and in India, in particular. Although many authors think that this adoption is universal, many local facts prove the opposite.

Chapter 12 analyzes, across the Chinese consumer market, the role and the importance of the cultural aspects: differences between Western countries and China, differences between Chinese customers according their values, their religion, or their habits.

Chapter 13 analyzes the perception of brands in general and in China in particular. The importance and the acceptance of counterfeit goods in this country have modified this perception and local, as well as global, companies have to integrate this aspect.

This book does not seek to be exhaustive and to analyze every aspect of global consumer behavior, but through the chapters, written by researchers living around the world, we wanted to prove that globalization is not uniformity and that it is still necessary to integrate the local characteristics to avoid misunderstandings, rejections or business failures.

PART 1

Topics of Themes

Chapter 1

E-Travel Agents Selling to Ethnic Customers

1.1. Introduction

Over the past decades, the travel and tourism sector has emerged as one of the most important sectors for developing, as well as developed, countries. The World Travel and Tourism Council[2] [2006] estimates that the relative importance of tourism will grow to approximately 11% of the global gross domestic product (GDP) in 2016. Tourism incorporates many of the features of the information society,[3] such as globalization, mobility and information richness. People from all nations, social ranks, professions and different ways of life are potential tourists.

Tourism as a global industry links a worldwide supplier community with consumers, equally distributed worldwide. Its physical and virtual networks enable worldwide traveling, bringing together very distant cultures and habits. The tourism industry is diverse and partly fragmented and the size of tourism principals varies from micro- to global enterprises. Only certain segments, such as airlines, are concentrated into an oligopoly of global alliances.

Chapter written by Euler G.M. de SOUZA and Tunc MEDENI.
1 This chapter resulted from research undertaken at Tokai University and ongoing work at the Japan Advanced Institute of Science and Technology.
2 The World Travel and Tourism Council is a global forum comprising the presidents, chairpersons, and CEOs of companies involved in the travel and tourism industry.
3 A society in which low-cost information and ICT (information and communication technology) are in general use, a society in which the creation, distribution, and manipulation of information is becoming a significant economic and cultural activity.

The growth in the development of transportation after the First World War enabled people to travel to previously inaccessible areas and, furthermore, technological innovations improved transportation and the cost of travel declined, meaning that tourism throughout the world expanded.

Historically, travel agents were tour planners, as well as sales agents, for travel suppliers. Not only would the travel agent sell transport, accommodation and tours for suppliers, they would organize travel plans for customers and provide advice, as well as specialized information on destinations and other travel related information.

In the 1950s and 1960s, airlines entered the era of the jet aircraft and this was soon followed by the rapid introduction of wide-bodied airplanes in the 1970s and 1980s. Airlines viewed the use of travel agencies as an inexpensive and effective method of widening their distribution network in order to reach these new and expanding markets, combined with high labor costs and difficulties in reaching the marketplace. This led to the use of travel agents as intermediaries, to act as sales agents for their products. Airlines soon came to rely heavily on travel agents – often as an extension of their own office – for distribution, airline reservations, ticketing, transactions, travel advice, market coverage, market presence and packaging.

In this chapter, information technology will be addressed as the main type of technology concerning the business interactions of e-travel agencies with customers and more specifically ethnic/immigrant customers. Lovelock and Wright [LOV 02] skillfully adapted the flower of service (see Figure 1.1) to the information technology (IT)[4] era, which illustrates ways in which a website can be used to deliver or enhance service for each part of the service diagram, comprehending information, consultation, order taking, hospitality, safe keeping, exceptions, billing and payment.

---

4 A term used to define a group of technological and computational resources applied to generate and manipulate information.

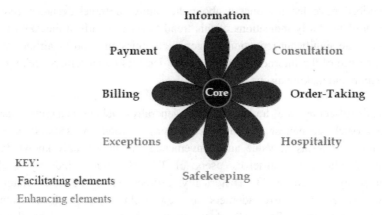

Figure 1.1. *The flower of service*

In most instances, there is an opportunity to improve productivity by encouraging customers to use self-service. For people who are optimists about the new paradigms in communication and distribution, IT enables firms to know more and to communicate more efficiently with their customers:

> More continuous connections with customers can provide information that focus groups and surveys cannot ... The knowledge of individual customer needs that companies can capture through technology harkens back to the days when the butcher, baker and candlestick maker knew their clientele personally ... In that setting, customer service relationships were built on face-to-face transactions ... Today's technology can recreate the conversation between the shopkeeper and the customer [MCK 95].

Our research aimed to investigate the impact of e-commerce in relationship issues. It considered ethnic communities and was based on a survey of Brazilian customers living in Japan. We address the market structure of travel agents, customer relationships through the Internet, services marketing, relationship marketing and then our findings and conclusions.

1.2. Market structure

The travel agent industry is coordination intensive; in other words, it is centered on the communication and processing of information. The commodity-like nature of products offered by travel agents and the ease with which many travel products can be described have led to concern about the future of travel agencies given the evolution of IT. Early indications of this trend towards a shift in the role of travel agents are the significant reduction in agency commissions paid by airlines and the increasing use of the Internet and other online services by customers seeking travel information and making airline reservations.

Trends affecting the travel industry generally include changing customer demands (such as interest in exotic destinations or travel by seniors), increased expectations in terms of value and convenience and increasingly knowledgeable consumers who are themselves users of IT. The travel industry is being fundamentally altered by IT. Historically, airlines and large hotel chains, for instance, have been early adopters of new technologies such as computer reservations systems (CRS).[5] The distribution network being used by the travel industry is in many ways outdated, relying on third parties such as CRS vendors or travel agents who have traditionally justified their presence through a specialized technology infrastructure and specific knowledge.

A frequently-cited impact of IT is that the emergence of electronic markets will promote the bypassing of intermediaries [LEW 96]. This hypothesis is principally based on the ability of IT to significantly reduce transaction costs [MAL 94]. A useful way to examine the specific impact of IT on a given type of intermediary may be to compare the value added by an intermediary under different transaction characteristics and determine whether the role of the intermediary is likely to be enhanced or diminished [CHO 97].

The advent of the Internet and other online services, combined with widespread adoption of personal computers by businesses and consumers, has led to a growing role for electronic commerce[6] in the world economy. The emerging electronic commerce marketplace is expected to support all business services that normally depend on paper-based transactions.

Firms choose transactions that economize on coordination costs [STR 97]. These costs include the costs of the information processing that is necessary to coordinate the work of people and machines that perform a primary process, such as

---

5 CRS operations are also known as global distribution systems (GDS), such as Amadeus, Sabre, and Worldspan.
6 Electronic commerce is the buying and selling of information, products, and services through computer and telecommunications networks.

manufacturing a product or providing a service. IT allows buyers and sellers to communicate directly over data-rich, easy-to-use information channels. Where products take on a commodity-like nature and are easy to describe, decentralized electronic markets, rather than single-sources sales channels, may be an efficient form of coordination.

Travel products and services possess many characteristics needed to function in the electronic environment. The ease of description and commodity-like nature of many travel products, such as airline seats or hotel rooms, suggests that the travel industry exhibits the product attributes that are favorable for electronic commerce. The structural elements of the industry also support a shift towards more electronic means of carrying out transactions. The current travel agent market structure favors a centralized market configuration [MAL 87] among service providers, travel agents and consumers. Most consumers use a single or a very small number of travel agents for each trip, while most agents have access to all – or most – providers of travel services.

Within the travel agent industry, the traditional centralized market structure is currently under attack from many providers in the marketplace who are trying to access their customers directly. This trend is particularly evident in the airline industry where carriers sell most of their tickets without the use of travel agents. Even established airlines, such as American Airlines, are using more direct channels, such as online services, the Internet and toll-free telephone numbers, to reach customers. In fact, the structure is currently acquiring more decentralized market characteristics where each buyer/consumer has direct access to each seller/provider.

The ability to make travel-related reservations online directly with the provider significantly reduces fixed and variable coordination costs because there is no human intervention between the consumer and the travel provider. Human intervention can take the form of a travel agent or an airline employee in a telephone reservations office or city ticket office, but in either case eliminating human intervention minimizes costs to the airline. This is why many airlines are offering discount fares that are available exclusively to online users and promoting the use of electronic ticketing.

In the travel industry, the two factors mentioned above – product uniqueness and ease of description – have become critical factors in determining whether an intermediary, in most cases a travel agent, will be used by a prospective traveler. Some itineraries, such as a simple business round trip by air, may be just as easy to arrange when dealing directly with a carrier. However, a package tour or cruise is inherently complex to describe and will vary greatly in content and price depending on the different suppliers and options. Such leisure trips often involve pitfalls and uncertainties and the average consumer needs advice on these matters before making a decision.

A number of social and institutional factors mitigate against the elimination of intermediaries. Consumers may choose to continue to use traditional or online intermediaries because those intermediaries in fact represent multiple suppliers of travel products. It has also been argued that electronic markets do not become "disinter-mediated", but are facilitated by IT, with new intermediaries emerging in an electronic environment [BAI 96].

Travel agents do not have the same biases as the suppliers they represent, although the agents' behavior can be affected by such practices as commission overrides. Finally, aspects such as trust and social contact are important to many consumers, particularly when planning leisure travel. Face-to-face contact with an agent at a physical retail location will remain important for many travelers.

Travel agents currently play three key roles. First, they act as information brokers, passing information between buyers and suppliers of travel products. Secondly, they process transactions by printing tickets or forwarding money. Thirdly, they act as advisors to travelers [LEW 98]. It is probable that IT will affect the first two roles and force travel agents to focus on the third, advisory role. Travel agencies can play a valuable role by using IT to assist the consumer in dealing with the complexity of the market-place. Despite incentives to do so, travelers will not always want to approach travel suppliers directly. Some agencies have set up websites that allow prospective travelers to compare schedules and fares from different airlines, in effect repositioning the agencies as electronic intermediaries that offer significant added value.

Certainly the technology is changing the environment for travel agents and, considering O'Brien [OBR 98], these effects include:

– the intermediaries' (such as travel agents) role in the distribution channel is altered [POO 93];

– the development of cost-competitive and flexible travel products is enabled [POO 93];

– "assisting in transforming tourism and travel into a more flexible, individual-oriented, sustainable and diagonally integrated industry" [POO 93], as cited in [OBR 98].

Technology, particularly e-commerce, will impact on the travel agents' role as "transaction processors (ticketing and settlement) and suppliers of raw unprocessed, product information". They argue that these roles may easily be replaced by technology, as suppliers using technology can communicate directly with consumers.

There are many different views and opinions about IT being introduced to the travel agents' market. In fact, this kind of service is not a service from the Internet business era; it has been adapted to the new way of commercializing and there are many necessary adjustments to be made by travel agents. This is what we propose to examine throughout this chapter: how service and relationship marketing theories identify the threats and opportunities, especially the relationship aspect.

1.3. Customer relationship through the Internet

It is believed that successful services deliver responsiveness, empathy, assurance and reliability. In fact, services are all about relationships. Even in traditional retailing, the relationship behind the transaction has been demonstrated to influence customer loyalty more than any other aspect, including price. The majority of consumers in a recent survey reported that loyalty is based primarily on having a relationship with the store and with its staff [BLA 98]. Although consumers expect prices – at least for staple items – to be comparable across competing outlets, loyalty to a store is based on service and in-store details, while loyalty to brands is based on product performance.

If the service experience is consistently well executed, the service provider, over time, creates a "bond"[7] with the customer, which the customer values as much as the service itself.

Customers value their relationships with service providers, so long as they continue to satisfy their customers' lower- and higher-order needs.[8] As a result, customers often develop a "superordinate need"[9] to maintain their relationship with the service provider – a personal need that goes beyond the need to simply obtain whatever service or product is provided. As a result, the customer develops an ongoing desire to return to the service provider to maintain a valued relationship.

---

7 Nurturing a relationship through continuous contacts.
8 Lower-order needs are considered to be physiological and security needs. Higher-order needs are listed as social needs, esteem needs, self-actualization, and achievement.
9 Solid dependence.

Establishing this level of relationship with customers is harder to achieve in an e-commerce transaction because of the impersonal nature of the process, which makes it difficult to establish the of bond that is often enjoyed between other service providers and their customers.

This impersonal characteristic results from the e-commerce medium, which sets up a barrier between the service provider and the service recipient.

Because the Internet, as a medium, is less personal than other retail channels, surrogates for direct personal interaction must be provided in an e-retail transaction.

However, the task of establishing e-retail relationships that customers value may become easier as consumer values regarding Internet relationships evolve. As Internet users increase their use of communications media like e-mail and chat rooms, relationships developed over these media may become as readily valued as those arising from more direct personal interactions.

E-commerce has attracted consumers in many diverse industries, such as retailers, banks, telecoms and even b2b[10] operations. However, air travel and tourism are considered to be among the most important application domains on the World Wide Web (WWW). According to comScore,[11] online leisure travel bookings reached about US$51 billion in 2004, or 44% of all online sales. An estimated 30% of all travel bookings occur online, with the bulk of the market growth recorded between 2001 and 2003. Abundant information allows customers to compare services and prices, among the growing number of online competitors and globalization of the industry. These are challenges for the companies selling through the Web and they have to figure out ways to foster relationships.

1.4. Electronic distribution channel

E-commerce is defined as the strategic deployment of computer-mediated tools and information technologies to satisfy business objectives. As such, e-commerce offers fundamentally new ways of doing business, as opposed to mere extensions of existing practices. Indeed, the emergence of the "marketspace" – a virtual world of information paralleling the real marketplace of goods and services – enables

---

10 Business to business – a business model that focuses on providing services for other companies rather than individual consumers.
11 comScore Networks is a global information provider and consultancy.

marketers to manage content, context and infrastructure in new and different ways, thereby providing novel sources of competitive advantage [RAY 94: 145]. Electronic marketing channels use the Internet to make products and services available so that the target market with access to computers or other enabling technologies can shop and complete the transaction for purchase via interactive electronic means.

All marketing channel systems must perform three fundamental tasks: the exchange of goods, the exchange of money and the exchange of information [EHR 99: 3]. In terms of the generic functions that are provided, these tasks are referred to as physical distribution or fulfillment, transaction facilitation and communication, respectively. As an electronic marketing channel, the Internet is quite capable of replacing conventional distribution channels when it comes to communicating information and conducting transactions.

1.5. Services marketing

Services marketing became a specific field in marketing and has been in constant flux, reflecting the impact of developments in the service sector itself and most notably the impact of deregulation and technological change. While acknowledging the breadth and diversity of the service sector, it is possible to identify certain generic themes within the literature, although the relevance of such themes varies across the different components of the sector and are dependent on the specific nature of the service [CLE 00]. Two broad aspects may be regarded as providing the critical foundations underpinning services marketing. These are the management of the service delivery process and the nature of interaction between consumers and suppliers.

1.5.1. *Management of the service delivery process*

The concept of the service encounter is central to the marketing of services; indeed, it is the focal point of marketing activity. Reflecting the inseparability of production and consumption in service industries, the service encounter is the actualization of the service that is the intersection of service capacity and demand.

The service encounter can be seen as that point at which the consumer can evaluate the service offering and the service supplier can manage the consumer perceptions of the service [JOH 96].

The primary focus considered has been on the interpersonal interactions between consumers and service providers in terms of the management of service quality and consumer satisfaction [JOH 96]. For the consumer, the service encounter thus encompasses a number of interactions, both personal and impersonal and related experiences alongside their formal interaction with the organization providing the service. In this regard, many of the technological developments impacting on the service sector, in particular those facilitating "self-service" utilization of services, may be regarded as having significant consequences. The Internet-driven information revolution is widely perceived to be transforming the way that both businesses and consumers operate [DOC 99]. This is particularly seen to be the case in those areas of the service sector, notably financial or travel services, where transactions do not require interpersonal interaction. In such circumstances, the Internet effectively serves as a new distribution channel [ALE 98]. For such services, the Internet may be viewed primarily as an information resource, rather than as a distribution channel. Yet, the Internet in this capacity may have the potential to fundamentally change the way in which consumers interact with service providers. In turn, the established format of the service encounter, which is the "interactions between the customer and the organization that provides the service" [JOH 96], in such services is called into question by changes in consumer access to service information.

1.5.2. *Nature of interaction between consumers and suppliers*

The information revolution engendered by the Internet in terms of consumer access to specialist technical information has changed the informational asymmetries between consumers and enterprises. Professional dominance and power in the service encounter has conventionally been based on the existence of an imbalance in knowledge and expertise between the professional and the service user [WIL 95]. The Internet, with its breadth of information and more significantly its scope for interaction between consumers through providing virtual discussion forums and facilitating the emergence of consumer communities, has the potential to redress these informational asymmetries and empower consumers to challenge the established legitimacy of service providers. This empowerment of consumers arguably has profound implications, both for the management and design of the service encounter.

Such changes in the format of the service encounter will, in turn, inevitably impact on the nature of the interaction between the service provider and the consumer, given that over an extended time horizon:

> ... encounters provide the social occasions in which buyer and seller can negotiate and nurture the transformation of their accumulated encounters into an exchange relationship [CZE 90:13].

Successive consumer-supplier interactions, which are defined as service encounters, are widely viewed as providing the basis on which long-term relationships are established in both consumer and business-to-business service markets [ERI 00]. The development and maintenance of such long-term interactive relationships has constituted a central plank of the evolving body of services marketing theory from the early 1990s onward [GRÖ 94]. This reflects the impact of the underlying characteristics of services, most notably intangibility, heterogenity and inseparability, on consumer behavior in terms of both the selection and the evaluation of service providers. In this regard, long-term relationships are perceived as providing a critical means by which service users, both consumer and organizational, are able to reduce risk and uncertainty in the purchasing of services given the complexities of assessing service quality [GWI 98]. Below is a services marketing model that could be used to consider a virtual environment.

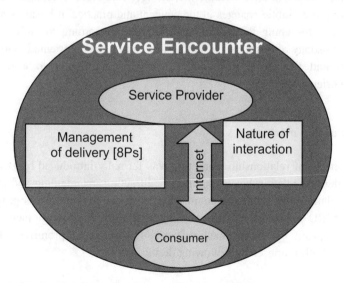

Figure 1.2. *Services marketing model for the Internet*

Yet, given increasing competition in many service industries as a result of deregulation and globalization, service organizations are confronted by the need to enhance customer retention, with the development of closer relationships being perceived as the route to achieving such retention [ERI 00].

However, this increasing emphasis on the centrality of close customer-supplier relations to the marketing of services can be viewed as being challenged, at least within consumer services, by the twin trends of technological mediation and commodification. One of the key developments in service industries over the past decade has been the increasing investment in technology in the service delivery process. From the introduction of ATMs through to online medical consultations, technology has revolutionized many areas of the service sector. Replacement of service staff with technology not only offers a means of addressing variability in the service delivery process, but also facilitates cost reduction through increasing the self-service component of the service delivery process. However, by reducing the personal interaction, that basic, social, building block of service relationships, such developments may be viewed as undermining the development of closer customer-supplier relationships.

The trend in marketing toward building relationships with customers continues to grow and marketers have become increasingly interested in retaining customers over the long run. Subtle changes in the concept and practice of business have been fundamentally reshaping the marketing discipline. According to Grönroos [GRÖ 89], the philosophy of business has shifted from a production orientation to a selling orientation and then to a marketing orientation and finally to a relationship marketing orientation.

1.6. Relationship marketing

The concept of relationship marketing was formally introduced by Berry [BER 83], who defined relationship marketing as "attracting, maintaining and enhancing customer relationships". Later, a more comprehensive definition was proposed by Grönroos [GRÖ 91] to include "establishing relationships with customers and other parties at a profit by mutual exchange and fulfillment of promises". Recently, Harker [HAR 99] proposed the following definition:

> An organization engaged in proactively creating, developing and maintaining committed, interactive and profitable exchanges with selected customers [partners] over time is engaged in relationship marketing.

Although the above three definitions differ somewhat, they all indicate that relationship marketing focuses on individual buyer-seller relationships, that these relationships are longitudinal in nature and that both parties in each individual buyer-seller relationship benefit. In short, from a firm's perspective, the relationship marketing concept can be viewed as a philosophy of doing business successfully or as a distinct organizational culture/value that puts the buyer-seller relationship at the center of the firm's strategic or operational thinking.

Services researchers argue that a consumer's satisfaction with a particular service is primarily an outcome of the interactive relationship between the service provider and the consumer [BER 93]. In fact, the findings of several studies on services marketing have suggested that in order to acquire and maintain a competitive edge, service organizations should develop long-term relationships with their customers [BER 83; GRÖ 91]. A relationship marketing orientation will be discussed below.

Given the importance of personal relationships in services businesses, RMO (relationship marketing orientation) should have a strong influence on the services industry, which is characterized by dyadic exchange processes in which a firm's employees interact directly with customers [BRO 89]. Building strong relationships between a firm and its customers can help the firm to increase the customer loyalty and/or commitment to the firm. Therefore, the adoption of RMO can help a service provider to design and offer a service mix that is perceived by core customers as superior, while at the same time helping the firm to make a profit and to build a competitive advantage.

Based on past related literature [MOR 94; WIL 95; YAU 00], it has been hypothesized that RMO is a multidimensional construct consisting of six components: trust, bonding, communication, shared values, empathy and reciprocity. In the figure below, we illustrate the relationship marketing components.

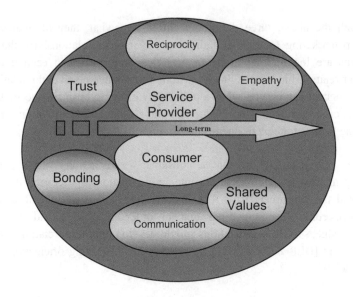

Figure 1.3. *Relationship marketing components [YAU 00]*

Trust is defined as a willingness to rely on an exchange partner in whom one has confidence. Trust is conceptualized as the dimension of a business relationship that determines the level to which each party feels that they can rely on the integrity of the promises offered by the other party. It is, in essence, the belief that an individual will provide what is promised. The inclusion of trust as a central variable in a relationship exchange has been examined widely in the marketing literature. For example, in services marketing, Berry and Parasuraman [BER 91: 144] find that "customer-company relationships require trust". It is theorized that the higher the level of trust between buyer and seller, the greater the probability of long-term relationships.

Bonding is defined as the dimension of a business relationship that results in two parties (buyer and seller) acting in a unified manner toward a desired goal. Bonding, as it applies to RMO, consists of developing and enhancing consumer loyalty, which results directly in a feeling of affection, a sense of belonging to the relationship and, indirectly, in a sense of belonging to the organization. Levitt [LEV 83] described a sale in the buyer-seller interaction as the "consummation of the courtship" in the sense of a relationship and made the distinction between single transactions as having, "as in modern life, an affair" and the intention to enter into a long-term relationship as having a "bonded relationship (to have a marriage)". Compared with trust, bonding, as a construct, has received a modest amount of attention from relationship marketing researchers in the West.

Communication is defined as the formal, as well as informal, exchanging and sharing of meaningful and timely information between buyers and sellers. Communication, especially timely communication, fosters trust by assisting in solving disputes and aligning perceptions and expectations. Research on relationship marketing also highlights the importance of information exchanges in business relationships. Communication is "the glue that holds together a channel of distribution" [MOH 90]. Additionally, some studies reveal that information exchange can help both buyers and sellers to respond better to new opportunities and threats. Also, the transmission of information through a contact network can stimulate technological development.

Shared values are defined as the extent to which partners have beliefs in common about what behaviors, goals and policies are important or unimportant, appropriate or inappropriate, right or wrong. Shared values have long been considered as an important dimension in building buyer-seller relationships and have been defined as a system in which people or groups are interrelated and in which they are engaged in reaching a shared goal and having patterned relationships with one another. Thus, when exchange partners have common goals or values, they will be more committed to their relationships.

Empathy is the dimension of a business relationship that enables the two parties to see the situation from the other person's perspective. Empathy is defined as seeking to understand somebody else's desires and goals. In business, this somebody else is often a relative stranger or, at best, a business connection. In the personal selling literature, it is the empathetic abilities of the salespeople that have been identified by a number of theorists as a prerequisite to successful selling. In service marketing literature, the dimension of empathy is used by Berry et al. [BER 90] in developing the SERVQUAL test instrument for service quality. Thus, it is clear that empathy is a necessary condition to foster a positive relationship between two parties.

Reciprocity is the dimension of a business relationship that causes either party to provide a favor or make allowances for the other in return for similar a favor or allowances to be received at a later date. Reciprocity can be summarized by three interrelated aspects of social interaction between two individuals: bilateral contingency; interdependence for mutual benefit; and equality of exchanged values. First, when a person does a favor for another person, he/she may oblige the recipient to repay the favor. This is a bilateral contingency. Secondly, the rationale for a person to give something to another person may be the giver's intention to obtain something else that is needed from the recipient. Thirdly, the reciprocal process will eventually approach a converged value. In other words, what a person gives will be the equivalent to what he/she receives from the recipient in the long run. These symmetrical aspects of reciprocity have been regarded as "sociological dualism" and "mutual legal obligations of repaying". The links of reciprocity to relationship marketing have been indicated as a basis for the interface between exchange transactions and marketing activities. This is further reinforced by Ellis *et al.* [ELL 93], who explains that relationship marketing is characterized by "… interactions, reciprocities and long-term commitments".

According to Yau *et al.* [YAU 00], the relationship marketing orientation has been positively associated with sales growth, customer retention, return over investment and overall performance in service firms. Besides, because of the intangible nature of services moving from a transactional orientation towards relationship orientation would be beneficial for both customers and firms. Therefore, service firms not only should take care of the satisfaction of the customers regarding commercial transactions but also should nurture the development of long term relationships with them. Travel agents usually combine the use of a website and telephone communication in e-commerce operations; there is no personal encounter in such transactions. Some travel agents, who market on the Internet in Japan, are organizing their customers like Japan Travel Bureau (JTB) which created virtual clubs where only members could buy and take advantage of the company's e-commerce that enabled the firm to better know their customers and to improve customer management. Another important factor is the participation of customers in producing desired services which bring them a high level of satisfaction. A deeper interaction through use of relationship marketing and customer relationship management tools has been noted as a big competitive advantage to firms in the marketspace [ZHA 04].

1.7. Hypotheses and findings

This study attempted to investigate the changes in technology that impacted on the roles of travel agents selling through e-commerce and customers' evaluations concerning their relationships with online travel agents. This research model was developed and based on Moutinho *et al.* [MOU 00], who researched travel agents' attitudes towards automation in Canada and New Zealand and identified different groups of travel agents and their perceptions on how automation influenced the performance of their businesses. The model was adapted to visualize the relation between technology and relationship aspect. The 8Ps services marketing model [LOV 02], which is integrated service management through 8 variables (product elements, place, promotion, price, process, productivity, people and physical evidence) seeks to make the service delivery process successful, thus guaranteeing satisfaction to customers, combined with the relationship marketing orientation components, which are items to be managed by the service firm with the aim of achieving a long and profitable relationship with customers. Thus, the firm should employ the components – trust, reciprocity, empathy, bonding, communication and shared values – as a philosophy and as core values in its business relationships [YAU 00]. The components are applied to the travel agents selling to the Brazilian community in Japan.

The marketspace has been substituted for the traditional marketplace [RAY 94] and this new approach to the interaction between customer and company leads us to make the following comments on the researched industry.

1.7.1. *Hypotheses*

Lovelock and Wright [LOV 02] and McKenna [MCK 98] have affirmed that information empowered the customers and reduced the knowledge asymmetry between the middlemen and the customers. Wilson [WIL 95] leads us to think that the Internet is a broad source of information capable of providing very detailed information about products and services and it also makes it possible to research prices and comparisons between providers. Hence, the following hypothesis is proposed.

H1: The impersonal character of e-commerce reduces the dependence of consumers on personal contact with travel agents.

It was suggested by Yau *et al.* [YAU 00] that the adoption of RMO can help a service provider to design and offer a service mix that is perceived by core customers as superior, while at the same time helping the firm to make a profit and to build a competitive advantage.

Gwinner *et al.* [GWI 98] researched the aspects that influence loyalty in different kinds of services and has concluded that nurturing relationships is the key to a long-term and loyal consumer.

Price is considered to be less important when the customer has all their needs supplied by the interaction with the service provider; therefore the following hypothesis is proposed.

H2: Relationships influence loyalty more than any other feature, including price.

A study, conducted by Zhang [ZHA 04], about the travel market in Japan concluded that the companies using Customer Relationship Management (CRM) systems and other information systems are more successful in organizing and marketing to their customers, instead of just waiting for the customers to come and buy through the Internet. Such companies interact with the customers and provide what the customers really need. Hence, the following hypothesis is proposed.

H3: Through the use of e-commerce, travel agents have more opportunity to better know the needs of their different consumers.

Based on the discussion in section 1.3, according to Bailey *et al.* [BAI 96], intermediaries in electronic markets assume very important roles while aggregating information, providing trust relationships and ensuring the integrity of the market, matching customers and suppliers and providing marketing information to suppliers. Hence the following hypothesis is proposed.

H4: Considering the expertise and knowledge of travel agents: they will not be extinguished by airline companies.

Hypothesis	Marketing components	Questionnaire questions (consumers)
H1: The impersonal characteristic of e-commerce reduces the dependence of consumers on personal contact with travel agents.		17. Through the Internet I can get all the information I need and can buy air tickets through my travel agent's website and I don't need constant personal contact with the agency.
H2: Relationships influence loyalty more than any other feature, including price.	trust	10. I fully trust my travel agent.
	bonding	11. I feel I am an important customer to my travel agent and I want to keep buying from him.
	communi-cation	12. I don't mind communicating with my travel agent only through a website or through email.
	shared values	13. I believe I share some similar values with my travel agent, for example: honesty (I will pay him and he will provide me the promised service).

	empathy	14. I could accept a mistake by my travel agent if I could see it was made by accident.
	reciprocity	15. I already received a favor from my travel agent, something that was in addition to the commercial obligation.
H3: Through the use of e-commerce, travel agents have more opportunity to better know the needs of their different consumers.	product elements	1. Provides me with additional services and benefits besides the air ticket itself; for example: a person helping with concerns at the airport before the flight.
	place	2. Is able to give me all the information I need to know to choose a flight and to send me the air ticket conveniently.
	process	3. Gives me confidence that the process of buying and traveling will happen as stated.
	productiv-ity	4. Generally sends me information and the air ticket at the promised time.
	people	5. Usually when I need to establish contact by telephone, e-mail or personally, the staff is willing to help me and really care about my needs.
	promotion	6. Has a very well built website with easy access for searches and instructs me about new offers.
	physical evidence	7. Has many offices or a big office with many workers.
	price	8. Offers me reasonable prices and treats me in a special way by giving me discounts.
	partners	16. I can see the partners of my travel agent are really committed to customers' satisfaction.
		9. Keeps a record of all my preferences and past purchases.
		19. I often receive useful information by e-mail from my travel agent, including special promotions.
H4: Considering the expertise and knowledge of travel agents: they will not be extinguished by airline companies.		18. When I buy through the Internet I can get a cheaper price than from my travel agent.
		20. I think that buying directly from an airline company could be cheaper, but I have better access with my travel agent and I care about this relationship.

Table 1.1. *Hypotheses-questionnaire linkage table*

Following the above we conducted a survey through a Likert-scale [12] questionnaire that was sent electronically to members of the Brazilian community residing in Japan who are regular customers of Brazilian travel agencies. 400 individuals were requested to answer the questionnaire and 146 fully answered it.

1.7.2. *Findings*

The findings related to the proposed hypotheses as follows.

The impersonal character of e-commerce reduces the dependence of consumers on personal contact with travel agents. Considering the results for this group, we assume that consumers still prefer to have the traditional personal contact with the agencies, whether by telephone or *in loco*. This could be explained by the need of Brazilian people for personal contact; although the opportunity to buy online is very useful, but usually they prefer to look in to the eyes of the person who is selling and be assured that the service will really be provided as promised.

Relationships influence loyalty more than any other feature, including price. It is hard to be definite about this hypothesis because the results are neutral and the data contains a strong standard deviation. It is interesting to note that although in the first hypothesis customers show an interest in personal contact, the relationship is not considered persuasive enough to influence loyalty in hypothesis 2. It is important to observe that shared values and reciprocity were highly valued by customers, therefore showing that it is critical for online travel agents to try to understand their customers' needs and to offer values that could provide benefits to their customers and generate the greatly desired loyalty.

Through the use of e-commerce, travel agents have more opportunity to better know the needs of their different consumers. The results of questions 1 to 8 (8Ps of services marketing) are significant in that they show through the management of customers that companies are allowed to provide the kind of services customers really need and desire. Product elements, or service itself and place (distribution) are considered the most important by customers. The use of IT by travel agents is perceived to be low by customers and thus companies could see it as a competitive

---

12 A type of psychometric scale often used in questionnaires, and is the most widely-used scale in survey research. It asks respondents to specify their level of agreement to each statement in a list.

advantage to start building intelligent databases of their customers allowing interaction with customers in a very personal way. Regarding partners, addressed by question 16, customers do not have a very strong perception of their commitment to services providers. In general, there is good evidence for the hypothesis, which should encourage companies to identify their weak points and improve in order to provide the expected service, delivering satisfaction and even amazing the customers through the use of IT

Considering the expertise and knowledge of travel agents: they will not be extinguished by the airline companies. It is hard to confirm this hypothesis because the results tended to be around the "not sure" point and the standard deviation was high. Therefore, this is another aspect that could be seen as an opportunity to improve by travel agencies because they have the capacity to provide services not provided by airline companies and that capacity could be a competitive advantage.

1.8. Conclusions, limitations and future research

Some interesting tendencies were observed regarding relationship between e-travel agencies and customers.

As McKenna [MCK 95] observed, IT enables firms to know their customers better and to communicate more efficiently with them, reminding us of the time when the butcher knew each customer's name and preferences, thus delivering a very personal service. The great challenge for firms is that by knowing and communicating better with their customers, the firms can become more effective and profitable.

We conclude that the use of e-commerce cannot compensate for the loss of personal contact itself. However, there is a very important point to mention: Brazilians, like many others from Latin cultures, have a great need for personal contact. This also shows a significant limitation of this study in that it was research done with one ethnic group and in one specific industry. Therefore, we suggest that further investigation concerning e-commerce and online relationships is needed, but with other ethnic groups and different industries.

It became clear that managing marketing services provided satisfactory results and that customers perceived the benefits offered by travel agents. One very important aspect observed is the limited use of databases for managing customers and the fact that customers noticed this. This shows that there is a huge opportunity for firms to analyze the viability of implementation of CRM systems. The extension of relationships with business partners is another prominent area where the perception of customers was low. In the management of the services marketing, the 8Ps could include "partners" as another P, but it is understandable that it is a difficult task to manage partners' behavior. The partners' participation in, and influence on, an e-commerce business could be another subject for future research, in order to measure the customer perception of the effects of partnering on satisfaction and loyalty.

By using IT, airline companies could reduce agency commissions and increase operations to sell directly to customers through their websites. However, there are still many opportunities to travel agents as they can act as advisors, something that the airline companies cannot do. In conclusion, customers' answers to the survey were neutral regarding their preferences, so we cannot precisely comment on the trends for the future of travel agents. Although airlines have taken decisive action in order to have direct access to consumers, travel agents still have significant knowledge and do not have the natural biases of airlines.

In short, Information and Communication Technology has been shown as a potential means to foster relationships between customer and company. A great challenge for travel agents, however, is to overcome the impersonal characteristics of e-commerce. We recommend future detailed research on the dynamics of relationships through e-commerce and the impact of the use of CRM systems.

Lewis [LEW 98] suggests that travel agents mainly play the role of information brokers, transaction processors and travel advisors. The first two roles could easily be performed by airline companies; however, the advisory task is something that needs to be well explored by travel agents. Thus, the adopted model suggests an analysis from the customer's or user's viewpoint, so it could aid firms in making decisions about the use of technology to obtain better results in their e-commerce operations concerning the relationship issue with customers. Being able to use the Internet for transactions is not enough for customers; they wish for more interaction and a personal touch in their contacts. This could be seen as another opportunity to add more value to the transactions by ensuring a personal slant to e-commerce operations.

Some decisions relating to the ethnicity of customers are based on globalization phenomenon that reduce international barriers and aid firms and entrepreneurs to identify new niches. We believe that travel agents need a deeper understanding of cultural necessities and behavior in order to overcome the challenges of marketing goods or services online and to successfully sell those goods or services, as well as keeping the customers' patronage. As an example, we researched the Brazilian community in Japan, which is the third-largest foreign population in Japan, numbering almost 300,000 people. We clearly identified that because of the language barrier and cultural features, customers preferred to buy from, and maintain a relationship with, co-ethnic-owned travel agencies. However, it is still a great challenge for travel agents to better understand their customers' needs and improve online operations in order to become more successful in delivering products and services that really satisfy their co-ethnic customers. Diasporas are not unusual and we could list several examples, such as Asians and Latinos in the USA, Turks in Germany and Latin Americans in Japan. Therefore, it is a great challenge for researchers to understand how ethnic or immigrant communities use or perceive e-commerce and for companies to design and deliver goods and services that meet the tastes of ethnic or immigrant customers.

1.9. References

[ALE 98] ALEXANDER, N and COLGATE, M (1998) "The evolution of retailer, banker and customer relationships: a conceptual framework", *International Journal of Retail and Distribution Management*, Vol 26, No 6, pp 225–36

[BAI 96] BAILEY, JP (ed) (1996) "Internet Economics" special issue of the *Journal of Electronic Publishing*, University of Michigan Press

[BER 83] BERRY, LL (1983) "Relationship marketing" in Berry, LL, Shostack, GL, and Upah, GD (eds), *Emerging Perspectives on Service Marketing*, Chicago: American Marketing Association, pp 25–38

[BER 90] BERRY, LL, ZEITHAML, VA and PARASURAMAN, A (1990) "Five imperatives for improving service quality", *Sloan Management Review*, Vol. 31, No 4, pp 29–38

[BER 91] BERRY, LL and PARASURAMAN, A (1991) *Marketing Services: Competing Through Quality*, New York: Free Press, p 144

[BER 93] BERRY, LL and PARASURAMAN, A (1993) "Building a new academic field – the case of services marketing", *Journal of Retailing*, Vol 69, No 1, pp 13–60

[BLA 98] BLACKWELL, R and BLACKWELL, T (1998) "Consumer logistics – a qualitative look at the shopping process" *International Mass Retail Association*, p 85

[BRO 89] BROWN, SW and SWARTZ, TA (1989) "A gap analysis of professional service quality", *Journal of Marketing*, Vol 53, pp 92–98

[CHO 97] CHOUDHURY, V, "Strategic choices in the development of interorganizational information systems" *Information Systems Research*, 8(1), March 1997, pp 1–24

[CLE 00] CLEMES, M, MOLLENKOPF, D and BURN, D (2000) "An investigation of marketing problems across service typologies", *Journal of Services Marketing*, Vol 14, No 7, pp 573–94

[CZE 90] CZEPIEL, JA (1990) "Service encounters and service relationships: implications for research", *Journal of Business Research*, Vol 20, pp 13–21

[DOC 99] DOCHERTY, NF, ELLIS-CHADWICK, F and HART, C (1999) "Cyber retailing in the UK: the potential of the Internet as a retail channel", *International Journal of Retail and Distribution Management*, Vol 27, No 1, pp 22–36

[EHR 99] EHRENS, S and ZAPF, P (1999) *The Internet Business to Business Report*, Bear Stearns Equity, Research Technology, http://www.bearstearns.com

[ELL 93] ELLIS, KL, LEE J and BEATTY, SE (1993) *Relationships in Consumer Marketing: Directions for Future Research*, Provo, UT: American Marketing Association, pp 225–30

[ERI 00] ERIKSSON, K and VAGHULT, AL (2000) "Customer retention, purchasing behaviour and relationship substance in professional services", *Industrial Marketing Management*, Vol 29, pp 363–72

[GRÖ 89] GRÖNROOS, C (1989) "Defining marketing: a market-oriented approach", *European Journal of Marketing*, Vol 23, No 1, pp 52–60

[GRÖ 91] GRÖNROOS, C (1991) "The marketing strategy continuum: toward a marketing concept", *Services Marketing Management Decision,* Vol 29, pp 7–13

[GRÖ 94] GRÖNROOS, C (1994) "Quo Vadis marketing? Towards a relationship paradigm", *Journal of Marketing Management*, Vol 10, pp 347–60

[GWI 98] GWINNER, K, GREMLER, D and BITNER, MJ (1998) "Relational benefits in service industries: the customer's perspective", *Journal of the Academy of Marketing Science*, Vol 26, pp 101–14

[HAR 98] HART, S and HOGG, G (1998) "Relationship marketing in corporate legal services" in Hogg, G and Gabbott, M (eds), *Service Industries Marketing: New Approaches*, London: Frank Cass, p134

[HAR 99] HARKER, MJ (1999) "Relationship marketing defined? An examination of current relationship marketing definitions", *Marketing Intelligence and Planning*, Vol 17, No 1, pp 13–20

[JOH 96] JOHN, J (1996) "A dramaturgical view of the health care service encounter: cultural value-based impression management guidelines for medical professional behaviour", *European Journal of Marketing*, Vol 30, No 9, pp 60–75

[LEV 83] LEVITT, T (1983) "After the sale is over", *Harvard Business Review*, Vol 61, No 5, pp 87–93

[LEW 96] LEWIS, I and TALALAYEVSKY, A, "Travel agents – threatened intermediaries?" *Transportation Journal*, 36(3), Spring 1996, pp 26–30

[LEW 98] LEWIS, I (1998) "The impact of information technology on travel agents", *Transportation Journal*, Vol 37, No 4, pp 20–25

[LOV 02] LOVELOCK C and WRIGHT, LK (2002) *Principles of Service Marketing and Management*, 2nd edn, Prentice Hall College Division, pp 142–53

[MAL 87] MALONE, TW, "Modeling coordination in organizations and markets" *Management Science*, 33(10), October 1987, pp 1317–331

[MAL 94] MALONE, TW and CROWSTON, K, "The interdisciplinary study of coordination", *ACM Computing Surveys*, 26, March 1994, pp 87–119

[MCK 95] MCKENNA, R, "Real-time marketing", *Harvard Business Review,* July–August 1995, pp 87–89

[MOH 90] MOHR, J and NEVIN, JR (1990) "Communication strategies in marketing channels: a theoretical perspective", *Journal of Marketing*, Vol 54, No 4, pp 36–51

[MOR 94] MORGAN, RM and HUNT, SD (1994) "The commitment – trust theory of relationship marketing", *Journal of Marketing*, October, pp 20–35

[MOU 00] MOUTINHO, L, DENG, S and LAWSON, R, "Travel agents' attitudes towards automation and the delivery of service", *Asia Pacific Journal of Marketing and Logistics*, Vol 12, No 4, 2000

[OBR 98] O'BRIEN, P (1998) "Electronic commerce, the Internet and travel cybermediaries", *Proceedings of the Australian Conference on Information Systems*, pp 462–73

[POO 93] POON, A (1993) *Tourism, Technology and Competitive Strategies*, Oxon: C.A.B International

[RAY 94] RAYPORT, JF and SVIOKLA, JJ (1994) "Managing in the marketspace" *Harvard Business Review* 72 (November–December), pp141–50

[STRA 97] STRADER, TJ and SHAW, MJ, "Differentiating between traditional and electronics markets: toward a consumer-based cost model", 1997, Association for Information Systems Proceedings

[WIL 95] WILSON, DT (1995) "An integrated model of buyer-seller relationships", *Journal of the Academy of Marketing Science*, Vol 23, No 4, pp 335–45

[YAU 00] YAU, OHM, MCFETRIDGE, PR, CHOW, RPM, LEE, JSY, SIN, LYM and TSE, ACB (2000) "Is relationship marketing for everyone?" *European Journal of Marketing*, 34(9–10), pp 1111–127

[ZHA 04] ZHANG, Z, "Organizing customers: Japanese travel agencies marketing on the Internet", *European Journal of Marketing*, September 2004, Vol 38, No 9–10, pp 1294–303

Chapter 2

Local Advertising over the Product Life Cycle: The Product-Consumer Relationship in the International Context

2.1. Introduction

In the contemporary international marketplace, consumer behavior in national markets is shaped by the cultural background of each market, as well as by the increasing influence of economic development and globalization. Consumers seem to be more able to fulfill their individual needs with increasing economic progress and these individual needs are deeply influenced by shared cultural values [DEM 98]. Similarly, empirical evidence exists that shows that the cultural differences still persist even in harmonized economic areas with common markets, such as the EU (European Union) [MAH 94]. Even in cases where convergence might be empirically demonstrated, people belonging to the same reference group internationally may buy the same products for different reasons depending on the value that those products carry within the culture [DEM 04a].

Global markets consist of national economies which show distinctively differing product-adoption dynamics while having characteristics of presenting general phases of the product-adoption life cycle, ie introduction, growth, maturity and decline ([DEK 00]; [HEL 93]; [TAK 91]). The influence of national characteristics on the dynamics of the product-adoption has been empirically verified in earlier research

Chapter written by Saku MAKINEN and Hanna-Kaisa DESAVELLE.

(eg [KUM 98]; [TEL 99]). Therefore, companies' actions and operations should differ from one national market to another. In addition, companies' operations, such as marketing communications, product designs and advertising messages, etc, should differ for the different phases of product-adoption dynamics (eg [MOH 01]). Consequently, designing locally-meaningful global marketing messages for each phase of the product life cycle is crucial to the successful targeting of local markets.

One way to build locally-meaningful marketing messages is to build a relationship between the consumer and the offered product by using linguistic strategies. The overall importance of language as a part of an effective advertising message has been acknowledged in earlier literature [HIT 88], [MEL 99]. However, simple translation of advertising text is not enough since the use of language is influenced by varying factors, such as culture and consumer behavior [DEM 04b]. Therefore, linguistic strategies, such as questions or the use of pronouns, need to be used in order to achieve meaningful and responsive local messages in advertising. Further, possessive pronouns can manifest expressions of emphasis or attenuation; as an example, in the case of "It is my belief" or "I believe", the personal belief is more strongly accentuated in the former than in the latter [MUL 90: 207–26]. Personal and possessive pronouns therefore build successively deeper relationship between the consumer and the product. However, research studying linguistic strategies used for creating the relationship by using pronouns in advertisements is, to a large extent, missing in existing literature.

In light of the above, the advertising text forms a significant part of the advertising message. In this chapter, we report results of a linguistic study on the relationship created by the marketer between the product and the consumer in an international setting. Specifically, we concentrate on how a locally-meaningful marketing message is created through the relationship that is built with personal and possessive pronouns and how the relationship changes temporally over the product life cycle in two national markets.

2.2. Background and objectives

Consumers' adoption of new products in the marketplace has long been known to follow the life cycle model [GOR 82]. Traditionally, the product life cycle has been divided into phases from the initial slow growth of the introduction phase to the accelerating growth phase through to the decreasing growth at maturity and finally ending with the decline phase [MAH 90]. Explanations for the evolutionary trajectory of adoption dynamics has been provided from both the demand and supply sides. On the demand side, the customer segments adopting new technology products vary in their characteristics during the evolution of life cycle. Similarly, in response to the changes in consumer behavior, the supply-side providers adapt their operations to respond to these market changes.

On the supply side, the basis of competition evolves from capacity and functionality at the introduction, to reliability and further to convenience at the growth phase and finally to the economies of scale matching the price decline as the technology matures [CHR 97]. Therefore, among other supply-side actions, marketing communications and the advertising message should be different for each of the phases of the product life cycle [MOH 01]. This would reflect the changes in the demand side of the adoption dynamics. On the demand side, the adoption evolves through diverse customer segments after the launch of a new technology product. First, the products are adopted by innovators and early adopters in the introduction phase. After this initial period, in the subsequent growth phase the mainstream customer segments, ie early and late majority present demand for the product. Finally, at the maturity phase, laggards finally adopt the products [ROG 95].

The importance of the innovators and early adopters in the introduction phase is that they validate the technical functionality of the new technology and they further validate the existence of basis for the markets for a new technological product [FEL 03]. The introduction phase is characterized by fear, uncertainty and doubt on the part of mass-market customers since they do not understand how the new technology might create value for them, or what its purpose might be [MOH 01]. The subsequent growth phase is characterized by entry into the mass-markets and is represented by increasing reliability, increasing price pressures and ease-of-use requirements by the main customer segments. The consumer preferences change from technical functionality to more marketing-oriented attributes, such as usability and availability [MOO 99]; [ROG 95]; [UTT 94]. Similarly, the change from the growth phase to maturity in the product life cycle signifies the increasing importance of price and technological commoditization as customers are already familiar with the products [MOO 99].

The evolution of product adoption has been found to be influenced by national-level characteristics in the international marketplace. Even the start of the product adoption, ie national launch timing, has been found to depend on various national-level attributes, such as economic and political conditions, time since the first global launch of a new technology, cultural characteristics, religious beliefs, language and lifestyles [GAN 97]. Further, these national attributes influence the evolution of the product life cycle and the marketing means and advertising messages should be designed to reflect these attributes [GAN 96]; [MOH 01].

Hofstede's cultural dimensions have been used in earlier studies to seek explanatory factors influencing cross-cultural variations, such as national-level differences in adoption dynamics or consumer behavior [DAW 96]; [DEM 00]; [HOF 01]. According to Hofstede, values form the core of culture and define tendencies to prefer certain states of affairs over others [HOF 97]. The four original cultural dimensions, ie power distance, individualism, masculinity and uncertainty avoidance, represent cultural variability and different value systems in cultures [HOF 80]. Power distance defines how members of a culture accept and give authority. Individualism is found to prevail in task-oriented societies where ties between individuals are loose and people look mainly after themselves and their immediate family. Uncertainty avoidance can be defined as the extent to which the individual feels threatened by uncertain or unknown situations [HOF 97] and it has been found that high-uncertainty-avoidance cultures are distrustful of new ideas or behavior [DAW 96]. Masculinity dimension has been traditionally associated with assertiveness, high competition, ambition and forms of materialism, such as money and earnings [HOF 97].

In order to cope with heterogenous national markets in global markets, companies have always, at least to some extent, tailored their marketing messages to local markets, at minimum translating their textual advertising components. The text in advertisements is one way to enhance responsiveness to local needs during the evolution of product adoption. The overall importance of language as a part of an effective advertising message has been acknowledged in earlier literature [HIT 88]; [MEL 99].

In the context of international marketing, a simple translation of advertising texts to the local language is not enough since the use of language is influenced by varying factors, such as consumer preferences, culture, local customs, etc [DEM 04b]. Therefore, linguistic strategies, such as orders or questions or use of pronouns, need to be used in order to achieve meaningful and responsive local messages in advertising. An example of incomparability between advertising texts and culture is the unsatisfactory advertisements of Western products in Russia in the 1990s. The deficient advertising texts were drafted according to the Western tradition of commanding and presenting questions to the consumer, which ignored the Russian cultural conventions of addressing the consumer [SIX 05].

The previous linguistic studies concerning advertisements have focused, eg on the usage of adverbs as discursive strategies in French advertising texts [GAR 96], the diverse forms of reference present in German and Australian advertising posters [GAR 00] and the usage of personal pronouns and possessive determinants in Russian and English advertising texts [SMI 04]. Previous research combining advertising and language in international marketing has considered, eg standardization and translation of brand names [FRA 02]; [HON 02]; [ZHA 01], the use of foreign words in global and local markets [NEE 95] and the role of language in international corporate visual identity [MEL 99].

The need for comparative analyses in cultural level, as well as in linguistic studies, has been solicited in earlier literature [MCQ 96]; [SAM 94]. More specifically, the linguistic studies concerning the use of pronouns and their functional issues have not been widely discussed and, similarly, attention has been given to the sentence level at the expense of the discourse level. Further, there is a lack of studies handling the pronoun use, especially for languages other than English [MUH 90: 13–14]. Consequently, this study considers the use of advertising language to create a relationship between consumer and product in the international setting. Additionally, we study the longitudinal aspects of the use of linguistic strategies to build the relationship with the data spanning from 1991 until 2005.

2.3. Theoretical framework

This study is grounded on discourse analysis. The focus of discourse analysis is on how people use language in order to communicate information about the world, themselves and their social relationships [SCH 94]. Advertising can be seen as a research object reflecting current phenomenon [POS 90], the social and cultural contexts in which it operates [KRE 87], as well as the needs of cultures and social groups [NEE 95]. When analyzing societal content through language, it is important to also focus on the form, ie the textual structuring of the language, as well as on the context as current societal situations are always realized in forms [FAI 92]. Therefore, this study focuses on an approach that combines both aspects of language as the focus is on the linguistic structuring of the advertising message, as well as on its realization in a specific context. More specifically, the theoretical frame is based on a French stream of discourse analysis – theory of enunciation, *théorie de l'énonciation* – which combines the communication situation and textual organization enabling a linguistic analytical approach [FIS 99]; [KER 80]; [MAI 87]; [MAI 00].

Enunciation and utterance form the central concepts of the theory of enunciation. Enunciation refers to the individual act of using language and utterance is the linguistic object resulting from the use of language [MAI 94]. An utterance, in contrast to a phrase, always carries a communicative intention as it must be transmitted orally or in writing [PER 00]. Different linguistic structures may function as strategies according to their communicative intention. This refers to a conscious or non-conscious choice on the addresser's behalf to choose one linguistic operation over another in a communication situation that is constrained by restrictions, rules or norms [CHA 02]. The main thrust of the theory concerns the articulation of the subject, the moods which express the addresser's attitude towards the utterance (declarative, imperative, interrogative, exclamation), the modalities that refer to the addresser's assessment of the probabilities and duties inherent in the situation and the deictic features (ie participants, time and place) [MAI 96].

We concentrate on the participants of the advertising discourse and on the relationship built by the advertiser between the consumer and the product. From the linguistic perspective, every utterance, written or oral, includes an addresser that enables us to constitute the other, the addressee [MAI 00: 86]. In the context of our study, the addresser refers to the advertiser, ie the company delivering the product. The addressee refers to the potential consumer portrayed in the advertisement. Pronouns can be used to constitute the relationship between the parties of the discourse and it is important to notice that the relationship between the two parties is produced only by and within the situation of enunciation [BEN 82].

2.3.1. *Pronouns as relationship building units*

The question of pronouns brings forth, on one hand, the conventions of the formal language and, on the other hand, the conventions of their use in various social contexts. First, according to the grammatical conditions, pronouns stand for nouns. Secondly, there are several classes of pronouns, such as personal, possessive, demonstrative and indefinite; and, thirdly, pronouns come in the first, second and third person [MUL 90]. In addition to the formal rules, there are many cultural and contextual prerequisites concerning the pronoun use, such as the degree of formality of discourse, the relationship of the parties and the formality of the situation. Our focus is on the two first classes of pronouns, ie personal and possessive and their use in the context of French and Finnish advertising texts.

The grammatical function of pronouns is to act as linguistic units that introduce objects that are to be mentioned in discourse or refer to already-mentioned objects in the discourse. However, pronouns as such do not reveal the total complexity of discourse. The full significance of the utterance and to what or whom the addresser refers to can only be understood by linking the utterance with its actual occasion of use [MUH 90], eg an utterance where the advertiser urges the consumer to use all his or her potential might seem inappropriate without a context in an advertisement. Thus, the meaning of an utterance varies according to the context. Therefore, the rules for use of pronouns are not self-explanatory and speakers need to acquire social rules in addition to the grammatical rules [MUL 90]. Pronouns make it possible to enlighten relations in discourse, such as who speaks to whom and what he/she has the right to say [MUL 90: 34]. Pronouns play a considerable role in defining social relations as markers of, for example, formality, level of politeness, or degree of intimacy [MUL 90: 132].

2.3.2. *Advertising and personal and possessive pronouns*

Advertising is about "talking to someone and not *about* someone" [BOW 05: 20). Generally, advertising seeks the personal touch by approaching numerous consumers as if they were addressed as unique individuals [MYE 94]. The advertiser can use straightforward or subtle ways in the search of a close relationship, such as directly addressing the consumer [MYE 94], or by assigning them a role in the advertisement [BOW 05]. In many cases, addressing the individual consumer is realized with the help of pronouns. Thus, pronouns play a significant role in constructing the relationship between the product and the consumer.

An advertising text is always destined for someone – the potential or existing consumer even though he/she may not be explicitly depicted in the advertising text. Many advertisers choose to emphasize the consumer as one of the most important parts of the advertising message [SMI 04]. Generally, the most common way of explicitly including the consumer in the advertising text is by the use of the second person pronoun. The personal pronoun "you" creates a one-to-one relationship between the advertiser and the consumer, but at the same time it can be applied to anyone. Thus the personal pronoun "you" is not exclusively a private way of addressing the consumer, but also one that theoretically enables anyone to be identified with the personal pronoun "you" [MYE 94].

The role of the second person in advertising texts is significant as it enables the advertiser to mark the social distinctions of the informal and formal "you" [MYE 94]. Many European languages make a "T/V" (informal *tu*, formal *vous*) distinction in their systems of address; the distinction depends on social factors in addition to formal rules [SMI 04]. The use of "T/V" is influenced by numerous rules, but in essence, the more alike the communication parties are and the more informal the situation, the more common it is that the informal "you" is used [MUH 90]. In English, "you" is used as both the informal and formal – singular and plural – forms of second person address, but both French and Finnish make the "T/V" distinction. In French, the informality is expressed by pronoun *tu* and it expresses either particular intimacy or, rarely, condescension. The formal address is expressed by *vous* which is also the second person plural, both formal and informal. The formal you, *vous*, is used as the pronoun of address for public, formal conversation or as the pronoun of respect [MUH 90: 135]. In Finnish, the pronoun *sinä* (informal singular "you") expresses informality and the pronoun *te* (formal singular "you", also plural "you") is used for formal address. In Finnish, the use of the personal pronoun, in addition to the conjugated verb, is grammatically compulsory, but when searching for a more neutral tone the personal pronoun can be omitted.

The function of possessive pronouns is to establish a relationship between possessor and possession. Possessive pronouns usually proceed or follow a noun and their main function is to modify a noun. Possessive pronouns can also show expressions of emphasis or attenuation, as an example in utterances "It is my belief" vs. "I believe", the personal belief is more strongly accentuated in the former than in the latter [MUH 90: 207–26]. Therefore, while personal pronouns build a relationship between the advertiser and the consumer and indirectly with the product, the possessive pronouns deepen the direct, more intimate relationship between the product and the consumer.

The marking of possession differs in the French and Finnish languages. In French, possession can be determined by a possessive pronoun or the genitive construction "*de* + noun", which is comparable to the English "of + noun". Finnish uses, in addition to the possessive pronoun, the possessive suffix according to the person in question attached to the object of possession [HAK 95:128], for example "*your book*" corresponds to *sinun kirjasi* (*sinun* = second person singular possessive pronoun + *kirja* = book + *si* second person possessive suffix). The omission of the possessive pronoun is not considered wrong in more informal situations and the use of only a possessive suffix is adequate.

2.4. Data and methods

Our mission is to study the level of the relationship between the consumer and the product with the usage of pronouns in the advertising text in an international setting. We have chosen France and Finland in order to obtain diverse cultural viewpoints inside the European Union (EU). According to Hofstede's cultural dimensions, the two countries differ from one another. To begin with, on the dimension of power distance, France is categorized as a high power distance culture and Finland as a low power distance culture. Similarly, the uncertainty avoidance is high in France and low in Finland. In addition, both countries are highly individualistic cultures, France having a slightly higher index value than Finland, while in the masculinity dimension France is relatively high and Finland has a low index value. Finally, in the long-term orientation, the countries do not differ significantly from one another.

The corpus, ie linguistic data, consists of advertising texts of three technology products (mobile phones, digital cameras and DVD (digital video disk) players) in France and Finland between 1991 and 2005. The evolutionary life cycle trajectories of the products were divided into three distinctive phases, ie introduction, growth and maturity. These phases are separated from one another by turning points in evolutionary trajectories, ie the takeoff point at the start of rapid growth and the slowing of the growth rate at the start of the maturity phase. The identification of the turning points from the adoption-time series was done by expert evaluation which has been shown to result in the most reliable separation of life-cycle phases [HAA 06]. The product-adoption life-cycle time-series data were obtained from ITU and Euromonitor. The advertisements were collected systematically from all the issues of the magazines during the mentioned time frame. The French advertisements were collected from two magazines, *L'Express* and *Le Nouvel Observateur* and the Finnish advertisements were gathered from *Tekniikan Maailma*.

This chapter concentrates on the linguistic structures building the relationship between the consumer and the product in different phases of the product life cycle. The unit of analysis is the use of the 2nd person personal and the 2nd person possessive pronouns and their occurrences in the French and the Finnish advertisements. The utterances containing personal and possessive pronouns were considered according to the linguistic rules in French and in Finnish. In contrast to French, in Finnish there are few variations for both the personal and the possessive pronouns. Therefore, we separately analyzed the occurrences of the conjugated verb with and without the corresponding personal pronoun. Further, we also analyzed the occurrences for the possessives expressed by the personal pronoun with the possessive suffix – *si* and the occurrences for the possessives expressed by the possessive suffix –*si* alone. The quantitative results of the Finnish advertisements on both personal and possessive pronouns were counted and reported as separate categories to facilitate comparison with the French quantitative results.

We calculated the occurrences of utterances that included personal and possessive pronouns and the total number of utterances according to the linguistic definition that an utterance entails every meaningful entity in the context of the advertising text (purposely designed for the textual organization). In the quantitative results we report the percentage of utterances, including personal and possessive pronouns, for each product life-cycle phase in order to reveal the trends in the building of the relationship between the consumer and the product.

2.5. Results and contribution

Table 2.1 presents our division of the time frames of the phases in all three product life cycles in France and in Finland.

	Introduction	Growth	Maturity
France, mobile phones	1996	1997–2001	2002 and ongoing
France, digital cameras	2002	2003 and ongoing	
France, DVDs	2000	2001 and ongoing	
Finland, mobile phones	1994	1995–2002	2003 and ongoing
Finland, digital cameras	2000	2001 and ongoing	
Finland, DVDs	2000	2001 and ongoing	

Table 2.1. *The time frames for the phases of the product life cycles*

In order to further explicate our linguistic analysis we will give examples of advertising texts from different life-cycle phases. The examples used depict the general tendencies of the linguistic trends. The texts from the original French and Finnish advertisements have been translated into English by the authors for the purposes of this study. While every attempt has been made to translate the content of the advertisements accurately, the main intention is to show the linguistic properties of the texts. Some advertising texts already contain English words and they have been identified by "# ... #". The product and the company names have been replaced with "PRODUCT" and "COMPANY", respectively.

2.5.1. *Mobile phones*

In our study, mobile phones represent products that are considered as having a highly personal use. Figure 2.1 gives an overview of the quantitative results of the study.

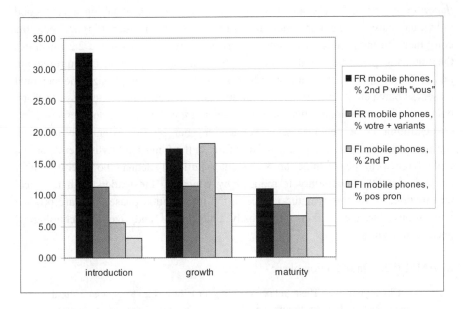

Figure 2.1. *The percentage of utterances containing pronouns in mobile phone advertisements in France and in Finland*

In the French advertisements for mobile phones, there is substantial use of the second person *vous* referring to the consumer. Even though the occurrences decrease gradually in the growth period and continue to do so moderately in the maturity period, they maintain their prominence in the advertising texts. The use of the possessive pronoun *votre* and its diverse forms that refer to the consumer remain at a similar level throughout the three phases. The Finnish advertisements during the introduction phase start with a limited use of the personal pronoun, the second person *sinä*. The use increases considerably in the growth phase and decreases again in the maturity phase. The use of the linguistic possessive constructs in the Finnish advertisements is limited in the introduction phase and increases during the growth phase remaining at this level also in the maturity phase.

Example 2.1 below, which represents the French advertisements in the introduction phase, depicts how the supply-side in the introduction phase strongly attempts to reduce the fear uncertainty and doubt on the part of the potential consumer by explicitly bonding him/her with the product. The French consumer has the use of the mobile phone personally explained in the second person. All the utterances are connected to the consumer with possessive pronouns such as *"your thumb* or *your hand"*. The advertiser gives the impression of taking a very good individual care of the consumer and strengthens the relationship between the consumer and the product with precise, private instructions. Example 2.2 illustrates the linguistic properties of the Finnish advertising texts used in the introduction phase. In this phase, the Finnish advertisements do not emphasize the personal closeness between the advertiser, the product and the consumer. The possible fears, doubts and uncertainties that the consumer may have are not lessened by concentrating on a personal level connection, but by the exhaustive technical information concerning the product. Therefore, in the Finnish advertisements, only a few references to the consumer are sufficient to build an adequate bond with him/her and subsequently uncertainty is reduced by educating the readers with technical information. Partly this is natural since in the introduction phase there are product innovations that the markets are mostly unaware of and overall technological uncertainty is high.

EXAMPLE 2.1: Introduction phase – France

> ... Close your fist. Then, relax your fingers a little bit. Now, make rapid movements with your thumb up and down. Finally, carry your hand to between your mouth and ear. Talk! It is as simple as that to communicate with the portable phone "PRODUCT" of "COMPANY". From the first time it is used you will realize its small size 147 x 62 x 30 mm and its lightness 295g. ... *Express* 1993.

EXAMPLE 2.2: Introduction phase – Finland

> A new period requires a new phone. "PRODUCT". When you need a real, international-requirements-fulfilling portable phone, it is here. "PRODUCT" is totally new, a pocket phone based on a new digital technology. It works in the fast growing European GSM system. GSM network (Global System for

Mobile Communications) will cover in the near future almost the whole of Western Europe. By the middle of the 1990s already almost 80% of Europeans will live under coverage area of the network. Every detail of "PRODUCT", even the design, has been designed to facilitate your everyday communication whether you are in Helsinki, London or even Berlin ... *Tekniikan Maailma* 1993.

Example 2.3 depicts the French growth phase where the bonding with the consumer is still present, but clearly in a less prominent style than during the introduction phase. The Finnish advertising texts of the growth phase, illustrated in Example 2.4, show an increase in the emphasis on the relationship created between the consumer and the product. The consumer is addressed frankly and the direct relationship with the consumer by the use of the second person has a higher priority than the purely technical features. Even though the Finnish introduction phase puts the consumer at the forefront, the relationship is not overwhelmingly protective or bonding when possessive pronouns are not used.

EXAMPLE 2.3: Growth phase – France

"PRODUCT" from "COMPANY". Offer yourself the smallest and the lightest of portable telephones. The know-how of "COMPANY" again pushes the limits of technology in order to propel you into the third millennium. At 100 grams, the "PRODUCT" is the smallest and the lightest of cellular phones that you could offer yourself. It offers you the most advanced functions (vibration mode, data transmission ...), user friendly interface ... *Express* 1997.

EXAMPLE 2.4: Growth phase – Finland

Minuscule. Forget the huge mobile phones of the past years. "PRODUCT" is even smaller than the smallest, so that it fits into your palm. Forget the weak audio quality: now you get a phone with which you sound like yourself also when heard by the receiver. Forget watching the talk time: with this phone you can speak for hours on end. "PRODUCT" is easy to use, even though it includes a large number of special functions. Choose the one you prefer from four subdued colors. *Tekniikan Maailma* 1997.

The French example, Example 2.5, from the maturity phase represents the consumers' awareness of the basic functions of the products. Some details are still explained, but the building of the closeness between the consumer and the product is to a lesser extent. Example 2.5 shows the decrease in the use of personal and possessive pronouns in the French advertisements which illustrates the diminishing role of the bonding with the consumer. In the maturity phase, there are a limited number of competitors left and branding becomes a crucial issue. The consumer has become aware of the product features and the time is right for more personalization of the advertising text, emphasizing the brand image. The Finnish maturity phase shows the same tendencies in advertising as the French one. Example 2.6 represents the advertising texts and the decreasing usage of personal and possessive pronouns through the Finnish maturity phase. The relationship to the consumer is created through action enabled by the product without being unnecessarily patronizing or explicitly linking the product to the consumer.

EXAMPLE 2.5: Maturity phase – France

> Now you see
> Guess the moment, capture the instant, reveal the emotion … with the "PRODUCT", now you see:
> - high definition auto-focus device
> - sensor of 2 million pixels
> - 2 hours of video recording of VHS quality.
> Take it everywhere … *Nouvel Observateur* 2005.

EXAMPLE 2.6: Maturity phase – Finland

> The world's smallest 3G-phone. "PRODUCT" is already recognized from the appearance. It seems almost amazing that it has been possible to fit in a 50MB internal memory and all the latest 3G functions. You can take pictures and send videofootage, make videocalls and take advantage of the subtlety of the mobile phone of the future. Finally, in a real pocket-size. www."COMPANY".fi … *Tekniikan Maailma* 2005.

In general, the results reveal detectable trends in building the relationship between the product and the consumer over the product's life cycle. A possible explanation for the difference between the countries in the trends on building the relationship in advertisements might be the uncertainty avoidance dimension. France is a high uncertainty avoidance culture and this might partly explain the use of the linguistic strategies in the advertisements to soothe consumers' fears, especially in the introduction phase when the technical uncertainties are high. In contrast, the Finnish advertisements do not use relationship building in the introduction phase of the product life cycle, which may be due to the low uncertainty avoidance index.

2.5.2. Digital cameras

In our study, digital cameras represent products that are less personal than the mobile phones, but still used by individuals. Figure 2.2 presents the overall results of our linguistic study.

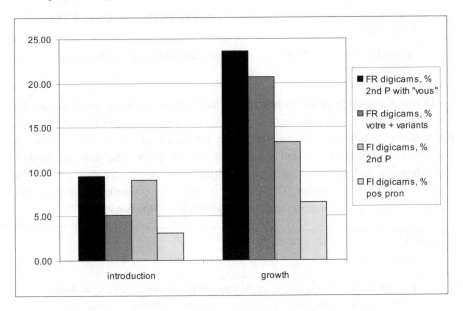

Figure 2.2. *The percentage of utterances containing pronouns in digital camera advertisements in France and in Finland*

In the French advertising texts during the introduction phase, there are limited occurrences of the personal and possessive pronouns referring to the consumer. Their use is at the lowest level when comparing the introductory phases of all the three products. In the growth phase, the use of both pronoun types increases dramatically. The Finnish advertising texts manifest a similar tendency to the French linguistic trend where the pronouns are used to a lesser degree in the introduction phase than in the growth phase.

The Finnish examples, 2.7 and 2.8, which are from the same company, are used to illustrate the tendencies in both countries during the introduction and the growth phases. The introduction phase of the digital camera depicts a lesser emphasis on the intimacy between the advertiser, the product and the consumer. This is notably observable from the more limited use of personal pronouns which results in a more distant connection between the consumer and the product. In an extreme case, the consumer can be completely erased from the advertising text, as illustrated in Example 2.7 where the consumer is faded out from the advertising text.

EXAMPLE 2.7: Introduction phase – Finland

"PRODUCT" a pleasure for the eye. #LONDON PARIS MILAN SILICON VALLEY#

"PRODUCT" www. "PRODUCT".com #Imaging across networks# *Tekniikan Maailma* 2000.

During the growth phase in both countries, there is a greater emphasis on the consumer. There is a change from the impersonal textual style in the introduction phase towards personal bonding with the consumer in the growth phase, as illustrated in examples 2.7 and 2.8. In the growth phase, the detailed product characteristics and general functionality of the product are important, as is the connection with the consumer. The intimacy between the consumer and the product is tied with the usage of the personal pronoun referring to the consumer.

EXAMPLE 8: Introduction phase – Finland

"PRODUCT"

This camera does not leave you cold. You will pay attention to its style, form, technology. A 7.1 megapixel cell and a 3x zoom hide beneath its steel cover. Don't be surprised if you feel an irresistible attraction to it. www."COMPANY".fi *Tekniikan Maailma* 2005.

The increasing trend of building a relationship between the product and the consumer from the introduction to the growth phase is similar for both countries, but Finnish occurrences of both pronoun types do not reach the French level. The similarity of the trend might come from the less personal nature of the product and industry specific factors, for example, digital cameras need complementary offering (memory devices, computers, printers etc). Therefore, the consumers' use of the complementary offering might have led the suppliers to think that there was a reduction in consumers' feelings of uncertainty about digital camera products.

2.5.3. *DVDs*

DVD (digital video disk) players are adopted, in most cases, by households rather than by individuals and are used by many people in contrast to the other two products which are more personal in nature. Figure 2.3 presents the overall results for our linguistic study.

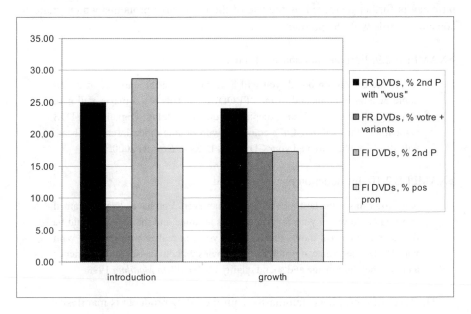

Figure 2.3. *The percentage of utterances containing pronouns in DVD advertisements in France and in Finland*

The occurrences of *vous* in French advertisements are high during both periods. The use of possession with *votre* increases considerably from the introduction phase to the growth phase. The occurrences of both the personal and possessive pronouns in the Finnish advertisements are frequent in the introduction phase. The tendency to use both pronouns decreases in the growth phase.

Example 2.9, which represents the French introduction phase, shows the strong emphasis on the consumer as an object or actor in the introduction phase when there is a limited use of the depiction of possession. The intimacy of the relationship and the familiarity with the product comes from the consumer being depicted as a participant in the advertising text. The introduction phase of DVDs does not represent a considerable depiction of possession following similar trend with the digital cameras' advertising texts. The Finnish introduction phase of DVD advertisements commences with a strong emphasis on the intimacy between the consumer and the product. This is apparent in Example 2.10 which shows the

Finnish introduction phase where the consumer is positioned in the advertising scenario by an omniscient advertiser, fully aware of the needs of the consumer. The intimacy is further increased by the use of the possessive pronouns which grant the consumer a role with the product.

EXAMPLE 2.9: Introduction phase – France

> … As the captain on board, you will have to explore the universe of digital home cinema in command of the "PRODUCT". This DVD player will give you digital images of an exceptional quality. Dolby Digital and DTS compatible, the "PRODUCT", equipped with double-diode laser read head, will also know how to read your CDs and CD-Rs… *Express* 2000.

EXAMPLE 2.10: Introduction phase – Finland

> Now you can see the best movies, better than ever! You have always dreamed that you could watch your favorite movies at home and the feeling would be the same as in a real movie theater. Now you can realize your dreams. With your DVD video you can watch feature movies without pauses and experience an overwhelming image and sound quality … *Tekniikan Maailma* 1998.

The level of consumers' familiarity with the DVD products is manifested in the French advertising texts with notably increasing manifestations of the possessive pronouns in the growth phase. The relationship between the product and the consumer does not necessarily become more intimate, but more direct and attaches the consumer to the product. The advertiser seeks to directly address the consumer with the product. However, the Finnish advertising texts move into more detached direction in the relationship between the consumer and the product. More emphasis is placed on the product and its features than on the consumer or the relationship between the product and the consumer. This also shows a greater tendency overall in Finland to concentrate more on the product itself.

EXAMPLE 2.11: Growth phase – France

> Record without counting. You are in command. Do you want to watch your favorite broadcasts whenever you want? Record programs for more than 300 hours? Save the best on a DVD? Get the advantage of an exceptional image quality? Not a problem, with the recording DVD with "COMPANY" hard drive, you are the director … *Nouvel Observateur* 2004.

EXAMPLE 2.12: Growth phase – Finland

> ... the "PRODUCT'S" unique appearance radically breaks traditional thinking
> and opens up an extraordinary world of music and movie experiences.
> "PRODUCT" is "COMPANY'S" new entertainment center in which is
> combined a FM-radio, a DVD and a CD player ... *Tekniikan Maailma* 2004.

The usage of personal pronouns maintains its level and the usage of possessive pronouns increases in the French advertisements from the introduction to the growth phase and therefore the relationship building is a constitutive part of French advertising of DVD players. In contrast, in the Finnish advertisements there is decreasing use of both personal and possessive pronouns which is peculiar when compared to the advertisements for mobile phones and digital cameras. The dissimilarities in the trends might be partially explained by the fact that DVD players are closely tied to the family-use and general group-type activities and since France is more collectivistic culture than Finland the use of high levels of relationship building is more appropriate in this cultural environment.

2.6. Conclusions and limitations

The advertising texts of both countries follow the communication conventions of the cultures – in French advertisements the consumer is always referred to with the formal "you", whereas in Finnish it is common to refer to the consumer with the informal "you" and still maintain politeness in the form of address. On the one hand, the formal address in French reflects the culture's high power distance maintaining. On the other hand, it is a question of convention and therefore it is not considered as distant as it could be, but more as a form of general respect. Also, the generally frequent use of possessive pronouns has a friendly way to affiliate the consumer with the product, despite the formal address.

As we witnessed, there is no one, straightforward, dominant trend in the usage of pronouns as linguistic devices for relationship building between the product and the consumer. Therefore, it seems that the industry-specific effects at least partially explain the dynamics of the relationship building. However, our results reveal some systematic tendencies. First of all, the most visible general trend over the product life cycle is the usage of personal pronouns as relationship-building devices which increases in one-half of the advertisements (FR – digital cameras; FI – mobile phones; and FI – digital cameras), decreases in one-third of the advertisements (FR – mobile phones; and FI – DVD players) and remains unchanged in one-sixth (FR – DVD players). Therefore, the phase of the life cycle does seem to have influence on the relationship building between the product and the consumer. Secondly, personal and possessive pronouns constitute a considerable part of the utterances of the texts advertising technology products in both countries. Thirdly, in general, the use of linguistic means to build the relationship between the product and the consumer is higher in France when compared to Finland. In addition, the explicit reference to the second person is more general in French and plays a considerable part in forming the advertising message in France. Finally, the uncertainty avoidance seems to be a plausible cultural dimension that explains the differences between France and Finland in the usage of pronouns as relationship-building linguistic devices.

In practice, for technology management and operations our results reveal interesting possibilities for the use of pronouns in different phases of the life cycle. For example, in the early phases of the life cycle, the use of pronouns might make the relationship between the product and the consumer more intimate. Therefore, in the technology management, more complex and functionally-advanced solutions might be offered to the consumers. However, the linkage of technology strategy with marketing strategy using pronouns as relationship-building devices needs to studied more closely to reveal the appropriate usage of the pronouns in different phases from the technology management point-of-view.

However, as with all research, our research has multiple limitations. First of all, our object is not to determine one, right way of addressing the consumer, but to reveal implications behind the linguistic strategies governing culturally-sensitive use of textual devices and enhance our understanding of linguistic matters in connection with consumer behavior and temporal evolution of product life cycles.

Our study was limited to the use of personal and possessive pronouns of the second person. There are also other linguistic strategies of building a relationship between the product and the consumer besides the pronoun use, for example, the imperative mood which also addresses directly the consumer.

The results of our study should not be interpreted as stating that the more personal pronouns used, the more intimate the relationship becomes. For example, the use of one personal and possessive pronoun in the middle of numerous, detailed, technical bullet points may have a major impact compared to their repetitive use. Also, social, economic and other trends may have influenced our results. However, this concern is limited since mobile phones were somewhat earlier in time than the digital cameras or DVD players. Similarly, only three of the Hofstede's cultural dimensions could be taken into account since only these three show differences between France and Finland.

In addition to tackling the limitations of this study, our results pave the way for promising avenues of future research. First, future research concerning the role of pronouns in advertising is needed, both quantitatively and qualitatively. The different manifestations of the first and the third persons should be taken into account, in addition to the second person. Also, the third person, when referring to the product, should be analyzed in the advertising text. Furthermore, the different roles of the possessive pronouns connecting the consumer and the product and the context should be studied in more depth. Finally, evolutionary longitudinal studies should continue to find the relationship between the life cycle and the usage of linguistic strategies and their appropriateness in the differing phases of the adoption life cycle. Especially vital for increasing our understanding of the appropriate use of linguistic strategies would be to study brands and companies utilizing different linguistic strategies. These studies could be further tied to the performance measures and find links between marketing actions and performance results.

2.7. References

[BEN 82] BENVENISTE, É (1982) "Problèmes de linguistique générale" *édit Gallimard*, France

[BOW 05] BOWERMAN, P (2005) "Writing better today: eight tips for instantly improving your marketing copy", *Public Relations Tactics* (February): pp 20–21

[CHA 02] CHAREAUDEAU, P (2002) "Stratégie de discourse", in Charaudeau, P and Maingueneau, D (eds), "Dictionnaire d'analyse du discourse", *Éditions du Seuil*, Paris, pp 548–49

[CHR 97] CHRISTENSEN, CM (1997), "Patterns in the evolution of product competition", *European Management Journal* 15(2), pp 117–27

[DAW 96] DAWAR, N, PARKER, PM and PRICE LJ (1996) "A cross-cultural study of interpersonal information exchange", *Journal of International Business Studies* 27(3), pp 497–516

[DEM 04a] DE MOOIJ, M (2004a) *Consumer Behavior and Culture. Consequences for Global Marketing and Advertising*, Thousand Oaks, CA: Sage Publications

[DEM 04b] DE MOOIJ, M (2004b) "Translating advertising: painting the tip of an iceberg", *The Translator* 10(2), pp 179–98

[DEM 00] DE MOOIJ, M (2000) "The future is predictable for international marketers: Converging incomes lead to diverging consumer behavior", *International Marketing Review* 17(2), pp 103–13

[DEM 98] DE MOOIJ, M (1998) *Global Marketing and Advertising – Understanding Cultural Paradoxes*, London: Sage Publications

[DEK 00] DEKIMPE MG, SARVARY M and PARKER PM (2000) "Global diffusion of technological innovations: a coupled-hazard approach", *Journal of Marketing Research* 37(Feb), pp 47–59

[FAI 92] FAIRCLOUGH N (1992) "Discourse and text: linguistic and intertextual analysis within discourse analysis", *Discourse & Society* 3(2), pp 193–217

[FEL 03] FELL DR, HANSEN EN and BECKER BW (2003) "Measuring innovativeness for the adoption of industrial products", *Industrial Marketing Management* 32(4), pp 347–53

[FIS 99] FISHER, S (1999) "Enonciation, manières et territories" Paris: Ophrys

[FRA 02] FRANCIS JNP, LAM JPY and WALLS, J (2002) "Executive insights: the impact of linguistic differences on international brand name standardization: a comparison of English and Chinese brand names of *Fortune*-500 companies", *Journal of International Marketing* 10(1), pp 98–116

[GAN 96] GANESH, J and KUMAR, V (1996) "Capturing the cross-national learning effect: an analysis of an industrial technology diffusion", *Journal of the Academy of Marketing Science* 24(1), pp 328–37

[GAN 97] GANESH, J, KUMAR, V and SUBRAMANIAM, V (1997) "Learning effect in multinational diffusion of consumer durables: An exploratory investigation", *Journal of the Academy of Marketing Science* 25(3), pp 214–28

[GAR 00] GARDNER, R and LUCHTENBERG, S (2000) "Reference, image, text in German and Australian advertising posters", *Journal of Pragmatics* 32, pp 1807–821

[GAR 96] GARRIC, N (1996) "Une stratégie discursive publicitaire: les averbes en -ment" *Langage & Société* 78 (December)

[GOR 82] GORT, M and KLEPPER, S (1982) "Time paths in the diffusion of product innovations", *The Economic Journal* 92(367), pp 630–53

[HAA 06] HAAPANIEMI, T and MÄKINEN, S (2006) "Determining the takeoff point in adoption of innovations: a comparison of content and discrimination analysis", *International Journal of Technology Marketing* 2(1)

[HAK 95] HAKULINEN, A and KARLSSON, F (1995) *Nykysuomen lauseoppia* Suomalaisen kirjallisuuden seura: Helsinki, Finland

[HEL 93] HELSEN, K, JEDIDI, K and DESARBO, WS (1993) "A new approach to country segmentation utilizing multinational diffusion patterns" *Journal of Marketing* 57: 60-71

[HIT 88] HITE, RE and FRASER, C (1988) "International advertising strategies of multinational corporations", *Journal of Advertising Research*, August–September, pp 9–17

[HOF 80] HOFSTEDE, G (1980) *Culture's Consequences: International Differences in Work-related Values*, Beverly Hills, CA, Sage Publications

[HOF 97] HOFSTEDE, G (1997) *Cultures and Organizations. Software of the Mind*, New York: McGraw-Hill

[HOF 01] HOFSTEDE, G (2001) *Culture's Consequences: Comparing Values, Behaviors, Institutions and Organizations Across Nations*, (2nd edn), Thousand Oaks, CA: Sage Publications

[HON 02] HONG, FC, PECOTICH, A and SHULTZ II, CJ (2002) "Brand name translation: language constraints, product attributes and consumer perceptions in East and Southeast Asia", *Journal of International Marketing* 10(2), pp 29–45

[KER 80] KERBRAT-ORECCHIONI, C (1980) *L'énonciation, de la subjectivité dans le langage*, Paris: A Colin

[KRE 87] KRESS, G (1987) "Educating readers: language in advertising", in Hawthorn, J (ed), *Propaganda, Persuasion and Polemic*, London: Edward Arnold

[KUM 98] KUMAR, V, GANESH, J and ECHAMBADI, R (1998) "Cross-national diffusion research: what do we know and how certain are we?", *Journal of Product Innovation Management* 15, pp 255–68

[MAH 90] MAHAJAN, V, MULLER, E and BASS, F (1990) "New product diffusion models in marketing: a review and directions for research", *Journal of Marketing* 54 (January), pp 1–26

[MAH 94] MAHAJAN, V and MULLER, E (1994) "Innovation diffusion in a borderless global market: will the 1992 unification of the European Community accelerate diffusion of new ideas, products and technologies?", *Technological Forecasting and Social Change* 45, pp 221–35

[MAI 87] MAINGUENEAU, D (1987) *Nouvelles Tendances en Analyse du Discourse*, Paris: Hachette

[MAI 94] MAINGUENEAU, D (1994) *L'énonciation en Linguistique Française*, Paris: Hachette

[MAI 96] MAINGUENEAU, D (1996) *Les Termes de Clés de L'analyse du Discour*, Paris: Seuil

[MAI 00] MAINGUENEAU, D (2000) *Analyser les textes de communication*, Paris: Nathan

[MCQ 96] MCQUARRIE, EF and MICK, DG (1996) "Figures of rhetoric in advertising language", *Journal of Consumer Research* 22 (March 1996), pp 424–38

[MEL 99] MELEWAR, TC and SAUNDERS, J (1999) "International corporate visual identity: standardization or localization?", *Journal of International Business Studies* 30(3), pp 583–98

[MOH 01] MOHR, J (2001) *Marketing of High-Technology Products and Innovations*, Upper Saddle River, NJ: Prentice-Hall

[MOO 99] MOORE, GA (1999) *Crossing the Chasm* (revised edn), New York: HarperCollins Publishers

[MUH 90] MÜHLHÄUSLER, P and HARRÉ, R (1990) *Pronouns and People*, Oxford: Basil Blackwell

[MYE 94] MYERS, G (1994) *Words in Ads*, London: Edward Arnold

[NEE 95] NEELANKAVIL, JP, MUMMALANENI, V and SESSIONS, DN (1995) "Use of foreign language and models in print advertisements in East Asian countries", *European Journal of Marketing* 29(4), pp 24–38

[PER 00] PERRET, M (2000) *L'énonciation en Grammaire du Texte*, Paris: Nathan

[POS 90] POSTER, M (1990) *The Mode of Information: Poststructuralism and Social Context*, Cambridge: Polity Press

[ROG 95] ROGERS, EM (1995) *Diffusion of Innovations* (4th edn), New York: The Free Press

[SAM 94] SAMIEE, S and JEONG, I (1994) "Cross-cultural research in advertising: an assessment of methodologies", *Journal of the Academy of Marketing Science* 22(3), pp 205–17

[SCH 94] SCHRIFFIN, D (1994) *Approaches to Discourse*, Oxford: Blackwell

[SIX 05] SIX, I (2005) "What language sells: Western advertising in Russia", *The Journal of Language for International Business* 16(2), pp 1–12

[SMI 04] SMITH, K (2004) "'I am me, but who are you and what are we?': the translation of personal pronouns and possessive determiners in advertising texts", *Multilingua* 23(3), pp 283–303

[TAK 91] TAKADA, H and JAIN, D (1991) "Cross-national analysis of diffusion of consumer durables in Pacific Rim countries", *Journal of Marketing* 55 (April), pp 48–54

[TEL 99] TELLEFSEN, T and TAKADA, H (1999) "The relationship between mass media availability and the multicountry diffusion of consumer products", *Journal of International Marketing* 7(1), pp 77–96

[UTT 94] UTTERBACK, JM (1994) *Mastering the Dynamics on Innovation*, Boston: Harvard Business School Press

[ZHA 01] ZHANG, S and SCHMITT, BH (2001) "Creating local brands in multilingual international markets", *Journal of Marketing Research* 38 (August 2001), pp 313–25

Chapter 3

Culture and Diversity:
A New Approach of Management

3.1. Introduction

In the actual process of globalization, culture has an essential role in the different management steps. To ignore this diversity would be a major risk; to integrate it badly or in an incomplete manner would create significant dysfunctions.

Trans-culture, or multi-culture, is becoming the norm in the modern economy. Business has moved outside the frontiers and companies have to integrate this fact in to the four stages of development:

– the national step: production for national needs;

– the exportation step: production surplus not consumed inside the producing nation is exported to culturally-closed countries to avoid a cultural gap;

– the multinational step: foreign markets are considered in a special way: specific products to satisfy specific behaviors and needs; power is concentrated and centralized and the local mangers have little power;

– the global step: the company is more settled in the local culture; power is decentralized and shared between the different countries.

Chapter written by Chantal AMMI.

However, it would be a mistake to limit the multiculturalism of a global process. Some countries have integrated cultural specificities for a long time, especially when these characteristics are a part of the national demographic.

We can distinguish two types of countries with diversified cultural demographic components:

– the countries with multicultural, religious, linguistic, or ethnic local diversities, eg India, China, Canada, Belgium, Switzerland. How do the local governments and companies manage these diversities in political, economical, or sociological terms? We will focus on two examples: China and India;

– the countries with a large immigration flux. How do these countries integrate the religious and ethnic differences in order to maintain national cohesion? We will focus on two examples with different orientations: France and the USA.

However, before we analyze the phenomenon of multiculturalism, it seems important to define the notion of culture and its major components

3.2. The notion of culture

Over the last 10 years the scientific community has formulated many definitions of culture. Despite their differences, all of them acknowledge two strong dimensions of culture:

– the content which includes the explicit and implicit elements; and

– the process which defines the properties and the characteristics.

3.2.1. *Definition, content and properties*

The content, which consists of the cultural elements, is divided into two levels according the degree of consciousness.

– the explicit elements, directly observable, include [TER 85]:

   - the verbal language (the languages) and non-verbal language (messages based on the objects, the communication, etc.),

   - the usual behaviors, such as food, clothes, hygiene, homes, etc.,

   - the know-how, such as the use of tools, artifacts, cultural codes, etc.,

- the organizational modes, such as family, schools, associations, religion, etc;

– the implicit elements, stemming from f the explicit elements [DUS 83] include:

- the norms explain the normality of the society,

- the values define the frame of the moral references,

- the mental states and cognitive operations: learning, memory, emotions,

- the myths, the beliefs and the social representations are at the roots of social identity and structure human behavior.

3.2.2. *Properties, functions and process*

Culture can be analyzed through specific functions and characteristics:

– Culture is collective and is the emanation of a society or a group.

– Culture is acquired, learned and transmitted subconsciously by a process of socialization and consciously by different agents, such as schools, families, religious groups, etc.

– Culture is exclusive and is based on an identification process from one person to a group.

– Culture is progressive and allows man to adapt himself to his environment and his social sphere.

– Culture produces norms, behaviors, etc.

– Culture helps to solve problems and is a reservoir of knowledge.

3.3. Culture and globalization

The origins of culture are diversified and are not the only explanation of human behavior[1]. The origins of culture make it possible to understand the main orientations of value (value orientations [GEE 73]; [KLU 61]) and the vision of the world and the people and the actors involved in the global process.

---

1 Charlat in his anthropological theory of organizations defines five levels: man, group, organization, society and world.

3.3.1. *Culture: orientation of values*

From the perspective of multicultural analysis, we are more interested in the relationships between the persons than the ones between the behaviors and the integration inside a group. Some of the different groups are components of the culture as the nation or are components of subculture as the family, the profession, the ethnic, the religion, the age.

3.3.2. *Culture: a solution for global problems*

Every people, every ethnic group, every religion has its own list of solutions to resolve the problems of mankind. These solutions change according the time, the situation and the purposes of the group. However, the type of problems is more or less the same:

– Relations with nature can be a dominant (occidental vision), harmonic (Japanese and Chinese vision), or subjugate (Indian vision).

– Relations with the time can be a monetarist one (in the case of the developed countries) or a factual one adapted to traditional cultures (in the case of underdeveloped or emergent countries).

– Relations with the persons explain the interaction with the referential group. Two main systems can be observed in two different types of society:

- a community vision based on the predominance of the family, the clan, the tribe, or the company can be found in the countries with a strong cultural tradition (Asia, Africa, Latin America, South Europe);

- an individualistic vision where people look after their individuality (Anglo-Saxon countries, Scandinavia, etc). Hofstede [HOF 80] has noticed in many studies that there is a positive correlation between the individualistic scores and income levels.

In communautarist societies, the relation with power is usually more hierarchic; with the rules being more personal and with the space being more public, the communication is more implicit and the decisions are more collective.

As to the relation with power, we can distinguish two ways by which power can be shared inside society [INK 69]):

– a vertical repartition based on a hierarchic system where the social differentiations depend on many criteria according the referential culture (age, gender, education, income, name, etc); these relations can be found in Asia and Africa;

– a horizontal repartition, where the relations are more egalitarian, can be found in Western countries.

As to the relation with the rules, the rules can be defined as norms that people have to follow throughout their lives. These relations can be particularistic or universalistic [TRO 93]:

– a particularistic vision is based on an adaptation to the rules according to the quality of the people; for this reason we notice a strong correlation between communautarism and particularism;

– a universalistic vision considers that the rules must be the same for everybody independent of their social level. This vision can be found in Western countries, except for in relation to some ethnic minorities.

Relations with space are valorized according to the type of culture. The strength of religion, the importance of the public area and the power of interpersonal relationships are the most usual criteria

Relations with action and activities can be based on two different methods: Do or Be. Western countries favor action and measure the value in money or in material properties. The non-industrialized countries favor the birth and the network of relationships.

Relations with the emotions change according the type of culture. Two fundamental questions have to be asked:

– Is it the habit to show personal emotions to the public?

– Is it the habit to mix personal emotions and business affairs?

The following table shows four types of societies according to the answers to these questions.

	Mix of emotions and business affairs	Separation between emotions and affairs
Exteriorization of emotions	Latino Semites Slavonics	Anglo-Saxon
Internalization of emotions	Asiatic African	Scandinavian

Table 3.1. *Relations between emotions and business affairs*

Culture and its different components play a fundamental rule inside each society and explain, to a great degree, the differences between human beings.

In this global economic system where the financial, technical, commercial and productive frontiers are disappearing or are decreasing, some local and cultural particularities are maintained. These characteristics have to be integrated in the marketing, commercial and managerial processes.

3.4. Multiculturalism and the global economy

We can distinguish three main types of multiculturalism around the world.

A universal culture does not exist. Of course we notice a predominance of Western culture and more specifically American culture, in the movies, the stars, the products, the value systems, etc. Although Coca Cola, rap music, the American language and the film *The Titanic* have invaded the planet, the particularities are still present and oblige the companies to integrate them

3.4.1. *Global companies*

A global company can be defined as a company settled in at least five different countries.

However, despite these differences, a global company has the following common purposes:

– delocalization of production or commercialization;

– development of income;

– integration of the cultural characteristics in marketing, sales and human resources.

In relation to the marketing aspects, the cultural determinants influence the purchase acts and the behaviors of the consumers. In an international environment this criteria becomes more important. Each culture and each country has its own characteristics. Trying to erase or to forget this fact would be a big mistake.

– *Global or adapted product?* According to the type of product, the level of development of the country, the profile of the firm, the state of local and international competition, the size of the market, the income of the consumers, the company has two options:

- a global product: the same everywhere because the differences are not so important that it becomes necessary to create a special product for each country (Coca Cola, Lewis, Nike, etc),

- an adapted product: with total or partial modifications to integrate the local differences (food products, cars, etc).

– *Local or global advertisement?* Cultural characteristics oblige global firms to modify their communications independently of the choice of the product. There are three possibilities:

- a global advertisement where the script, the music, the actors and the message are identical; only the language is modified and translations are used,

- a local advertisement addresses the local specificities and each country has its own advertisement,

- a "glocal" advertisement is based on a mix of the two previous possibilities: the message and the script remain the same, but the actors and the supporting elements can change to be more efficient according to the local characteristics.

In relation to the commercial aspects, the local characteristics influence the commercial actions in the following areas:

– the negotiations and the relations with the suppliers, the distributors, the partners (banks, insurance companies, press agencies, ad agencies, etc) can be different according to the country;

– the choice of local agreements, of the selling methods and of the places to sell will depend on both the local characteristics and the strategy of the firm.

In relation to the human aspects, globalization creates a cultural diversity inside the organization. All the subsidiaries are involved at different levels: budget, advertisement, research, remuneration and staff recruitment.

3.4.2. *Countries with ethnic, cultural, religious and linguistic diversity*

No country is completely homogeneous and in most of them we can find some significant differences. However, some countries have a very diversified demographic composition. Their governments and local companies have integrated these characteristics at different levels, eg political, economic, commercial, or social. The most significant differences appeared in three different areas:

– linguistic;

– religious;

– ethnic.

In relation to the linguistic differences, in the case of multi-linguistic countries, for example Canada, Belgium and Switzerland, the linguistic cohabitation is generally harmonious. The political and administrative organizations integrate the different national languages. The economy takes the phenomena into consideration according to the weight of each linguistic minority in the country. For example, the French language is used extensively in the province of Quebec in Canada, but is less used in the West coast province.

In relation to the religious diversities, rare are the countries – except those where one religion is considered as the official and unique religion – with only one religion. According to the degree of religious liberty and the level of secularism, countries integrate the religious differences into the common life, for example religious holidays, public subsidies for religious buildings, dietary requirements, adapted clothes, etc:

– In India, where there is great religious diversity, most restaurants do not serve pork or beef to respect the religious rites of the dominant religions in the country (Islam and Hinduism).

– In some African countries where the religious repartition seems balanced (eg Benin, divided into three equal parts, Christians, Muslims and Animists), the different religious days and rites of each community are integrated into the life of the country.

– Lebanon has 18 official religions, although some of them predominate. Political power is equally distributed between Muslims and Christians. However, the economy seems unconcerned by this aspect. The physical size of the country, the limited number of its inhabitants (3 million) and the lack of specific religious behavior does not encourage integration of religious characteristics.

– In France, there is a mixture of a religious tolerance for all religions and an extreme secularism. This duality has lead to a prohibition of external religious signs in the administration and the public schools. The right to establish religion-based schools and religious places is total, but there are no public subsidies to finance them. It is forbidden to use the national media to promote religious facts, places, clothes, food, or schools. The increasing number of Muslims has created a new and lucrative market for halal meat, special clothes and religious artifacts.

In relation to the ethnic communities, before developing this point, it seems important to define the term "ethny". Ethny integrates two notions:

– the first is the notion of race, a notion not used in Occidental countries for reasons of political correctness;

– the second is the notion of tribes; ethny has its own characteristics, such as habits, norms, values, dietary requirements, religious practices, physical representations (tattoos, scarifications, etc).

In this section, we will only analyze the countries with representative and local ethnic minorities. As for the religious aspects, few countries are completely homogenous and we can find ethnic diversity in every continent:

– In Central and South American countries, the percentage of native tribes in the population varies from country to country (up to 80% in Bolivia for example).

– In Asia, the place of the ethnic minorities depends on the country: ethnic minorities are ignored in Burma, integrated in Indonesia (Javanese), assimilated in China (Tibetans and Ouzgourh), pursued in Sri Lanka (Tamils), etc. Their recognition of ethnic minorities inside the national community is most of the time limited to the protection of linguistic heritage and cultural patrimony. Their potential differences of behavior are rarely integrated in the economy.

– In sub-Saharan Africa, decolonization, with the creation of arbitrary frontiers, has generated, first, a fragmentation of some tribes into different countries and, secondly, the emergence of multiethnic countries. Some tribes have only a few thousand people (the Fons in Benin, for example), others have expanded into many countries (the Yoruba in Benin, Nigeria, etc). Whatever their importance, few of them have any real political power. Moreover, protection of the cultural and linguistic characteristics is rare.

3.4.3. *Countries with imported ethnic minorities*

The periods of industrialization in Western countries have brought waves of immigration. The first waves arrived at the beginning of the 20th century, but the number of waves has exploded in the last 30 years. The newcomers have brought with them their cultures, their religions, their education, their values and their languages.

3.4.3.1. *Integration or assimilation?*

Depending on the host country and its immigration policy, the length of stay, the level of education, the linguistic knowledge and the level of differentiation between the origin and the host countries, the immigrants are more or less integrated or assimilated. Three attitudes can be observed:

– an integration/assimilation in the host country with a rejection of the culture of origin;

– an integration with a maintenance of the values of the culture of origin, which leads to the two cultures living together;

– no integration with a maintenance of the values of the culture of origin.

Even if it seems impossible to establish an accurate mapping of the integration, we can nonetheless distinguish three types of criteria which make it possible to understand this phenomenon:

– objective socio-demographic factors of the people:

  - level of education,

  - origin language,

  - religion,

  - age when immigrated,

  - income level,

  - occupation,

  - family size,

  - level of urbanization in the country of origin.

– characteristics of the host country:

  - immigration policy,

  - quota per origin,

  - special or historic links with the country of origin.

– personal aspects.

3.4.3.2. *Ethnic marketing*

Considering the differences of behavior according to ethnic origins, some companies, always in the search of profitability, have developed specific marketing and commercial policies (products, prices, places and methods of commercialization) for these minorities.

We will analyze two different countries. Both of them have important ethnic minorities, but they have chosen different immigration and integrative policies: the USA and France.

The USA classifies all citizens by their ethnic background. Each citizen has to choose the ethnic group or groups to which they belong. Five ethnic groups are registered:

– Caucasian;

– African-American (12% of the population);

– Hispanic-American (13% of the population);

– Asian-American (6.5% of the population);

– Native-American (1% of the population).

The Caucasian population is divided into many sub-groups according to their origin, but these subdivisions, even if they contain many thousands of people, do not generate political or economic actions.

For the other minorities we can distinguish two types:

– The people born outside of, or to parents born outside of, the United States or who have recently come to the USA (Asian- and Latin-Americans). Their behaviors, values, religions, languages and consumption modes are different from the majority. Their childhood was spent outside the USA and this fact has greatly influenced their way of life or their children's way of life, even many years after their arrival in the USA. Some specific products, advertisements, places and methods of commercialization can be proposed.

– The people, mostly the African-Americans, born and raised inside the USA for many generations (95% of this community; the others came from Caribbean islands or from Africa). Their values, behaviors, religion and way of life are the same as the majority of Americans, except in relation to some cosmetic products for skin/hair. However, a specific marketing technique has been developed. It is not based on real, specific characteristics, but more on a communautarist feeling.

France is characterized by a multiethnic society based on recent or ancient waves of immigrants. The origins of these immigrants are very diverse, but we can distinguish three important groups:

– North Africans (Algerian, Moroccan, Tunisians), mostly Muslims, speaking Arabic and French;

– sub-Saharan Africans coming from West or Central Africa, Muslims or Christians, speaking their national languages and French;

– Asians who came from Vietnam, after the war in Vietnam, for political reasons, or from China during the last 10 years for economic reasons;

– other nationalities that have recently immigrated to France; for example Turkish nationals in the east of the country and more recently East Europeans with the expansion of the European Union.

Despite the existence of these ethnic minorities it seems difficult to develop an ethnic marketing in France for many reasons. First, French law does not authorize the development of advertisements targeted at specific ethnic groups and ethnic references in the census data. These minorities, as they are not concentrated in specific and geographic areas, are very hard to reach. For all these reasons, companies are still hesitant to develop special products. Only food products (eg halal food) or cosmetic products (eg skin and hair care) have benefited from these real opportunities.

3.5. Conclusion

Culture is a new factor in global marketing, not only outside country frontiers, but even within them. Even if we assist in a globalization of the economy and a multiplication of the exchanges, people maintain their differences: values, behaviors, ways of life, methods of purchase, etc. To increase their profit and to reinforce their positions, companies need to integrate these differences and to adapt their products, their prices, their commercialization, their advertisements, their strategy, etc.

The purpose of this chapter was to present different and actual cases of multiculturalism around the world. It had no ambition to be exhaustive and it needs to be verified by empirical studies. Two studies will be done during 2007 one in France, the purpose of which will be to the behavior of immigrants according to the length of time that they have been in France. The other will be undertaken in India and will analyze the behaviors of the two main communities, the Hindus and the Muslims.

3.6. References

[AJZ 80] AJZEN, I and FISHBEIN M (1980) *Understanding attitudes and predicting social behavior,* Englewood Cliffs, NY: Prentice Hall

[AJZ 88] AJZEN, I (1988) *Attitudes, personality and behavior,* New York: Dorsey Press, p 175

[DUS 83] DUSART, C (1983) *Comprendre le consommateur et stratégie marketing,* Montréal: McGraw-Hill

[FIS 75] FISHBEIN, M (1975) *Belief, attitude, intention and behavior: an introduction to theory and research,* New York: Addison Wesley Publishing Company

[GEE 73] GEERTZ, C (1973) *The interpretation of culture,* New York: Basic Books, p 5

[HEN 76] HENRY, AW (1976) "Cultural values do correlate with consumer behavior?" *Journal of Marketing Research*, 13, pp 121–27

[HOF 84] HOFSTEDE, G (1984) *Culture's consequences: international differences in work-related values*, Beverley Hills, CA: Sage Publications

[HOF 94] HOFSTEDE, G (1994) *Vivre dans un monde multiculturel: comprendre nos programmes mentaux*, Paris: Les Editions d'Organisation

[INK 69] INKELES, A and LEVINSON, D (1969) "National character, the study of modal personality and sociocultural system" in Linzey, G and Aroson, E (eds), *The Handbook of Social Psychology*, vol 4, Reading, MA: Addison Wesley

[KLU 61] KLUCKHON, E and STRODTECK, E (1961) *Variation in value orientations*, Evanston, NY: Row Peterson

[KRO 48] KROEBER, AL (1948) *Anthropology*, New York: Harcourt, Brace and World

[MUR 77] MUNSON, J and MACINTYRE, M (1977) "Personal values: a cross-cultural assessment of self values and value attributes to distant cultural stereotype" in Hunt, H (ed) *Advances in Consumer Research*, Association of Marketing Research, pp 48–52

[RIC 95] RICE, C (1995) *Consumer behaviour: behavioural aspects of marketing*, Oxford, UK: Butterworth Heinemann, pp 242–53

[ROK 73] ROKEACH, M (1973) *The nature of human values*, New York: Free Press

[TER 85] TERPSTRA, V and DAVID, K (1985) *The cultural environment of international business*, Cincinnati: South Western

[TRI 80] TRIANDIS, HC (1980) "Values, attitudes and interpersonal behaviour" in Howe, HE (ed) *Symposium on Motivation, Beliefs, Attitudes and Values*, Lincoln University of Nebraska Press, pp 195–259

[TRO 93] TROMPENAARS, T (1993) *Riding the waves of culture*, London, The Economist Books

[USU 91] USUNIER, JC (1991) "Business time perception and national cultures: a comparative survey", *Management International Review*, 31:3, pp 197–217

Chapter 4

Is Behavior Prone to Social Influence?

4.1. Introduction

The concept of "social network", a notion regularly used in the studies of the individual behavior, was borrowed from sociology. It underlines the fact that the individual is embedded in a fabric of social relations and that his behavior is appreciably prone to those. This concept, which appeared in the 1920s, ensues from works on the understanding of societies and cultures, by insisting more on the complex relations between individuals belonging to social groups and on the behaviors which ensue from this [RUM 98]. From this concept was born, some years later, the notion of "social capital", which was defined as the "reward" expected from the individual after investment in the social relations and whose behaviors belong to the value system [BOU 80; LIN 99]. In social psychology, the social influence often calls upon the concept of intermediarity which underlines the existence of individuals, with weak individual influence, but these individuals are important because of the cumulative effect [FRE 79] and its social impact which governs behaviors. Indeed, the individual is the target of a set of signals, emitted by this social unit (a compound of a multitude of individuals with weak influence); in a relative measurement, those signals finish by being considered by the individual in his decision-making process and his actual behavior. So, the concept of intermediarity underlines the cumulative character of the individual influences which, taken separately, are insufficient to urge the individual to change his position toward the decision to behave in one way or another.

Chapter written by Toufik KHARBECHE and Kaouther JELASSI.

4.2. The problem

This chapter aims to underline the importance of social influence on behavior, by stressing the social values, which are certainly subjective but which preserve all their importance in the determination of the behaviors; many sociologists agree that not all behavior is rational – far from it – and that Adam Smith's behavioral objectivity (with the theory of the "invisible hand"), centered on the self-interest of the individual, would not find its place in the very complex "social" systems; the "social vacuum/space", marking behavioral individualities, is not easily conceivable at the era of interactionism [GOR 68].

4.3. Theoretical view: a psychoanalytical "interactionist" diagram

With this intention, in this chapter we will use an interactionist diagram of reflection based on a psychoanalytical literature. The consideration of the social customs, the social standards, the codes and the beliefs is indispensable to the understanding of the behavior of the individual in his social environment; this set of elements, however subjective they are, are upstream from acting and behavior of the individual. To be interested only in the behavioral unit of the individual without referring to his culture, his direct environment and, more precisely, to the influence exerted by his social system would be equivalent to ignoring the existence of the social and environmental influence on the actual behavior of the individual; the study of the irrational social elements which compose the behavioral appreciation of the individual are undeniably a part of him and his social identity within his community "because the individual does not always behave as he would have wanted in the heart of himself" [BOU 80], particularly in the social systems which we define as "collectivists" where the social values and the culture dominate the individual in the perceptions and behaviors.

We will thus consider, in this chapter, that the behaviors are just like the social individuals and that these same behaviors are the outcome building of a sociocultural identity.

The culture is a concept which draws its origins from social sciences and the aim of which is the understanding of the social experience within a community. This community being considered as a society "in miniature" (Silverman, 1970), it holds characteristics connected to its history and to the lives of the individuals and assumes an influence on the social practices of the social group. Therefore, to mark the anchoring of the culture in its social environment, the term "sociocultural" has the role of reporting sociological phenomena which are explained by reference to the culture which prevails in the social group.

4.4. Culture in the sociological sense

In this chapter, we will retain the sociological sense of the word "culture" as defined by, amongst others, Hofstede [HOF 80]:

> The culture is a set of values and beliefs, shared by a group in its most general aspects, but being able to be supported by variations corresponding to the individual specificities, which make it possible to decide, to act or not to act. The culture thus includes an undeniable set of symbols which are at the same time explicit and implicit listed and scheduled in the mind of each group of individuals.

From a sociological point of view, culture constitutes all the material and ideological phenomena suitable/appropriate for a given group; it groups together the values, the standards and the practices acquired and shared by the members who compose the society. In this way, the sociologists recognize three essential determinants of the culture [CAP 02]: values, standards and cultural practices, which are strictly correlated because the values, which are intangible by definition, particularly take form in the concrete practices.

The values can be defined, in a given social system, as being the subjective mental capacities, accepted and wished by the members of a society. These members view these values as ideals. They appear in two ways:

– In the way of thinking, of making judgments, representations and symbols.

– In the way of acting (norms, rituals, rules, customs, religion, traditions, etc). In a society there is a whole hierarchy of federative values.

The social standards constitute an essential component of the culture. It is about rules of conduct such as the customs within a group, the laws and regulations, morals etc. All the standards are the subjects of judgments on behalf of the community; sociologists use the term "penalty" to qualify these judgments.

Rockeach [ROC 60] highlights the existence of two main categories of values: those known as "instrumental' which constitute tools pushing the individuals to resort to certain precise behaviors; for example, the moral values and the competences values; and the values known as "terminal" and which can be associated to principles. Terminal values can be subdivided into two categories:

– personal values, which arise from individual experiences and from family education (we will call this "personal identity"); and

– social values, which characterize the social systems (concerning "the social identity" through which individuals recognize their perceptions and their behavior).

4.5. Does behavior result from social identity?

"Social" identity positions the individual within his social group, place where individual functioning coordinates itself with social functioning. Social identity allows the "individual" and the "social" to be coordinated, in order to draw the behaviors and functioning of the individual in his social sphere. From a psychoanalytical point of view, Sigmund Freud [FRE 21] introduced the concept of identification to explain the existence of the emotional link to the object, or the individual. In other words, the identification can be defined as being the mental and behavioral process by which an individual develops a link with a person or a group. In this field, psychoanalysis played a significant role in considering the importance which is granted to the subjective aspects (or emotional) of the individual identity, in a social context.

4.6. Behavior and collective conscience

Durkheim [DUR 1893], through his sociological approach, was one of the pioneers on the subject of identity, in particular due to the concept of "collective conscience". We cannot speak about socialization ([WEB 46]; [PAR 51]; [BOU 80]) or about deviance ([MER 65]; [GOF 59]; [BEC 85]), without using the concept of "collective conscience".

Durkheim emphasized the increased importance of the social link and the collective conscience that he defined in the following way: "representative, cognitive and emotional state which embraces, besides the person itself, all individuals of the group, as well as the interests and the sociocultural values." Furthermore, he adds that society plays the part of an institution and defines deviance as being a wound of the collective conscience.

The concept of identification was also raised by Parsons who associated it with a cornering of the values of a model shared by the members of a social system. As the social actor is not at all individualist, not only his own interests determine his behavior but also the system of standards and federative rules.

The role can be defined as being a position or a function in the social system. Identity thus leads to the integration of the status and the roles of the individual in accordance with the status and the roles of the others who constitute his social environment.

This concept of status and roles was also addressed by Mead [MEA 34]. He developed the concept of the individual ("oneself") as being indissociably social; this concept contributed much to the development of symbolic interactionism, which consists of the analysis of interaction through behaviors known as "symbolic". The interactionist models of the social individual (or of "the social self") thus allow the determination of the importance of the exercise of the roles, an inescapable social stage for the construction of the identity and the determination of the behaviors.

4.6.1. *Social psychology*

Whereas social psychology granted more and more importance to the study of psychology in a social context, it was only with the rise of cognitive psychology that a growing interest in the study of the individual ("the self") and of his social identity was born in the 1970s.

Identity is built, defined and studied in the relationships with and the behavior towards, others. It exists only in the relationships of a subject (individual or collective) to *an another* (individual or collective) and towards an object (real or imaginary, physical or social). Identity is indissociable from social and environmental links.

The ways in which individuals and groups are defined and behave, are closely related to other individuals or the other groups in an environment. Consequently, identity can be also dreaded as a lasting process and as an unstable function due to its evolving character. Identity can then be defined as an abstract symbolic appropriation of the individual, enabling him to be defined as another (a mirror image) in an environment [BAU 88]. This definition effectively makes it possible to advance the main and constituent elements of the identity process which are the faculty to show itself, to behave, to be identified and to maintain a link and a social existence.

4.6.2. Cognitive approach of the individual: the personal and mechanical behavior of the individual

This approach was born in the USA in 1975 and developed in the 1980s as being a social cognition under the influence of cognitive psychology. It is characterized by the concept of the relatively independent individual, the social sphere being relegated to a lower level, or even eliminated (hence our interest in "the phenomenological approach of the social individual" which regards the social factors as being the cornerstone of the individual and his social identity).

In the phenomenological approach, the individual is studied using concepts drawn from cognitive psychology and introduced in the social psychology to permit the social cognition. In this approach, the individual is defined as a cognitive structure. He acts using cognitive processes dominated by individualism: the individual being seen as a schema [MAR 77] and the individual being seen as a prototype [KUI 79]. The individual is then likened to a "machine" ("the machine man") because of his individuality. His intellectual functioning and his appreciations being appropriate for an individual, his social environment, hardly influence him at all. Gordon [GOR 68] criticizes this approach as being "excessively" linear and cognitive of the individual and underlines the "social emptiness" object of this approach.

4.6.3. Phenomenological approach of the individual: individualist dominant of the behavior

The phenomenological approaches are characterized by the prevalence of the "personal" perception of the individual, without denying the existence of the social environment. [COM 59; LEC 75]. They privilege the way how the individual perceives what happens and organizes this set of perceptions in his social environment. They insist (not as much as the cognitive approach) on the central position of the individual which reflect an introspection of self. So, is the phenomenological approach characterized by the domination of the intrapersonal experience?

Phenomenological psychology is interested in the concept of the individual. It is based on his experiences, such experiences being the starting point of the phenomenal reflection.

4.6.4. *Phenomenological approach of the social individual: priority of the interests of the group*

Contrary to the two previous approaches which advance the central role of the individual, the phenomenological approach of the "social" individual insists on the prevalence of the "others" [GOR 68; ZIL 1973] in the concept of the individual.

Gordon, with the model of the "configurations of the individual", defines the individual as a structured set of perceptions linked together. These perceptions (personal, social and environmental) gradually organize themselves into a hierarchy according to the interactions tied to other mental structures (other individuals). We find in these conceptions of the individual various elements, such as:

– attributive characteristics (objective social identity, subjective social identity, etc);

– roles and memberships;

– individuality of the person.

Moscovici [MOS 70] underlines the existence and the increased weight of the social dimension which influences in an undeniable way the formation of judgment, perception and behaviors. The factor which regulates the perception and the doings of the individual is assuredly social, the "oneself" being relative to others by the existence of social relations and federative social standards of perceptions and behaviors.

4.7. Behavior: from individual identity to social identity

Identity is permanent and singular at the same time; permanent, because the identity of the individual enables him to be himself regularly. Moreover, the singularity of identity enables the individual to be single. Thus, identity is strongly correlated with individuality, in particular when we talk about individual identity (or personal identity). Nevertheless, it would be simplistic to have an endogenous vision of identity. As the individual evolves in a social context and in a given environment, his intellectual and behavioral paradigm is modulated by the relations which he maintains with others (individuals, groups). The identity of one individual and his behavior are thus dependent on his social environment.

Various currents of research in social psychology make a distinction between personal identity and social identity that constitute the cornerstone of many studies. Personal identity exists, depends on and evolves according to its position in the social sphere. This presents the problem related to the distinction between individual and social identity in studying behaviors variables.

The group and collective constructions result from psychic mechanisms of the individuals. The collective phenomena and the individual phenomena are not so different by their nature, but are different because these phenomena are carried out in a determined way within the framework of standards and rules which govern the group. From there the question of the social link and the interactionist perspective becomes crucial, which raises the relationship between the individual and his group.

As "the individual identity" and "the social identity" are two different concepts, Tajfel and Turner [TAJ 86] contend that there are undeniable links between these two concepts and a "continuum individual-group":

. – The pole relating to the individual. As individuals are defined by their interpersonal relations, the individual characteristics are not affected by their social memberships. This pole is seldom activated in the individual's social life: it is the pole of personal identity which surpass (such as we can find in the cognitive approaches).

– The social pole. Individuals exist initially through their membership in their group – not through interpersonal relations within this group, but by their relations inter-groups. It is about the social identity pole. This social identity is constructed thanks to other social groups.

As these two types of identity EW strongly connected, it appears that they evolve in a symmetrical way. Indeed, the more the social identity is present in behaviors, the less the personal identity is important and, conversely, the stronger the personal identity, the less the individual is subject to a social identity. Social identity is often a supplement when personal identity does not bring satisfaction to the individual. Finally, social identity tends to occult the personal identity and is accompanied by a disindividualization in behaviors.

4.7.1. *Covariance model*

The model of covariance nuances the binary and proportioned character of the continuum "individual-group". In this sense, Jean-Claude Deschamps [DES 87] emphasizes that sometimes the individual asserts their personal identity as well their social identity.

The covariance model establishes a certain balance of the types of identity by identifying the existence of differences intragroup (personal identity) and intergroup (social identity): "the ability of assimilation and integration (which refers to the social similarity) and the ability to be different (which corresponds to the individualism and the individual difference), presume this balance." As the balance is no perfectly proportional, one identity is stronger and dominates the other one [DES 91]. This type of "cognitive centrism" can show itself:

– either in favor of the individual's membership group which aims to value him in relation to the other groups; we referring to "sociocentrism"; or

– in favor of the self who has for objective to differ from the other members of the same group; it is about a form of "egocentricity".

Codol [COD 79] adds that by virtue of the PIP (*primus inter pares*) effect these two forms of cognitive centrism evolve in the same direction. According to him, the more the individual is bound to the standards of a group, the greater the tendency to differ from the other members of the same group. The individual looks for the most representative normative symbol, both inside and outside the group.

The model of the continuum individual-group and the model of the covariation both require the social and cognitive character of the links between personal identity and social identity. The emergence of the individual is subjected to the particular conditions of the membership group in a frame of intergroup relations.

4.7.2. *Social identity: the origin of social behavior*

Zavalloni [ZAV 84] defines social identity as the representation of the social environment, which means the various groups to which he refers (both the membership groups and the non-membership groups, more commonly called "opposition groups"). This definition differs from the design of the social identity raised by Tajfel [TAJ 86] in the processes of social categorization.

Tajfel stresses that "the social identity of an individual is related to the knowledge of its membership of certain social groups". In other words, its social identity is related to the individual conscience of belonging to a group, whereas in Zavalloni's definition, the social identity is the fact of referring to the social group (in perceptions, behaviors, etc) and of being detached from the groups at which the individual does not belong.

Zavalloni adds that social identity is the reflection of a subjective position of the individual because it is based on the individual's interests (material as wells as immaterial). This subjective position is generally strong and depends on its participative intensity within this group, which Merton [MER 65] underlined by the concept of "reference group".

As the representation of the individual is not always the image of objective social reality, Zavalloni makes a distinction between these two concepts by qualifying them respectively as "the subjective social identity" and "the objective social identity".

The objective social identity (or "social matrix") rises from the social reality, which means the various groups that the individual confronts – those with which he maintains actual relations – in other words his real social identity [GOF 59].

The subjective social identity relates to only the representations which the individual makes of these groups. Those sometimes are not identical to the objective and displayed social position of the individual.

Finally, the virtual social identity proposes the importance of appearance (in conformity with social expectations of the social group).

The appearance overrides reality; the manner overrides the deep inside and the physics overrides the personality of the individual. In this case, it is the displayed behavior of interaction which overrides the individual essence [OGI 89].

4.7.3. *Social identity and membership group*

Mead [MEA 34] raises two interesting points in the definition of the social identity. Initially, he defines the social identity as the social membership (endogenous vision), but later he widens its conceptual approach by a more exogenous view by stressing the importance of the existence of the other groups reflecting the existence of the social group of reference.

Tajfel [TAJ 86] underlines the existence of cognitive and social dimensions of identity by the process of social categorization which is the origin of the social identity theory. Categorization allows the adhesion to one of the social groups and the emergence of a social identity because categorization is the result of social environment division.

Beyond the cognitive process, categorization also constitutes a social and cultural process which results in behaviors, practices, respect of society and the social organization standards whose dichotomic categorization (behavior good/bad) enables the follow-up of the cognitive process, in the form of social rewards or sanctions and social behavioral readjustments.

The separation and the categorization of the individuals generate an increase in the similarity of those inside each category (similarity intracategory) and an increase in the difference between the categories (difference intercategory), in particular in the behaviors (and practices). It is these elements of similarity and differentiation which give place to subdivision into groups and the importance of membership in social identity definition.

4.7.4. *The social link: regulator of community behavior*

"The social link constitutes an element by which sociology tries to determine, either the fact that beforehand separate individuals can link themselves to form a community, or the fact that being linked, the individuals continue to live in common The social link is a dynamic element because of its evolutionary character" [FAR 93].

"The social links being multiple for the individual and the group in relation to his environment, the psychological and behavioral paradigm comes from the systems of values which have a certain conformity to certain social models and from the abstract contractual component of the society" [LEA 97].

The abundance of social links, variable in their intensity and evolutionary in time, testifies to the diversity of the social forms of membership to which standards and federator values of behaviors are attached.

The social link can thus be associated to a process of complex social construction and not as a factual element (which would suppose the absence of federator or generating variables).

As the study of social dimensions is inevitable, it highlights the existence of various natures of the social link: from major social relationships to more superficial relationships ([DUR 1893]; [WEB 46]; [FAR 93]; [XIB 93]; [MAR 99]). Even authors having worked on the gift paradigm ([MAU 85]; [CUR 98]; [GOD 92]) refer to the question of the nature of links in social systems. These authors distinguish the nature of the social links (deep versus superficial) depending on the existence or not of different kinds of relations like interest, reward or social recognition. Thus, does the diversity of social links of an individual lead to him the individual to go towards an independence or dependence of his behaviors?

In this same way, Granovetter [GRA 73; 82), Henning and Lieberg [HEN 96], and Kearns and Forrest [KER 00] define the "strong links" as being major relationships which bind the individual to his first environmental sphere (family, friends, etc) and as "weak links" which correspond primarily to more superficial relationships (trade, professional contacts, etc), but which are as important to the individual in the overall balance in his social environment.

Godbout [GOD 92] adds a terminological distinction to these two concepts by defining the "primary sociality" as being a social register where the person imports more than her functions (or "major relationships" such as those mentioned above) and "secondary sociality" as being a social field where the functions occupied by the individual override his person (interest relationships of a superficial nature). These two forms of sociality are accompanied respectively by two types of links: the primary link associated to the intrinsic value of the other (strong link) and the secondary link where we consider only the individual status or the functions that he occupies within his group (weak link).

4.7.5. The social status of the individual: factor of specific behaviors

We cannot ignore the influence of social status on the individual's life, on his behaviors and on his personal and collective development. The individual's social status is at the origin of a great number of choices and decisions which direct the individual's life and the life of the individual's group.

The norms that govern the stratification systems are not recognized by all. Some authors emphasize that stratification comes from conflicts between people and does not exist in well-organized systems. Conversely, other authors agree with the idea that the stratification is needed in the good working of a group, a community, or a society. They add that stratification enables the assignment important collective responsibilities to the most competitive and qualified individuals.

On this subject, Blumer [BLU 69], in "the interactionism symbolic", proposes the importance of social dimension in the analysis of behaviors and relations between the individual and his group. Blumer develops the idea according to which the interaction with others helps the formation of the individual status.

This principle, launched originally by Mead [MEA 34], constitutes a conceptual approach which helps with the comprehension of the social individual (or of the "social self"). This later is conceived as an entity closely related to the social processes. Mead considers that the individual conscience results from the social behavior while the individual organization is subordinated to the social interaction. These conscience and organization appear in the symbolic behaviors. As the social identity builds itself on federator collective values and representations through the interactions between the individual and society, we cannot ignore its evolutionary character due to communication processes. These processes, registered in time, allow the individual to position himself in his social group and to be conscious of what he is and what he represents compared to others. Finally, he is the result of the social processes [MEA 34].

4.7.6. Social status: conformist behavior – a source of social cohesion?

According to sociologists, conformist behavior of individuals ensures a certain social cohesion within the group, which exerts a pressure on its members. We cannot ignore certain social benefits related to conformism, in particular in the organization context and social structure, which thus ensures the avoidance of social anarchy and destruction of the group.

The act of conforming to the standards of its membership group (or reference group) is an active will of the individual. To achieve this goal, the individual has to show a personal, moral, or collective satisfaction.

Three cases can be underlined indeed in this way: the individual will agree to conform his behavior to the value system of his group and to the associated constraints provided that he feels that it is a potentially positive act for him (personal interest, hedonist motivation), or the conformist behavior enables him to be accepted by the others in the group (membership need), or to be respected (regard need), or it is his moral duty as an individual.

4.7.7. *Deviance facing social standards: non-conformist behavior*

Non-conformism is a concept which was raised by one of the pioneers, Thoreau [THO 1854], in the study of individual behavior with a social dimension. This concept was adopted by sociologists and known as "deviance". It means the tendency not to conform to the laws and the standards of the group and, thus, to be marginalized from the reference group or society. In other words, it means each member of society having to conform to the collective rules governing individual behavior.

To achieve its goals, society inculcates in its members codes which, for society, have an essential value for the proper functioning of the community. For this reason, the sociologist Merton stresses that "any social group has cultural objectives and the existence of coherent codes and rules, more commonly called 'the standards', is essential to get successful objectives" [MER 65].

On this subject, Lemert [LEM 72] makes a distinction between what he describes as "positive standards" and "negative standards". The purpose of the positive standards is to define what the individual must do – in particular, "positive" behaviors regarding the group vision. The negative standards draw up a framework of restrictions by indicating, to the members of the group, the prohibited behavior.

Thus, could someone note the evolution of societies, since the "Middle Age". In these societies, the "positive" standards seemed to dominate the social systems thanks to the collective interest and the social code which draws up the importance of the work and the practice of religion, etc. Conversely, we must note that modern societies mainly consist of "negative" standards because they warn individuals against behaviors that are contrary to law and to good morals, etc.

4.8. Conclusion

The majority of contemporary research agrees that identity, given by the mental structures and the psychological processes, does not have to be regarded as a substance or as an immutable attribute of the individual, but rather as a "dynamic" image of the individual (or "image of oneself") built on the interactions between individuals, groups and their ideologies.

The concept of individual identity can appear simple to define; but it is a multidimensional concept that integrates several concepts.

First, it has an objective significance. As each individual is unique because of his genetic makeup, intellectual inheritance, etc, the identity of the individual is characterized by his behavioral singularity.

However, identity also has a more subjective direction because it is built on collective representations: the similarities and the social behaviors which we find in any social group. This semantic paradox denounces a certain form of contradiction which characterizes identity. Identity can, at the same time, be single (because each individual has his own particular behavior) and similar to others (common and shared system of values). In other words, the identity of each individual is made up of a contradictory set of singular individuality and, at the same time, social individuality. For this reason, social psychology shows us that identity is built in an opposite movements of assimilation/differentiation and identification/distinction compared to others.

The individual builds his identity gradually, through a long process. His image, his beliefs and representations of self constitute a psychological structure which is used by him as a reference in his behavior and in his social roles. Identity construction is thus a major progressive stage in the life of the individual and his environment.

The work of social psychology on the topic of identity development and the study of subjective behaviors contends that identity is not a factual element, but a process.

Lipianski [LIP 91] adopts this principle in the study of individual behavioral identity by emphasizing the progressive character of this "non-linear" concept (because it is marked by rupture, crisis, reaffiliation, etc.). This principal was also developed by L'Ecuyer [LEC 75], who indicated that identity construction – the basis of the behavior – is carried out by successive stages in the confrontation of the individual with his social environment. This identity construction – mixing the cognitive aspects, affects and social interactions – is the result of behavioral and similarity difference.

4.9. References

[BAU 88] BAUGNET, L (1988) "Sentiments d'appartenances et representations" in *l'Identité politique*, CURAPP, PUF, Paris

[BEC 85] BECKER, H (1985), *Outsiders. Etudes de sociologie de la deviance*, Paris: Métailié

[BEN 06] BENNAMA, M (2006), *Psychologie sociale de Boukerche et du Javelot*, Ed. Paris: Bonneuil

[BLU 69] BLUMER, H (1969), *Symbolic Interactionism: Perspective and Method*, Englewood Cliffs, NJ: Prentice Hall

[BOU 80] BOURDIEU, P (1980), "Le capital social: Notes provisoires", *Actes de la Recherche en Sciences Sociales* 3

[CAP 02] CAPUL, JY and GARNIER, O (2005) *Dictionnaire d'économie et de sciences sociales*, Paris : Hatier

[COD 79] CODOL, JP (1979) "Semblables et différents : recherches sur la quête de la similitude et de la différenciation sociale", Doctorate thesis, Aix en Provence, Université de Provence

[COM 59] COMBS, AW and SNYGG, D (1959) *Individual Behavior* (revised edn), New York: Harper & Row

[CUR 98] CURD, M and COVER, JA (1998), "The problem of justification", in Curd, M and Cover, JA (eds) *Philosophy of Science:*, New York: The Central Issues

[DES 87] DESCHAMPS, JC (1987) "Social and personal identity: analysis of some theoretical models", *Social Identity Conference*, University of Exeter

[DES 91] DESCHAMPS, JC (1991) "Identité et processus socio-cognitifs", Università di Napoli, Facoltà di Lettere e Filosofia, Napoli

[DUR 1893] DURKHEIM, E (1893) "Représentations individuelles et représentations collectives", in *Sociologie et Philosophie*, Paris: PUF

[FAR 93] FARRUGIA, F (1993), "La crise du lien social, essai de sociologie critique", Paris: L'Harmattan

[FRE 21] FREUD, S (1921) "L'inconscient", in Freud, S, *Métapsychologie*, Paris: Gallimard

[FRE 79] FREEMAN, L (1979), "Centrality in social networks – conceptual clarification", *Social Networks* 1

[GOD 92] GODBOUT, JT (1992) "L'esprit du don", Paris: La Découverte

[GOF 59] GOFFMAN, E (1959) "La mise en scène de la vie quotidienne, présentation de soi", Ed. Paris: *De minuit*

[GOR 68] GORDON, C and GERGEN, K (1968) *Self-Conceptions, Configurations of Content*, New York: Wiley

[GRA 73] GRANOVETTER, MS (1973) "The strength of weak ties", *American Journal of Sociology*, vol 78, no 6, May 1973, pp 1360–380

[GRA 82] GRANOVETTER, MS (1982) "The strength of weak ties: a network theory revisited", in Marsden, PV and Lin, L (eds) *Social Structure and Network Analysis*, Beverley Hills: Sage Publications

[HEN 96] HENNING, C and LIEBERG, M (1996) "Strong ties or weak ties? Neighbourhood networks in a new perspective", *Scandinavian Housing & Planning Research* 13, pp 3–26

[HOF 80] HOFSTEDE, G (1980) *Culture's Consequences: International Differences in Work-Related Values*, Beverley Hills, Sage Publications

[KEA 00] KEARNS, A and FORREST, R (2000) "Social cohesion and multilevel urban governance" *Urban Studies*, 37 (5–6), pp 995–1017

[KUI 79] KUIPER, NA and ROGERS, TB (1979), "Encoding of personal information: self-other differences", *Journal of Personality & Social Psychology* 37, pp 499-514

[LEA 97] LEANDRO, ME (1997) *Le lien social dans la pensée sociologique classique*, Paris, L'Harmattan, pp 41–54

[LEC 75] L'ECUYER, R (1975) *Genèse du concept de soi*, Naaman: Sherbrooke

[LEM 72] LEMERT, EM (1972) *Human Deviance, Social Problems, and Social Control*, New Jersey: Prentice-Hall Inc

[LIN 99] LIN, N (1999) "Building a network theory of social capital", *Connections* 22 (1)

[LIP 91] LIPIANSKI, EM (1991) *Représentations sociales et idéologies*, DelVal, Switzerland

[MAR 77] MARKUS, H (1977) *The Cognitive Perspective in Social Psychology*, New York: Random House

[MAR 99] MARTUCELLI, D (1999) "Sociologie de la modernité", *Gallimard,* Paris

[MAU 85] MAUSS, M (1985), "Sociologie et anthropologie", PUF, no 58, Paris

[MEA 34] MEAD, GH (1934), "L'Esprit, le soi et la société", PUF, Paris

[MER 65] MERTON, RK (1965) *Social Theory and Social Structure*, New York: Free Press

[MOS 70] MOSCOVICI, S (1970) "La psychanalyse, son image et son public", PUF, Paris

[OGI 89] OGIEN, A (1989) "La décomposition du sujet", in Joseph, I, *et al.* (eds.) *Le parler frais d'Erving Goffman*, Paris: Editions de Minuit

[PAR 51] PARSONS, T (1951) *The Social System*, New York: Free Press

[ROC 60] ROCKEACH, M (1960) *The Open and Closed Mind*, New York: Basic Books

[RUM 98] RUMSEY, D (1998) "Connecting the past with the present: on ties to the early years of social network research", *Connections* 21(1)

[SIL 70] SILVERMAN, D (1970) *The Theory of Organizations*, London: Heinemann Educational Books

[TAJ 86] TAJFEL, H and TURNER, JC (1986) "The social identity theory of inter-group behavior", in Worchel, S and Austin, LW (eds), *Psychology of Intergroup Relations*, Chicago: Nelson-Hall

[THO 1854] THOREAU, HD (1854) "Walden, or a life in the woods", reprinted in Thomas, O (ed) (1966) *Walden and Civil Disobedience*, New York: W. W. Norton

[WEB 46] WEBER, M (1946), *Essays in Sociology*, Oxford: Oxford University Press, pp 77–128

[XIB 93] XIBERRAS, M (1993) "Les modèles sociaux de la solidarité", Colloque de l'Institut International de Sociologie (IIS, San Diego), Paris-Sorbonne

[ZAV 84] ZAVALLONI, M and LUIS GUERIN, C (1984) *Identité sociale et conscience*, Montréal and Toulouse: Presses Universitaires de Montréal-Privat

[ZIL 73] ZILLER, RC (1973) *The Social Self*, Oxford: Pergamon Press

PART 2

Applications at the National Level

Chapter 5

The Gender Approach to Understanding Time-Saving Durables Buying: Tunisian Women in 2000

5.1. Introduction

The evolution of the roles of men and women, a social and cultural fact, inevitably has implications on consumption behavior. Indeed, the arrival of women on the labor market obviously modified their household-management practices. Currently, one sees a true metamorphosis of the gender ideologies by the confusion and the reduction of the distinction of the roles achieved by men and women. This social, economic and psychological revolution gave birth to the analyses and research on the influence of gender on consumption. During the 1960s, researchers in marketing studied the impact of gender roles and their distribution on purchasing behaviors and strategies.

The research on the gender differences of purchasing behaviors is old, but it is only in the past 10 years that gender was applied when studying these differences. The few studies of the influence of gender on the behavior of the consumer analyzed the social and political implications on consumption marked by the gender in relation to topics of the capacity within households, communities and society in general [EDI 2000].

Chapter written by Rafika BEN GUIRAT.

This chapter does not fit into the field of gender-distribution research on the roles which rests on the male-female relationship, but rather in fields of research on gender and women's purchasing behavior. The most important current research on the concept of gender in marketing is interested in the influence of gender on behavior in relation to consumption, more specifically on the analysis of the evolution of women's purchasing behavior.

The gender roles are connected to the variations of influence in the decisions in relation to purchases, the allocation of the tasks, in relation to the responsibilities for purchasing and household life. A revolution in the gender roles implies a revolution in the models of consumption. However, to date, marketing research is sometimes obsolete in its vision of the woman as the consumer. Marketing researchers continue paradigms in relation to decision-making which do not make it possible to understand certain phenomena, however obvious, as the influence of the social change on the behavior of consumption of women.

The poor specification of the framework of analysis and the assumptions of research questioning shows that the field of consumer research is dominated by a male perspective, thus running the risk of ignoring the interests of women.

Thompson, Heisley and Holmes stress that the social context must be studied to obtain a better comprehension of the interaction between gender and consumption, thus making it possible to better understand women's behavior [THO 92: 3–18]. Before social change, a new paradigm appeared demanding new methods and new procedures. These researchers use an interdisciplinary feminist approach which is based on the ideology of gender. It is possible to recognize the social revolution and to wonder about its implications in changes of women's behavior.

In Tunisian society, the change of orientation is significant for women, as well for the level of the future consumption. Today, a large majority of Tunisian women carry out more than two lives between their work, the education of the children and the life of the household. The revolution induced a new structure of the roles, but the segregation of the roles and the gender-based division of work still persists. Indeed, women always carry many constraints – moral, social and temporal.

Time becomes a key factor in the organization of their life and new time-saving technologies are needed to help women discharge their responsibilities. The evolution of the role of women created a need for new time-saving durable goods and new services that were better adapted to their way of life.

This chapter is a contribution to the analysis of the purchasing behavior of the Tunisian woman in a context marked by a social change through a new framework of analysis. It attempts to answers the following questions:

1. Does not considering gender make it possible to better understand the purchasing behavior of women?

2. Does not the gender ideology of the Tunisian woman determine its purchasing behavior, for example, through the choice of the time saving device (TSD)?

3. Would not a woman supporting a modern gender ideology be more inclined to develop an attitude favorable to the TSD?

In this chapter, we have two aims:

– to highlight the relevance of the prospect for gender in the analysis of the purchasing behavior of women; and

– to explore, envisage and compare the determinants of the intention to purchase TSD for each group of women.

In response to the objectives of the research, two general assumptions were developed:

– the gender ideology of the Tunisian women makes it possible to explain their purchase;

– the explanatory variables of the purchase intention of the TSD differ according to women's behavior.

In a first part of this chapter, we will try to understand the gender approach in marketing

5.2. Gender approaches in marketing

In marketing, many researches on gender were developed from a feminist point of view. From this perspective, American feminists employed gender. All the feminist approaches recognize the impact of economics, teaching, the media and the family. In the exploration of the topic of gender, women had more influence of research on consumer behavior than in any other subcategory of marketing [COS 00: 95-97].

It is by this permanent interaction that the gender is built [TIS 02: 55-69].

Gender stresses the relational aspect of the normative definitions of femininity. It is used to mean that female thought can transform the disciplinary paradigms.

Bristor and Fischer [BRI 93] adopt a feminist prospect to criticize scientific objectivity and the theoretical approaches in the behavior of the consumer by underlining the objectivity generated by the male approaches. Bristor considers that consumer research largely ignored women [BRI 93].

The critical discussion of consumer research, in light of the feminist theories, identified several false assumptions which are anchored. The several false assumptions which are based on stereotypes and relations of the traditional gender marketing research on consumers (where only the man is the economic provider and the woman must perform her roles in the household, etc) leads to two situations:

1. Research questions do not suitably reflect in the interests of women.

2. The distortion of research results, such as concluding that there is no relation between the remunerated work of the woman and the purchase of the TSD.

To understand and analyze the purchasing behavior of women, Roberts and Wortzel note the importance of a multidimensional approach which allows for the multiple facets of the attitudes and behaviors of the current market rather than a simple neutral analysis of women who work outside the home and housewives [ROB 79: 28–39]. Only analyzing the one-dimensional role of women is likely to lead to unimportant correlations and/or false conclusions.

The determining factors of the purchasing behavior of women are divided into socio-demographic factors and ideological factors. In this chapter, we propose to study the impact of work and the economic situation of the household and the ideological variables. We will analyze the influence of the attitudes of Tunisian women with regard to feminism, status, autonomy, male-female ratios, remunerated work and housework on the intention to purchase the TSD.

5.2.1. *Gender orientation of the roles/ideology of gender*

The debate on the roles of the sexes is connected to the change of roles of women in the household, work and society. Usually, one speaks about the attitudes towards the roles of the sexes or the ideology of gender roles. This ideology is the result of intensive socialization by parents, teachers and all of society.

Gender orientation of the roles refers to the adoption of male and female characteristics on certain occasions. Gender becomes a variable of personality and can be regarded as the "total filter through which the individuals discover their social environment" [BRI 93: 18-36]. The theories on family roles reveal that gender roles differ between couples where the man and the woman both work outside the home and couples where only the man occupies a position outside the home. It is then obvious that the socialization of the gender role contributes to a differentiation in the behavior of the man and the woman in the household or other situations.

The orientations or the preferences of the roles of the sexes appear during adulthood and are influenced by marriage (domestic tasks, remunerated work performed by women, etc). These preferences in turn influence and determine (without forgetting the tangible variables such as intangible resources and variables such race and age) the decision-making processes [SCA 80: 743–756]. They influence the roles in the household, such as financial resources management, the performance of household tasks and the purchasing process [KIM 93: 52–59].

Several research projects studied the relation between the roles of the sexes and the purchasing process for durable products as well as for nondurable products. They revealed that the traditional models of decision-making are insufficient for understanding the purchasing decisions and behaviors of households. According to many feminists, the absence of a relationship between the remunerated work of women and the purchase of the TSD is simply due to the fact that the assumptions of the model are traditional.

Certain researchers were interested in the analysis of the consequences of changes in the gender roles on the decision-making processes. Others stressed the effects of the gender orientation of the roles on the strategies and the models of consumption. Some researchers have suggested that constructs of attitudes are more relevant than the professional status of the woman to explain her purchasing behavior [ORO 93: 567–80].

The changes that marked the roles of women greatly influenced gender relations. They were at the same time stimulative and alarming. The change of orientation is not without implications for marketing, products and the reasons for consumer purchases. Marketing researchers agree that the changes of roles led to substantial changes in the models of purchasing behavior. Thus, in the case of durable purchases, they stress the importance of gender by confirming the influence of gender orientation on the roles in the decision-making process in relation to household purchases. Women who choose a modern orientation are naturally different in their lifestyles and their purchasing behavior, so the researchers must explain the change of attitudes by the introduction of new products which go with these changes (for example, time-saving goods) and by repositioning existing products.

Green and Cunningham showed differences in contributions for the groups of women (liberal, moderate and traditional) in the case of domestic machines [GREE 96: 85-95]. Roberts and Wortzel note that it is necessary to approach contemporary women through the attraction of saving time, which explains women's tendency to adopt the TSD [ROB 79: 28–39]. Venkatesh, for her part, found that, generally, American women do not consider the TSD to be essential [VEN 80: 189–97]. However, traditional women show a greater appreciation for washing machines. Bristor and Fisher confirm that if the woman who works outside the home does not buy more TSDs than the housewives, it is because they try to satisfy the social role in accordance with the standards of society [BRI 93: 18-36]. It should be expected that women buy these goods whatever their occupation. For Firat [FIR 96: 78-81], for women do not produce but consume, the TSD in a traditional gender ideology. Women consume more of these products and undertake the physical pressure of housework and the purchasing decisions [FIR 96: 378–81]. Women, as they have important family roles, are more likely to buy the TSD [JOA 91: 666–72].

5.2.2. Women's remunerated work

The change of lifestyles and models of consumption due to women's remunerated work greatly motivated marketing researchers such as Strober and Weinberg, Bartos, Reilly and Oropesa to design, examine, interpret and revise the models which explain the manner in which women's work and occupation influence their purchasing behavior [STR 77: 141–47]. Work determines the income and the level of household consumption and naturally influences the choice of products.

Sociologists say that the paid activity of women cannot be dissociated from her family and society. Through the gender role model, women's remunerated work is perceived as the final link in a causal chain in which socialization leads to the development of a leveling ideology which replaces the traditional division of the responsibilities within the household [POT 93: 548–58].

Generally, marketing researchers did not succeed in finding a significant relationship between women's remunerated work and the purchase and possession of durable goods. Many of them confirm this link. Two general assumptions underline the work on the relationship between women's remunerated work and the purchase of durable goods. Argawala and Drinkwater, along with Mincer, suggest that a large proportion of women's income is regarded as transient if the women's work is regarded as secondary in the household and that the income of the man is more important than that of the woman [ARD 72: 89–96]. In this case, women tend to save their proportion of the income or to use it to purchase durable goods (which is regarded as a form of saving). The second assumption, advanced by Gabraith and Becker, who base themselves on the household production approach, concludes that the durable goods and the time that women devote to the housework are complementary [GAL 96]. Women who work devote less time (or less interest) to household purchases than housewives. They then buy fewer TSD "wife-operated-and-maintained machines" [GAL 73]. As women's remunerated work becomes increasingly important, the assumption of the household production approach becomes more common.

The results of Bryant's empirical study showed a negative and significantly different impact [BRY 88: 37–47]. Women who spend more time in remunerated work spend less time in domestic activities. Time and goods are complementary and do not act as a substitute for each other. This result contradicts research that concluded that women's time and the possession of TSDs are substitutes. It also rejects the suggestion that there is no relation between women's remunerated work and expenditure on durable goods. Indeed, several researchers stress that women's remunerated work does not determine important decisions about the purchase of and expenditure on, TSDs [STR 77: 141–47]. The purchase of these goods depends more on factors like the age of the product, the income of the family and the type of work performed by the woman. Moreover, these researchers confirm that there are no significant differences between women who work outside the home and housewives in relation to the expenditure on TSDs if the income, goods and other variables are constant.

Strober and Weinberg note that neither women's remunerated work nor their entry in the market constitute significant determinants for the purchase and possession of TSDs, such as microwaves and dishwashers [STR 77: 141–47]. It should be noted on the other hand that the scarcity of time among women who work can indirectly influence their purchases and expenditure. The expenditure on durable goods and the time that woman devote to the household are substitutes for each other. In other words, the more the woman works, the more she tends to spend on durable goods.

Many studies on household durable goods suggest that income and possession of durable goods are related. However, a French study showed that this is true up to a certain income level above which the rate of possession tends to reach a maximum, especially in the case of televisions and washing machines: "income does not explain all then!" Certain researchers wonder about the lack of existence of a relationship between the status of women's work and the purchase of TSDs. According to McCall, the request for services and the suitability of products are in direct proportion to the entry of women into the labor market [MCC 77: 55–65]. When women work, there is a certain replacement of the time devoted to the household by products and services. Herpin notes that the women who work outside of the home buy more equipment and services to save time than the others [HER 80: 599–628]. Thus, women have the additional income necessary to acquire the goods and they make up for part of the time that a woman would otherwise devote to the household tasks.

Oropesa stresses that the studies carried out did not confirm the assumption that there is no relationship between women's remunerated work and the purchase of TSDs [ORO 93]. For households where the woman works outside of the home, time constraints cause the need to buy TSDs. Reilly concludes that the woman who works outside of the home buys more TSDs because, on one hand, she has the means with which to buy them and, on the other hand, because of the pressures of housework additional to her role outside of the home [REI 82: 407-418].

5.3. Housework

Most women (whether they work outside of the home or not) take care of the home, the education and the socialization of the children. This reality is not without implications for women's purchasing behavior.

The sociological approach is an alternative to the economic approach which failed to explain the inequality of the allocation of the domestic tasks [GRE 96: 585-95]. Mederer has advanced a new definition of housework which binds the housework to the stratification of gender in society [MED 93: 133-45]. She conceptualizes housework as all of the activities of the household (such as laundry and cooking), of the house (such as cleaning and maintenance) and of the transactional tasks (such as the making of medical appointments and the payment of bills).

The perception of the scarcity of time that faces the woman who has a double working-day led to the development of the concept of "the purchase of time by the consumer". This concept leads automatically to the idea of "saving time" by allocating time effectively between the various activities or by substituting products and services for the lack of time.

Often marketing research does not regard housework as an explanatory variable in the issue of purchasing of TSDs. The possession (and not the use) of time-saving apparatuses does not significantly affect the time devoted to the domestic tasks. Nicols and Fox concluded that women who work tend to reduce the time allocated to domestic tasks rather than buying TSDs [NIC 83: 197–208]. For Verger, domestic machines assist the housewife in the majority of her daily tasks, but the possession of such machines always depends on the income and the size of the household. However, certain researchers, such as Rubin, Riney and Molina, showed the tendency of women to reduce the quantity of housework and to replace it by products and services [RUB 90: 43–53]. Soberon, Ferrer and Dardis stress that time determines the household expenses on durable goods and that is what explains the differences in the models of expenditure of women who work outside the home and housewives [SOB 91: 385–396]. Ferber and Birnbaum state that the best solution to combat the disadvantages of women's remunerated work (thus with the pressure of time) is to reduce the hours of the household tasks [FER 80: 263–71]. Thompson and Walker say that the new tendency to use TSDs emerges mainly from the new design of housework [THO 95: 847–65]. They advance the proposition that a change of the roles of men and women is favorable to the adoption of TSDs in order to reduce the weight of domestic tasks.

5.4. Assumptions of the research

Explanatory variables		Scientific assumptions
F1: Feminism – women's remunerated work	H1	The more this attitude is favorable, the more the probability of choice of TSDs is high
F2: Feminism – birth control	H2	The more this attitude is favorable, the more the probability of choice of TSDs is high
RAHM: differences between men and women	H3	The more women have a modern orientation with regard to their relationship with men, the more they buy TSDs
Auno: request autonomy	H4	The more dependent women are, the less they adopt TSDs
ST: social and professional status	H5	The more the woman realizes her underprivileged situation, the more the probability of choosing a TSD is high
D1: Domestic work is a burden	H6	The more a woman perceives housework as a form of exploitation, the more the probability of choosing a TSD
D2: Division of domestic work	H7	The more the woman wants the participation of her husband in the domestic tasks, the more the probability of choice of the TSD increases

Research methodology

By adopting the gender approach as the framework for the analysis of this work, we conceptualized the TSD purchase intention model. The objective was to show the most significant determinant factors.

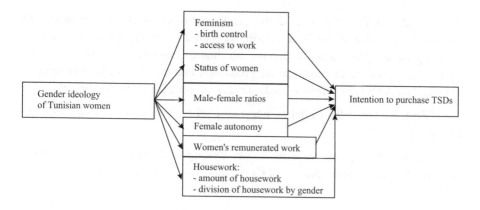

Figure 5.1. *Model forecasting the intention to purchase TSDs*

The quality of each factor was evaluated through Churchill's paradigm (Appendix: Note 3).

Within the framework of an exploratory analysis of the model, we started by specifying the groups of women who emerged.

A typological analysis made it possible to retain four homogenous groups of women.

The "family addicted" women	They strongly believe in the importance of the household and reject the participation of their husbands in household activities.
The resigned women	They do not believe that housework is a form of slavery and refuse to share the domestic tasks with their husbands even if the women carry out their underprivileged situation.
The consensual women	They do not carry out most of the housework, but approve of sharing the task with their husbands.
The "avant-gardist" women	They regard housework as the most modern form of exploitation and require the assistance of their husband in the drudgery.

To highlight the relevance of the gender approach in the understanding of purchasing behavior of Tunisian woman, we showed how the variables of gender ideology make it possible to forecast the intention to purchase TSDs. We proceeded by logistic regression to determine the probability and the force of each variable to explain the intention to purchase TSDs and did this for each group of women:

1. First, we tested the model by integrating all the variables of gender ideology (Table 5.1).

2. In the second phase, we used the step-by-step method to retain only the most significant variables in the process of choosing TSDs (Table 5.2).

Complete mode	"Family addicted" Women	Resigned women	Consensual women	"Avant-gardist" women
coefficients	ST $\beta = 1.41$ wald = 10.83 E $\beta = 4.10$ D1 $\beta = -0.87$ wald = 3.42 E $\beta = 0.41$ D2 $\beta = 1.41$ wald = 10.83 E $\beta = 4.10$	F2 $\beta = 0.660$ wald = 5.190 E $\beta = 1.935$ RHM $\beta = 0.458$ wald = 3.020 E $\beta = 1.582$ ST $\beta = 0.672$ wald = 8.121 E $\beta = 1.96$		F1 $\beta = -22.9$ F2 $\beta = -70.8$ D1 $\beta = 0.856$ wald = 1.455 E $\beta = 2.354$
Indicator of adjustment	χ^2 model = 0.045 χ^2 HL = 0.104 83.16%	χ^2 model = 0.00 χ^2 HL = 0.1140 78.72%	χ^2 model = 0.45 χ^2 HL = 0.165 78.52%	χ^2 model = 0.074 χ^2 HL = 0.201 94.41%

Table 5.1. *Model forecasting the intention to purchase TSDs*

Step-by-step model	"Family addicted" women	Resigned women	Consensual women	"Avant-gardist" women
Coefficients	ST $\beta = 1.592$ $-2LR = 14.222$ D1 $\beta = -1.025$ $-2LR = 4.923$ D2 $\beta = 0.699$ $-2LR = 7.759$	F2 $\beta = 0.653$ $-2LR = 5.55$ RHM $\beta = 0.573$ $-2LR = 5.154$ AUNO $\beta = -0.362$ $-2LR = 3.086$ ST $\beta = 0.610$ $-2LR = 8.685$	AUNO $\beta = -0.544$ $-2LR = 3.347$	F1 $-2LR = 4.851$ F2 $-2LR = 5.716$ D1 $\beta \beta = 1.407$ $-2LR = 4.066$
Indicator of adjustment	χ^2 model = 0.00 χ^2 HL = 0.10 83%	χ^2 model = 0.00 χ^2 HL = 0.13 77.78%	χ^2 model = 0.06 χ^2 HL = 0.49 77.69%	χ^2 model = 0.013 χ^2 HL = 0.7658 94.85%

Table 5.2. *Model forecasting the intention to purchase TSDs: analysis method*

5.4.1. *"Family addicted" women*

Among "family addicted" women we recorded the variables of status, amount of housework and the division of domestic labor as the most significant determinants of the intention to purchase TSDs. The results of the logistic regression show that the more the "family addicted" woman refuses the domestic assistance of her husband, the more the probability of choosing TSDs increases. The perception of the status of women also maintains a significant and positive effect on the probability of choosing TSDs with $\beta = 1.592$ and $p = 0.00$. Nevertheless, the more the "family addicted" woman does not regard housework as a form of slavery, the less she will plan to buy these goods (Table 5.1). The method, which retains only the variables judged as most significant, confirmed the importance of the variables of status, amount of housework and the division of the housework by gender to a threshold of significance of 0.05. The matrix also shows the capacity of these variables to propose more than 83% in terms of intention to purchase TSDs. The results confirm a strong positive association between the status variable and the positive attitude toward TSD variable. In addition, the refusal to divide the domestic tasks with her husband significantly increases the probability that a woman intends to purchase TSDs. The women in this group substitute these goods for their husband's domestic participation. However, the women in this group would not choose TSDs as a means of avoiding the oppression of housework (Table 5.2).

5.4.2. Resigned women

Each of these three variables (control birth, unprivileged status, male-female inequalities) is presented with a positive β (respectively: 0.66, 0.46 and 0.67) and a threshold of significance lower than 0.10. The impact of the status of women is most significant. A unit increase in this variable multiplies its effect by 2 (Exp $\beta = 1.96$) (Table 5.1). The step-by-step method improved the forecast of the intention to purchase TSD (93.68%). The results confirmed the intervention of the variables raised by the Wald method. The resigned women's negative perception of their autonomy plays a part in the forecast of their intention to purchase TSDs to a significance of 0.10 and about β −0.36. There are reservations about this result because the variable of autonomy arises with a threshold of Log R = 0.08 higher than the recommended limit (0.05) (Table 5.2).

5.4.3. Consensual women

First, the logistic regression revealed a problem with the model's specification. None the variables are able to predict the intention of the group of consensual women to purchase a TSD (Table 5.1). The step-by-step method made it possible to correct the model. Using the Wald criteria, the autonomy variable is the only one likely to predict the intention of this group to purchase TSDs. A weak association can be seen starting from the examination of the total model where we located very low coefficients of determination (lower than 0.05). This model has a relatively good predictive capacity (77.69%) and shows that the autonomy variable makes it possible to predict 100% of the positive attitudes to these goods. The more dependent the consensual woman is, the less she tends to choose TSDs ($\beta = -0.54$; p = 0.07; Exp $\beta = 0.058$). As we noted, the autonomy variable can predict the intention to purchase TSDs (Log R = 0.06) (Table 5.2).

5.4.4. *"Avant-gardist" women*

Among "avant-gardist" women, the adjustment of our model forecasting the intention to purchase TSDs notes a poor impact but it showed that two dimensions of feminism and the amount of housework make it possible to predict the intention to purchase TSDs. The variables of feminism (F1 and F2) influence the intention to purchase TSDs (Log R are respectively 0.027 and 0.017), but we did not succeed in evaluating either the force or the direction of their impact. For the amount of housework variable, the coefficients logit (β) and Log R show that the more women compare housework to a form of exploitation, the greater the probability that they will choose TSDs; β is ($\beta = 1.40$; $p = 0.04$; Log R $= 0.04$) (Table 5.2).

5.5. Summary of results

In this research, we corroborated some scientific assumptions through the four groups of Tunisian women.

For the "family addicted" women, three variables of the gender ideology determine the intention to purchase TSDs. Thus, the more favorable the attitude of the "family addicted" woman to her situation, the greater the probability that she will choose these goods. Our research did not check H5. In this group (where the family objectives are important) we confirm the conclusions of Bristor and Fischer [BRI 93]. Moreover, the more the "family addicted" woman does not consider housework to be a form of exploitation, the probability of her choosing TSDs decreases. This woman assumes the entire responsibility for domestic tasks. She refuses TSDs. Lastly, the more the attitude of the "family addicted" woman is unfavorable to the division of domestic labor, the greater the probability that she will adopt TSDs. We did not check H7. The only objective for women who choose TSDs is to avoid the pressure of housework. This result confirms the assumption of Thompson and Walker that the woman does not adopt TSDs when she supports a traditional gender ideology [THO 95].

Regarding resigned women, we find that the more the resigned woman does not believe in the intervention of feminism in birth control, the greater the probability of her choosing TSDs. We did not check H2. In addition, the more the resigned woman disagrees with the idea that the male-female ratios are discriminatory, the greater the probability that she will choose TSDs. We did not check H3. Resigned women choose goods which preserve family comfort like the TSD to show that they react in accordance with traditional values of society. Moreover, the more the resigned woman is unhappy with her status, the greater the probability that she will choose TSDs. H5 is selected. Resigned women are devoted to their families and carry a heavy load of many roles. Consequently, they desire TSDs. Lastly, the more the resigned woman is unhappy with her autonomy, the greater the probability of that she will choose TSDs. H4 is selected. When the resigned woman is happy with her dependence on a man, she also appreciates her superiority in decision-making processes such as purchasing decisions. She will be the only one to make decisions in relation to purchases. This result shows that even if resigned women support traditional roles, they do not reject modern products. This confirms the reflection of Venkatesh stipulating that traditional women appreciate the advantages of the TSD [VEN 80].

Among consensual women, many of them are unhappy with autonomy and they are less likely to choose TSDs. H4 is selected. These women give their husbands the responsibility for the purchase of TSDs.

We find that the variable of feminism is determinant only for the avant-gardist group of women. Another result revealed that the more the avant-gardist woman believes that housework is a form of exploitation, the greater the probability that she will choose TSDs. H6 is selected. The avant-gardist woman refuses to assume the responsibility for the housework. Thus, she chooses TSDs as the solution. For avant-gardist women, TSDs make it possible to reduce the housework burden [THO 95]. On the other hand and contrary to the views of Roberts and Wortzel [ROB 97: 28–39], we did not note that saving time was important for these contemporary women.

These results reveal the relevance of gender ideology in the analysis of the purchasing behavior of women. The variables of gender ideology intervene in the forecasts of the intention to purchase TSDs, which corroborates the third general assumption.

From these results we also deduced that the explanatory variables of the intention to purchase TSDs vary according to gender ideologies of the groups of women. For each type of gender ideology there is a particular process of purchase. Indeed, the variable of the status of women justifies the TSD choice in the first two groups of women, but not for the same reasons. If TSD preserve the objectives of the family and/or support an image of modernism among "family addicted" women, they seem to bring comfort to resigned women. Moreover, housework is as significant for "family addicted" women as it is for "avant-gardist" women. If "family addicted" women do not choose TSDs in order to avoid the pressure of housework tasks, they accept them as a substitute for the participation of their husbands in this activity. The "avant-gardists" choose TSDs only to avoid lessening the demands of housework. The differences in gender ideologies show that Tunisian women do not all choose TSD for the same reasons, which confirms the fourth general assumption.

Finally, we recorded that, overall, all Tunisian women appreciate the benefits of TSDs whatever their gender ideology. Liberal women are not the only ones to develop a favorable attitude towards the purchase of TSDs. There is an inconsistency between women's gender ideologies and their intentions to purchase TSDs, which infirm the general hypothesis. If a Tunisian woman holds a modern gender ideology, it does not imply an intention to purchase TSDs.

5.6. Conclusion

This research tries, in its exploratory aspect, to analyze certain features of the changing roles of women and their significance for consumer research. It enabled us to show differences in the factors that influence the intention to purchase TSDs among Tunisian women.

This research is of great interest. It provided implications, as well as limits, thus paving the way for future research. On the theoretical level, this work showed the range of gender approaches. The research makes it possible to design a model rich in latent variables, providing a robust theoretical basis for the development of theories on women's purchasing behavior.

On the methodological level, this work also enabled the construction of forecasting models of intention to purchase TSD, thus creating an advantageous empirical base for consumer research.

On the managerial side, this research encourages experts to consider the variables of gender ideology as reliable. Women are new targets for companies in search of new consumer sectors. Marketers must carry out differences among women related to their gender ideology with the objective of enabling them to offer products which appeal to the interests of women. Nevertheless, some limits mark this research.

On the methodological side, we emphasize the absence of longitudinal-type studies and qualitative or experimental approaches as recommended by certain researchers (Bartos [BAR 77]). Future research will need to extend and transcribe the results of the logistic regression in other cultural contexts to be sure of their validity in time and space.

5.7. References

[ARG 72] ARGWALA, R and DRINKWATER, J (1972) "Consumption functions with shifting parameters due to socio-economic factors", *Review of Economics and Statistics*, no 75, pp 89–96

[BAR 77] BARTOS, R (1977) "The moving target: the impact of women's employment on consumer behavior", *Journal of Marketing*, no 41, pp 31–37

[BEC 65] BECKER, GS (1965) "A theory of allocation of time", *The Economic Journal*, vol 75, no 299, pp 493–517

[BER 00] BERGADAA, M (2000) "La mutation de la recherche en marketing: l'analyse du genre comme exemple", *Décisions Marketing*, no 20, pp 23–34

[BLA 92] BLAIR, S and JOHNSON, M (1992) "Wives' perceptions of the fairness of the division of household labor: the intersection of the housework and ideology", *Journal of Marriage and Family*, vol 54, pp 570–81

[BRI 92] BRISTOR, J (1992) "Insider versus outsider: reflections of a feminist consumer", *Advances in Consumer Research*, vol 19, pp 843–49

[BRI 93] BRISTOR, J and FISCHER, E (1993) "Feminist thought: implications for consumer research", *Journal of Consumer Research*, vol 9, pp 518–36

[BRY 88] BRYANT, K (1988) "Durables and wives' employment yet again", *Journal of Consumer Research*, vol 15, pp 37–47

[CHE 99] CHENG-NAN C., MENGKUAN L., DAVID D. C. T. (1999) "Feminism orientation, product attributes and husband-wife decision dominance: A Taiwan-Japan cross-cultural study", *Journal of Global Marketing*, vol 12, no 3, p 23-39

[COS 00] COSTA, JA (2000) "Les raisons du courant de recherche sur le genre en marketing", *Décisions Marketing*, vol 20, pp 95–97

[CUN 75] CUNNINGHAM, ICM and GREEN, RT (1975) "Feminine role perception and family purchasing decisions", *Journal of Marketing Research*, vol XII, pp 325–32

[EDIT 2000] Editorial (2000) "Marketing et genre", *Décisions marketing*

[FEL 81] FELDMAN, LP and HORNIK, J (1981) "The use of time: an integrated conceptual model", *Journal of Consumer Research*, vol 7, pp 407–19

[FER 80] FERBER, MA and BIRNBAUM, BG (1980) "One job or two jobs: the implications for young wives", *Journal of Consumer Research*, vol 7, pp 263–71

[FIR 96] FIRAT, F (1996) "Gender and consumption: transcending the feminine", in Janeen Costa (ed) *Gender and Consumer Behavior*, Salt Lake City: University of Utah Printing Service, pp 378–81

[GAL 96] GALBRAITH, JK (1969), *Economics and the Public Purpose*, Boston: Highton Mifflin

[GRE 96] GREENSTEIN, T (1996) "Husbands' participation in domestic labor: interactive effects of wives' and husbands' gender ideologies", *Journal of Marriage and Family*, vol 58, pp 585–95

[HER 80] HERPIN, N (1980) "Comportements alimentaires et contraintes sur les emplois du temps", *Revue Française de Sociologie*, vol XXI, pp 599–628

[JOA 91] JOAG, S, GENTRY, J and EKSTROM, K (1991) "An investigation of a role/goal model of wives' role overload reduction strategies", *Advances in Consumer Research*, vol 18, pp 666–72

[KIR 36] KIRKPATRICK, C (1936) "The construction of a belief pattern scale for measuring attitudes toward feminism", *Journal of Social Psychology*, vol 7, pp 421–37

[KIM 93] KIM, C, LAROCHE, M and ZHOU, L (1993) "An investigation of ethnicity and sex-role attitude as factors influencing household financial task-sharing behavior", *Advances in Consumer Research*, vol 20, pp 52–59

[LEO 01] LEO YAT-MING, S and OLIVER HON-MING, Y (2001) "Female role orientation and consumption values: some evidence from Mainland China", *Journal of International Consumer Marketing*, vol 13, no 2, pp 49–75

[MAR 79] MARY LOU, R and WORTZEL, L (1979) "New life-style determinants of women's food shopping behavior", *Journal of Marketing*, vol 43, pp 28–39

[MCC 77] MCCALL, S (1977) "Meet the 'work wife'", *Journal of Marketing*, vol 41, pp 55–65

[MED 93] MEDERER, H (1993) "Division of labor in two-earner homes: task accomplishment versus household management as critical variables in perceptions about family work", *Journal of Marriage and Family*, vol 55, pp 133–45

[MEN 95] MENARD, S (1995) *Applied Logistic Regression Analysis: Quantitative Applications in the Social Sciences*, London: Sage Publications

[MIN 60] MINCER, J (1960) "Labor supply, family income and consumption", *The Economic Journal*, pp 574–83

[ORO 93] OROPESA, R (1993) "Female labor force participation and time-saving household technology: a case study of the microwave from 1978 to 1989", *Journal of Consumer Research,* vol 19, pp 567–80

[POT 92] POTUCHEK, J (1992) "Employed wives' orientations to breadwinning: a gender theory analysis", *Journal of Marriage and Family,* vol 52, pp 548–58

[PRE 94] PRESSER, H (1994) "Employment schedules among dual-earner spouses and the division of the household labor by gender", *American Sociological Review,* vol 59, pp 348–64

[QUA 84] QUALLS, W (1984) "Sex roles, husband-wife influence and family decision behavior" *Advances in Consumer Research,* pp 270–75

[REI 82] REILLY, MD (1982) "Working wives and convenience consumption", *Journal of Consumer Research,* vol 8, pp 407–18

[ROB 79] ROBERTS, ML and WORTZEL, LH (1979) "New life-style determinants of women's food shopping behavior", *Journal of Marketing,* vol 43, no 3, pp 28–39

[RUB 90] RUBIN, RM, RINEY, BJ and MOLINA, DJ (1990) "Expenditure pattern differentials between one-earner and dual-earner households: 1972-1973 and 1984", *Journal of Consumer Research,* vol 17, pp 43–53

[SCA 80] SCANZONI, J and FOX, S (1980) "Sex roles, family and society: the seventies and beyond", *Journal of Marriage and the Family,* vol 42, pp 743–56

[SEX 89] SEXTON, C and PERLMAN, D (1989) "Couples' career orientation, gender role orientation and perceived equity as determinants of marital power", *Journal of Marriage and Family,* vol 51, pp 933–41

[SOB 91] SOBERON-FERRER, H and DARDIS, R (1991) "Determinants of household expenditures for services", *Journal of Consumer Research,* vol 17, pp 385–96

[SPI 86] SPITZE, G (1986) "Women's employment and family relations: a review", *Journal of Marriage and Family,* vol 48, pp 595–618

[STR 77] STROBER, MH and WEINBERG, CB (1977) "Working wives and major family expenditures", *Journal of Consumer Research,* vol 4, pp 141–47

[THO 92] THOMPSON, L (1992) "Feminist methodology of family studies", *Journal of Marriage and the Family,* vol 54, pp 3–18

[THO 95] THOMPSON, L and WALKER, A (1995) "The place of feminism in family studies", *Journal of Marriage and Family,* vol 57, pp 847–65

[TIS 02] TISSIER-DESBORDES, E and KIMMEL, AJ (2002) "Sexe, genre et marketing, définition des concepts et analyse de la literature", *Décisions Marketing,* vol 26, pp 55–69

[VEN 80] VENKATESH, A (1980) "Changing roles of women: a lifestyle analysis" *Journal of Consumer Research*, vol 7, pp 189–97

[WEI 83] WEINBERG, CB and WINER, RS (1983) "Working wives and major family expenditures: replication and extension", *Journal of Consumer Research*, vol 10, pp 259–63

[ZEI 00] ZEÏTOUN, H (2000) "Pertinence et valeur stratégique de la cible 'femme' telle que traitée en recherche marketing", *Décisions Marketing*, vol 20, pp 89–93

5.8. Appendix

NOTE 1: Strober and Weinberg [STR 77] say that anything equalizes in addition.

NOTE 2: type II error: believing that the indicator in regression is insignificant whereas it is. The researcher tends to eliminate the insignificant coefficients. Menard [MEN 95] warns researchers of the very high β, where the standard error is inflated and the value β^2 of regression indicator is lowered.

NOTE 3: Tunisian women's gender ideology scale was developed starting with focus groups and the use of scales like Arnott's autonomy scale and Kirkpatrick's feminism. I am the author of this scale and this typology.

Construction of women gender ideology

– Four items measure two dimensions of feminism: F1 "remunerated work" and F2 "birth control".

– Five items measure dimension "reports/ratios: male-female".

– Four items measure dimension "autonomy".

– Six items measure dimension: "the woman's status".

– Five items measure two dimensions of built housework: D1 "work domestic – burden and D2 "work domestic – division".

The scale of gender ideology of Tunisian women is a reliable and valid multidimensional scale within the Tunisian context. Except for the first dimension of housework, the convergent validities of the other dimensions of the model could not be proved.

Typology

To qualify and interpret the groups of women retained of typology, we called upon two types of analyses. The first is an analysis of the multiple correspondences which enabled, by factorial analysis, the determination of the gender ideology variables. The second is a discriminate analysis which made it possible to determine, on the basis of discriminate factors relating to each factor in each group, the significant differences in the groups and to validate the selection of classes. The results showed that the differences are significant.

Chapter 6

The Cultural Impact on Changes in Consumption: Lithuania and Bulgaria

6.1. Introduction: globalization and culture

Globalization is the way in which national economies of the world are now becoming increasingly open and related to one another in economic, political, legal, cultural, social and information spheres. Globalization – the unification of goods, services, capital and labor into a single global market – based on free trade, comparative advantages and economies of scale created a really radical force for economic development. Globalization speeds and expands the strengths, but also the weaknesses, of the market system: its efficiency, instability and inequality [GLO 01]. The impact of globalization on each country is double: on one hand, there is the possibility for population welfare and cultural development, but on the other hand, it does not create equally sustainable economic and cultural development in each country. Globalization means that economic resources are used on market-based principles and this often creates legitimacy.

Some authors state that globalization has led to a proliferation of global brands and an alleged homogenization of cultures in driving regions: "Europeanization", "Westernization" or "Americanization", but much of this criticism is based on political grounds.

Chapter written by Jadvyga CIBURIENE and Anastasiya MARCHEVA.

The main external environment elements that influence consumer behavior are: psychological, situational, marketing mix and sociocultural factors. Two countries – Lithuania and Bulgaria – are compared in this chapter. National culture is one of the most important elements that condition sociocultural patterns of purchasing in a society. Sociocultural patterns reflect consumer perception of the strengths and weaknesses of the economy via favoring or disfavoring goods produced in their country. Consumer behavior patterns involve problem recognition and decision-making processes, the search for information and alternative evaluation and purchasing decisions and post-purchasing behavior.

Culture is a characteristic feature of each society. It is the values, religion, behavior norms and material products which determine lifestyle. ([MAC 98: 980]; [SCH 97: 19]). Culture is transmitted from one generation to another – in the same way as the genetic code of each separate nation is transmitted from one generation to another. It is always related to traditions. In a broad sense, all human behavior or shared patterns of behavior can be considered as culture ([STI 88: 55–56]; [MEA 53]). A common and detailed explanation is given by Schein [SCH 85]: it is a set of basic assumptions – shared solutions to universal problems of external adaptation (how to survive) and internal integration (how to stay together), which evolve over time and are transmitted from one generation to the next. The broadest view to understanding culture is as the sum total of the beliefs, rules, techniques, institutions and artifacts that characterize human population ([BRA 75: 1]; [BAR 75: 5]). Thus, culture can be characterized as a material (materialism) and spiritual (post-materialism) form of culture, as well as consumption.

Culture changes over a period of time. Culture is characterized by two aspects: some things are obvious and some things cannot be seen: the latter can only occur in certain situations. In accordance with the diversity of the problems which arise, the interacting cultural spheres of influence are divided into the following levels [SCH 97: 47–49]:

– national/regional (geography, history, political and economic forces, climate, religion, language);

– functional (external environment, time horizons);

– professional (education, training, selection, socialization).

All these spheres penetrate the processes renewal of labor force reproduction, which includes such as stages: manufacture, distribution, consumption and exchange.

Consumer goods and services show each culture's ability to create impact, because:

– culture is learned, not innate;

– culture is shared;

– culture's various aspects are interrelated;

– culture defines the boundaries of different groups.

6.2. Material determinant for consumption

Incomes are very important, but they are not the only determinant of consumption. Gross domestic product (GDP) is one of the main indicators that shows the economic situation in the state or region and helps to evaluate the achieved level of economic development and living standards. It is possible to compare the results of economic development of states of different sizes with different price levels and currencies, based on GDP per capita (GDPpc) in purchasing power (PPS), at current market prices (Table 6.1).

State/region	1996	1997	1998	1999	2000	2001	2003	2004	2005
EU-25	15,200	16,900	17,700	18,500	19,800	20,500	21,400	22,300	23,100*
EU-15	16,900	17,700	18,600	19,400	20,400	21,700	23,200	23,000	24,300*
change, in %	1.8	2.7	2.9	2.6	3.3	1.7	-	-	-
Lithuania	5,200	6,300	6,900	7,000	7,600	8,300	9,800	10,,700	11,600*
growth, in %	100.0	121.2	132.7	134.6	146.2	159.6	188.5	205.8	223.1
change, in %	4.7	7.0	7.3	-1.7	3.9	6.4	10.5	7.0	7.5
GDPpc, in %	35	37	9	38	39	41	46	48	50.7
population in millions		3.575	3.549	3.524	3.5	3.481	3.4542	3.4356	3.4143
Bulgaria	4,700	4,400	4,700	4,900	5,300	5,800	6,400	6,700	7,500*
growth, in %	100.0	90.4	100.0	104.3	112.8	123.4	136.2	146.8	159.6
change, in %	-9.4	-5.6	4.0	2.3	5.4	4.1	4.5	5.6	-
GDPpc, in %	28	26	26	26	27	29	30	30	32
population in millions	8.385	8.341	8.283	8.230	8.191	8.149	7.846	7.801	7.761

* - Forecasts; GDPpc, in % – GDP per capita (EU = 100%)
Sources: [EUR 05:142]; [BUL 05a: 78]; [EUR 04]; [ECO 06: 19]

Table 6.1. *GDPpc in PPS, at current market prices*

The data show that GDPpc growth, both in Lithuania (223.1%) and Bulgaria (159.6%), is higher then in EU-25 (152.0%) or in EU-15 (143.8%). The GDPpc produced in EU-15 during 1995–2005 increased and in 2005 it reached 24,300 PPS per capita; the same trend in observed in Lithuania – 11,600 PPS – and in Bulgaria – 7,500 PPS.

6.3. National culture values

The culture of an individual state is related to its implicit beliefs, norms, values and customs that underlie and govern society. These values are common to both former and current generations and are taught at all educational, training and economic institutions. Important historical events modify values in economic, political, institutional and cultural development. Common and specific features of Lithuania and Bulgaria are be revealed by structural and dynamic analysis of cultural and psychological values.

Culture involves a set of values, customs, traditions, attitudes and ideas that a society possesses and hands down from parent to child. Due to cultural elements, society becomes a meaningful social unit.

Psychological values are related to personality and lifestyle. Lithuania is a small country with a settled population. On the other hand, Lithuania has been recognized as a market economy country since 2002, though it has one of the lowest living standards in the EU. Bulgaria is one of two newly acceded countries; its GNP per capita is lower than that of Lithuania. Due to these factors, lifestyle (good quality of life, equality, freedom, happiness, family security) and purchasing behavior in Lithuania and Bulgaria are different and marketers have to consider these variables when targeting certain segments of the market. Appendix 1 shows the different characteristics on which we based the differences between culture and consumption.

Differences in national culture are based on the four Geert Hofstede values, which make it possible to understand behavior patterns [HOF 84: 81–84]:

1) individualism versus collectivism;

2) large versus small power distance (when members of society accept the unequal distribution of power among individuals);

3) strong versus weak uncertainty avoidance (the degree to which members of society feel threatened by ambiguity and are reluctant to take risk);

4) masculinity versus femininity.

National culture values, according to Hofstede, are shown for Lithuania and Bulgaria in Table 6.2.

Value	Lithuania	Bulgaria
1. individualism versus collectivism	individualism	strong collectivism
2. large versus small power distance	large	very large
3. strong versus weak uncertainty avoidance	strong	very strong
4. masculinity versus femininity	masculinity	moderate femininity

Table 6.2. *National cultures values in Lithuania and Bulgaria*

Large power distance and strong uncertainty avoidance in enterprises and firms, individualism and masculinity characterize Lithuanian culture values. Bulgaria is characterized as a country with very large power distance, strong collectivism, very strong uncertainly avoidance and moderate femininity culture values.

Globalization and the enlargement of the EU bring new challenges to countries' main features of culture and especially for new EU-27 State members. The main features of Western culture and Central-Eastern culture and their changes are shown in Table 6.3. In essence, these changes are the reason for Central and Eastern European countries' participation in the EU enlargement processes and the four freedoms principle (free movement of goods, people, services and capital). Western culture obviously has a tremendous influence on the cultural changes taking place in the countries that are analyzed.

Features	Features of Western culture	Features of Eastern culture	
		1990	2006
Individual	aggressive, individualist, self-expressive, social climber, strong-willed, motivated to succeed, smart, tolerant, optimistic, socially active, individual freedom, initiative	quiet, collectivistic, thoughtful philosophically and religiously, realistic, intolerant, not socially active, egalitarian	realistic, shift to more individualistic and socially active behavior rather than collectivistic, more self-expressive, aggressive, consumerist
- values	logic, knowledge, historical precision	harmony with nature, emotional, sentimental, prone to fantasizing, poetic	harmony with nature, emotional, sentimental, prone to fantasizing, poetic
- slight	emotional, sentimental, superstitious beliefs	inactive, disparaging of outsiders	inactivity, disparaging of outsiders
Attitude towards luck	material world	seeking to manage themselves and to find constant and eternal worth	seeking to manage themselves and to find constant and eternal worth

Sources: [BIE 99]; [LAU 97]; [SAV 04]

Table 6.3. *The main cultural features of Western and Central-Eastern countries*

These specific results show the changes in cultural differences which lead to differences in consumer consumption. The process of Westernization in Lithuania and Bulgaria is based on the fact that the population of these countries is characterized by a strong cultural drive towards the imitation of Western models of behavior [SAV 04: 70].

6.4. Material culture

Material culture involves all man-made objects and services that are used for consumption by individuals who purchase (or are given), use, maintain and dispose of products and services in their final form while attempting to achieve the highest level of satisfaction possible within their income limitations. The results of the European Values Studies (EVS) conducted in 1990 and 1999, which present the distribution of materialists, post-materialists and population with mixed values in different income groups in Lithuania, are shown in Table 6.4.

Year	Value	Income group				
		Lowest 20%	20-40%	40-60%	60-80%	Highest 20%
1990	Materialism	41	36	32	22	25
	Mixed	53	56	58	63	61
	Post-materialism	6	8	10	15	14
1999	Materialism	33	29	23	17	-
	Mixed	64	67	69	70	90
	Post-materialism	3	4	8	13	10

Source: [SAV 04: 105]

Table 6.4. *Percentage changes of cultural values distribution in Lithuania*

Cultural values are closely related to income. Materialism is less and mixed tendencies increase in each higher income group. This tendency is confirmed by the changes in cultural values. The highest income group population tends towards mixed- and post-materialism cultural values.

6.5. Changes in consumption

Households buy commodities and services to satisfy immediate needs. Consumption is a large part of the total expenditure in a country and is the most important determinant of GDP. The changes in consumption as a proportion of GDP size, both in Lithuania and Bulgaria, are shown in the Table 6.5. Durable consumer goods and services, such as computers and cell phones, the relative price of which tends to fall and new services, medical care and recreation, have boosted spending. Consumption as a proportion of GDP, which follows a growth pattern in Lithuania and Bulgaria, confirms the changes in aspects of quality of life in these countries.

Country	1996	1997	1998	1999	2000	2001	2002	2003	2004
Lithuania	70.2	65.0	63.0	65.3	64.3	63.5	63.6	64.6	65.8
Bulgaria	76.3	69.9	72.4	74.3	68.8	69.0	68.4	68.3	67.8

Sources: [LIT 02: 6]; [LIT 04: 6]; [BUL 00: 145]; [BUL 04: 194]

Table 6.5. *Percentage changes of consumption as a proportion of GDP*

The structure of consumption shows the priorities by place of residence (urban and rural areas) and the main structure of consumption expenditure (Table 6.6). All average consumption expenditures in Lithuania, except food, non-alcoholic beverages and alcoholic beverages, shows a growth tendency, both in total and when considered by place of residence.

Expenditure	Total		Urban areas		Rural areas	
	1996	2005	1996	2005	1996	2005
food and non-alcoholic beverages	55.2	36.6	51.7	32.2	65.3	49.4
alcoholic beverages	2.5	2.4	2.5	2.5	2.7	2.3
tobacco	1.2	1.4	1.2	1.3	1.1	1.7
clothing and footwear	7.8	8.6	8.4	9.1	6.2	7.2
housing, water, electricity, gas and other fuel	11.8	12.0	12.9	13.1	8.9	9.1
furnishings, household equipment and routine household maintenance	3.6	4.5	3.8	4.7	3.0	4.1
health care	2.6	5.1	2.7	5.1	2.4	5.2
transportation and communication	5.2	8.8	5.6	9.0	4.2	8.3
communication	N/A	5.0	N/A	5.5	N/A	3.8
recreation and culture	2.5	4.7	2.7	5.2	1.7	3.0
education	0.9	1.2	1.0	1.4	0.6	0.5
hotels, restaurants, cafes, canteens	3.4	5.0	3.9	5.9	1.9	2.4
miscellaneous goods and services	3.2	4.6	3.7	5.0	1.9	3.1
consumption expenditure in cash	78.9	88.6	84.7	93.5	62.5	74.5
consumption expenditure in kind	21.1	11.4	15.3	6.5	37.5	25.5

Sources: [HOU 96: 16–18]; [HOU 05: 42–44]

Table 6.6. *Average percentage changes in consumption expenditure in Lithuania*

The average consumption total expenditure changes, by social group and place of residence, in Bulgaria, in %, are shown in Table 6.7. The largest consumer expenditure in Bulgaria, on food, as well as being the largest overall expenditure of all households in 2004, decreases to 39.3% (the lowest values during the observed period). The shares of expenditure for housing, water, electricity, gas and other fuels, health and communication increase rapidly.

Expenditure groups	Total			Urban areas		Rural areas	
	1996	2004	2005	1996	2004	1996	2004
Total expenditure	100	100	100	100	100	100	100
Total consumer expenditure	85.2	85.3	86.3	N/A	85.2	N/A	85.8
foods and non-alcoholic beverages	48.2	39.3	38.6	46.9	36.8	51.2	46.1
alcoholic beverages and tobacco	3.9	4.2	4.2	3.8	4.0	4.1	4.9
clothing and footwear	6.2	3.4	3.4	7.0	3.6	5.3	2.6
housing, water, electricity, gas and other fuels	9.1	13.8	14.0	N/A	14.5	N/A	12.0
furnishings and household maintenance	3.5	3.2	3.3	3.8	3.3	3.0	3.0
health	1.9	4.5	4.7	N/A	4.4	N/A	4.7
transport	6.4	5.3	5.6	8.1	5.6	6.4	4.5
communication	0.9	4.8	5.1		5.2		3.8
recreation, culture and education	2.3	3.5	3.6	2.9	4.1	1.5	1.8
miscellaneous goods and services	2.8	3.3	3.8	N/A	3.7	N/A	2.4
consumption expenditure in cash	N/A	N/A	N/A	N/A	95.2	N/A	81.0
consumption expenditure in kind	N/A	N/A	N/A	N/A	4.8	N/A	19.0

Source: [HOU 04: 69–72]

Table 6.7. *Structure of the total consumer expenditure by group and place of residence in Bulgaria, in %*

The comparison of the percentages of average consumption expenditure in Lithuania and Bulgaria shows that food and non-alcoholic beverages expenditures in total are less in Lithuania (36.6%) in comparison to this expenditure in Bulgaria (38.6%). The total expenditure for clothing and footwear, furnishings, household equipment and routine household maintenance, health care, transportation and communication, recreation and culture is greater in Lithuania than in Bulgaria. The changes in expenditure for clothing and footwear, furnishings, household equipment and routine household maintenance, transportation and communication have been following a growth pattern during the 1996–2005 period in Lithuania. The fact is that this expenditure growth satisfies the European welfare-state requirements. These expenditures have decreased in Bulgaria during the period that was analyzed. It is likely that in the future this expenditure will increase in Bulgaria. Bulgaria has a higher consumption of alcoholic beverages and tobacco, which can be explained as being part of the Balkan culture. Communication and health expenditures are rapidly increasing in Bulgaria because of new communication trends (cell phones, Internet, etc) and health reform and new opinions about health care.

A very important indicator is the average consumption expenditure changes per capita per month. The comparison of this indicator in Lithuania and Bulgaria is shown in Table 6.8.

Country	1995	1996	1997	1998	1999	2000	2001	2002	2003	2004
Lithuania	100.0	143.0	159.6	175.3	174.8	166.1	168.8	171.0	200.2	210.5
Bulgaria	100.0	81.5	59.8	84.6	92.7	89.5	88.3	95.6	101.4	106.8

Sources: [BUL 05b, 4–5]; [HOU 02: 54]; [HOU 04b: 45–46]

Table 6.8. *Index numbers of real changes of cash household consumer expenditure per capita (1995 = 100%)*

The real change of real changes of cash household consumer expenditure per capita shows the long term trend of growth. In Lithuania this expenditure more than doubled over the 1995–2004 period. The decrease of Lithuania's index in 1999–2001 was a result of the Russian financial crisis. The real change of cash household consumer expenditure per capita in Bulgaria was related to economic and structural changes.

Each country is characterized by its main sociocultural variables: demographics, culture and subcultures, social classes and reference groups. Emerging market countries in Europe now face many new issues in their economic development and these issues modify cultural values in those countries. Direct (supranational institutions: World Trade Organization (WTO), European Union (EU) regulate national markets) and indirect (competitive pressure, stricter regulations, higher capital investment, loss of some national identity) changes in the economic development of individual countries are ripples triggered by changes in global economic development.

At present, on a global level, the issue of cultural values and consumption convergence between states emerges. Thus, it is important to note that:

– key cultural values (esthetic, attitudes and beliefs, religion, education, material culture) have an impact on a nation's consumer behavior and expenditure related to these values is growing;

– producers understand and meet cultural needs and values of a nation and the markets of national art, needlework, stoneware, etc, are growing;

– cultural values of families, folklore, educational and research institutions are both stable and dynamic at the same time; a shift to spending, instead of saving, leads to greater use of credit for housing and leasing (cars, furniture, computers and other durable goods);

– cultural values of different income groups are distinct in Lithuania and Bulgaria.

These changes are in line with Maslow's hierarchy of human needs (physiological, safety, belonging, esteem and self-actualization). Internal factors such as independence movements, traditions and materialism, have important impact on culture. Cultures have influenced one another through the global market and labor force reproduction and migration process, as shown in Figure 6.1.

Purchasing and the amount and structure of consumption are important to society because consumers:

– maximize utility or live according to the theory of rational choice; thus consumption shows materialistic values in a society;

– decide on products which are, and will be, produced inside the nation's economic sphere;

– markets are therefore the result of consumer demand and government regulation;

– follow a behavior pattern, which is driven by technological change.

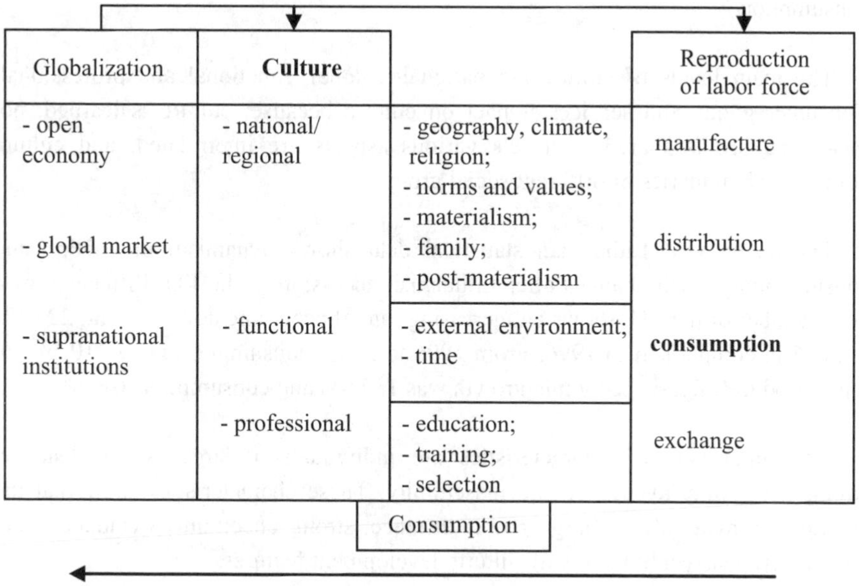

Globalization	Culture		Reproduction of labor force
- open economy	- national/ regional	- geography, climate, religion; - norms and values; - materialism;	manufacture
- global market		- family; - post-materialism	distribution
- supranational institutions	- functional	- external environment; - time	**consumption**
	- professional	- education; - training; - selection	exchange
		Consumption	

Figure 6.1. *Interaction of culture and consumption*

New and powerful technologies can bring enormous benefits and, at the same time, threats to the environment and human health. Democratic societies actively deal with the further development of environmentally unsafe technologies (fertilizer and cement industries, genetically modified organisms).

It is important that consumers become involved in the production of values, products or services and thus an element of synergy between culture, consumption, government and firms is created.

The economies of Lithuania and Bulgaria grew in 2004–05; this will lead to the increase in consumption expenditure, including direct and indirect expenditures on recreation and culture. Further growth of wages, economic and monetary relations with the EU and emigration was expected in Lithuania and Bulgaria in 2006.

6.6. Conclusion

Cultures influence each other through global markets and supranational institutions. Changing culture both obviously and imperceptibly influences consumption.

The main levels of culture are national/regional, functional and professional. Consumer goods and services impact on culture because: culture is learned, not innate; culture is shared; culture's various aspects are interrelated; and culture defines the boundaries of different social groups.

The analysis of Lithuanian statistical data shows dynamism in GDPpc and consumption-growth changes after Lithuanian accession to the EU. Lithuania, as a new member of the EU, shows an increasing rate of economic development: 223.1% in 2005 in comparison to 1996. From 1996 to 2005, consumption grew 210.5%. In this period in Bulgaria economic growth was 150.6% and consumption 106.8%.

Lithuanian national characteristics are individualism, large power distance, strong uncertainty avoidance and masculinity. These characteristics show that the country has materialistic (large power distance, strong uncertainty avoidance) and post-materialism (individualism) culture-development features.

Bulgarian national characteristics are a very large power base, strong collectivism, very strong uncertainly avoidance and a moderate femininity culture.

In both countries the younger and more educated people, who have higher incomes, share a post-materialist orientation.

6.7. References

[BAR 75] BARNOUW, V (1975) *An Introduction to Anthropology*, Homewood, IL: Dorsey Press

[BIE 99] BIELIAUSKAS, Z and JUKNEVICIUS, S (eds) (1999) *Culture and Civilization*, Vilnius: Gervele

[BRA 75] BRADY, I and ISAAC, B (1975) *Reader in Cultural Change*, vol 1, Cambridge, MA: Schenkman Publishing

[BUL 00] BULGARIA (2000) *Statistical Yearbook 2000*, Sofia: NSI

[BUL 04] BULGARIA (2004) *Statistical Yearbook 2004*, Sofia: NSI

[BUL 05a] BULGARIA (2005) *Comprehensive Monitoring Report*, Brussels: European Commission, SEC (2005) 1352, 25 October 2005

[BUL 05b] BULGARIA (2005) *Statistical Yearbook 2005*, Sofia: NSI

[ECO 06] *Economic and Social Development in Lithuania*, No 2, (2006) Vilnius: Statistics Lithuania

[EUR 05] *Europe in Figures*, (2005) *Eurostat Yearbook*, Brussels: European Commission, Ch 3

[EUR 04] *European Economy Annual Report* (2004): Commission of the European Communities

[GLO 01] "Global policy without democracy" (2001) speech by Pascal Lamy, EU Trade Commissioner

[HOF 84] HOFSTEDE, G (1984) "Management and planning", *Asia Pacific Journal of Management*, January 1984, pp 81–84

[HOU 97] *Household Budget Survey Results, 1996* (1997) Vilnius, Statistics Lithuania

[HOU 03] *Household Income and Expenditure 2002* (2003) Vilnius: Statistics Lithuania

[HOU 04a] *Household Budgets in the Republic of Bulgaria* (2004) Vilnius: Statistics Lithuania

[HOU 05] *Household Income and Expenditure 2004* (2005) Vilnius: Statistics Lithuania

[HOU 06] *Household Income and Expenditure 2005* (2006) Vilnius: Statistics Lithuania

[LAU 97] LAURISTIN, M (1997) "Contexts of transition", in Lauristin, M, Vihalemm, P, Rosengren, KE and Weibull, L (eds), *Returns to the Western World. Cultural and Political Perspectives on the Estonian Post-Communist Transition*, Tartu: Tartu University Press, pp 25–40

[LIT 96] *Lithuania Statistics Surveys* (1996-2005) Vilnius: Lithuania Statistics

[LIT 02] *Lithuanian Economy Review* (2002) Vilnius: Statistics Lithuania, no 1

[LIT 04] *Lithuanian Economy Review* (2004) Vilnius: Statistics Lithuania, no 1

[MAC 98] MACIONIS, J (1998) *Sociology*, New Jersey: Prentice Hall

[MEA 53] MEAD, M (1953) *Coming of Age in Samoa*, New York: Modern Library

[SAV 04] SAVICKA, A (2004) *Postmaterialism and Globalisation: The Specificity of Value Change in the Post-Communist Milieu*, Vilnius: Research Institute of Culture, Philosophy and Arts

[SCH 85] SCHEIN, EH (1985) *Organizational Culture and Leadership*, San Francisco: Jossey-Bass

[SCH 97] SCHNEIDER, S mad BARSOUX, J (1997) *Managing Across Cultures*, London: Prentica

[STI 88] STIMSON, J and STIMSON, A (1988) *Sociology: Contemporary Readings*, Illinois: FE Peacock Publishers

Appendix 1: Lithuania and Bulgaria basic characteristics in 2004

Basic characteristics	Lithuania	Bulgaria
population	3,615,200	7,518,000
birth rate per 1,000 population	8.8	9.7
death rate per 1,000 population	12	14.3
urban population	66.7%	70%
population density (persons per square kilometer)	52.8	68
population age	0–15 years: 19.2% working age: 60.9%; retired: 19.9%	0–15 years: 15.1% working age: 61.6%; retired: 23.3%
immigration (1990–2005)	500,000	800,000
family size	3.18	3.5
net migration rate (people per 1,000 population)	-3.1	-4.6
ethnicity	83.5%: Lithuanian; 6.3%: Russian; 6.7%: Poles; 3.5%: Belarussians, Ukrainians, Jews, etc.	83.9%: Bulgarian; 9.4% Turks; 4.7% Roma; 2.0%, Russians, Ukrainians, Armenians, Jews, Greeks, etc.
languages	Lithuanian is the official language; 80% (1998) are native speakers	Bulgarian is the official language; it is the first language of 84.5% of the population; 9.6% speak Turkish; 4.1% speak Romany
religion	Roman Catholics: 79%; Eastern Orthodox: 4.1%; Irreligious: 14.9%; Others: 2%	Christians: 83.7% (95% of which are Eastern Orthodox); Roman Catholics: 1.7%; Muslims: 12.2%; Jews: 0.8% Others: 1.6%
literacy rate	99%	98.6%

Chapter 7

Country of Origin: Perceptions and Attitudes of Portuguese Consumers

7.1. Introduction

Globalization impacts upon various facets of consumer behavior. It enables firms that were previously tied to their national markets to enlarge their reach to consumers worldwide. The consumers now have access to a much wider variety of goods and services offered by firms across the globe. However, the added variety makes the buying experience far more complex. Complexity further increases when consumers are choosing products for which they have limited, perhaps partial, information. In these instances, how do consumers decide which products to purchase? One possible avenue is for consumers to do extensive market research and product comparisons. This may be viable for some types of purchases, possibly those of big ticket items that represent a significant expense. An alternative is to simplify the buying experience by inferring the missing information. The use of heuristics to simplify the buying experience and the choice among alternative product offerings is, in fact, a likely outcome. The brand of the product and the signal provided by the country of origin are two known criteria that ease the choice among alternative products and services.

Chapter written by Ana LISBOA.

Although globalization could bring added homogenization of consumer preferences, lifestyles and patterns of consumption, as suggested by [LEV 83], there is some specificity of consumption and consumer behavior which is inherent to the country of origin. Understanding country of origin effects and their impact on consumer behavior may shed clarifying insights that are capable of supporting public policy and firms' marketing strategies. In particular, additional research on the relationship between the country of origin of a given product and the consumers' attitudes toward the products made in that country may partly explain consumers' choices, at least under conditions of uncertainty.

It is important at the outset to clarify what we refer to as country of origin effects in the study of global consumer behavior. The first related concept known and generally referred to as "made in" was proposed by Nagashima [NAG 70, 77] to represent the image, the reputation and the creation of a stereotype that executives and consumers associate with the products manufactured in a given country; that is, there are many descriptive, inferential and informational beliefs that an individual has about a country that build a "country image" [MAR 93] and that consumers extrapolate to the products made in that country. These two concepts, "made in" and "country image", are likely to have an effect on consumers' behavior – these are known as country of origin effects.

In this chapter, we study country of origin effects and their relation to consumer behavior. The perception of some products' country of origin may influence consumer behavior, leading consumers to purchase (or not) products made in that country. This influence can be observed in the perceptions of products' attributes and should be reflected in the marketing strategies that firms deploy. The influence of country of origin may be noted in product evaluations, with products made in more developed countries attaining more favorable evaluations than products made in developing countries. For example, products made in Germany tend to be associated with high quality and reliability; conversely, products made in China have been featured as low priced and poor quality items. Not only are the buying intentions influenced by the country of origin perception, but also the consumers' willingness to pay a premium for products made in specific countries. Hence, we focus on the attitude toward the country of origin and its products and the factors influencing that attitude. According to the country of origin studies (eg, [WAN 83]), there are three types of factors influencing the attitude toward countries and products; these are: consumer-related factors, market-related factors and factors related to the conditions of nations. Consumer-related factors, namely ethnocentrism [SHI 87; SHA 95] and familiarity [PAR 81] or experience with a country's products, are those associated with the consumers' profile or characteristics. Market-related factors are those associated with the products or the specific markets considered. The nations' conditions are related to the specific characteristics of the country, such as level of economic development, political and cultural environment and presence in the global markets [WAN 80, 83]. Prior research has noted that all these factors influence the attitude towards the country of origin.

In our study we discuss and differentiate the perceptions towards a country and the perceptions towards a country's products, its independent or interactive effects. Our study is empirically supported by primary data collected from Portuguese Internet-user participants. We surveyed participants about the image of nine countries: Portugal, the USA, Japan, Spain, France, Italy, the UK, China and Poland. We assessed the Portuguese consumers' perceptions and attitudes toward these nine countries and toward the products made in each country. To this end we employed a scale of general country attributes [NET 91]. The results show that the attitude toward each country and the attitude toward products made in those countries are highly related. Moreover, the attitude toward the nine countries appears to display a hierarchy shaped by the state of development of the countries. A discussion and some avenues for further research are presented.

7.2. Country of origin effects on consumer behavior

7.2.1. *Country of origin effects defined*

The country of origin effects are largely based on two related concepts: the concepts of "country image" and "made in". These two effects are actually used indistinctly in most country of origin studies. Nagashima [NAG 70] described the "made in" effect as the image, the reputation and the stereotype that executives and consumers associate with the products of a certain country, which involves the representative products of a country, the national characteristics, the economic and political environment, the history and the traditions of that country. Bilkey and Nes [BIL 82] defined "country image" as the general perceptions of the products made in a country. According to Martin and Eroglu [MAR 93], "country image" is the total of all descriptive, inferential and informational beliefs that an individual has about a country. Shimp *et al.* [SHI 93] described "country image" as a function of several influences, such as political and military hostility, nationalistic attitudes, habits, music, food and tourist attractions. Roth and Romeo [ROT 92] presented prestige (meaning the brand exclusivity, status and reputation) and workmanship (represented by the reliability, durability, ability and production quality) as country image dimensions. Place image [KOT 93] is the sum of all the emotional and esthetic qualities such as the experience, beliefs, ideas and impressions that consumers have of a place. For this study, we conceptualized country image as involving what consumers know (or think they know) about the production ability, the style, the design skills and the technological innovation of a country. The country of origin effects will then be analyzed through consumers' perceptions of these country image dimensions and through consumers' attitudes toward the country and the country's products.

It is worth noting that the increased regional economic integration, the formation of regional integration areas, such as the Association of Southeast Asian Nations (ASEAN), the North American Free Trade Agreement (NAFTA), or the European Union (EU), may partially dilute the country of origin effects. The label "made in the EU" as the place of origin is being encouraged, particularly in southern European countries, to overcome a possible unfavorable image and replace the "made in country X" label. Notwithstanding this, it is likely that the place of origin will continue be an important source of information and cues for consumer decision-making.

7.2.2. Halo or summary

Consumers, generally, do not perceive all the foreign products or all the products of a country similarly. Existing research points to the possibility of a difference between the stereotypes formed for products of a nation and the idiosyncratic attitude toward a specific product originated in that nation.

The country image can act as a halo or as a summary [HAN 89]. A halo effect occurs when consumers are not able to evaluate the true qualities of a product before the purchase and instead they need to rely on the indirect cues that a country image perception provides; that is, the halo effect refers to the inferential beliefs that consumers use to indirectly assess a product's attributes and which are based on the country [IVE 01]. The halo effect consists of the transfer of favorable (or unfavorable) perceptions about a country to the favorable (or unfavorable) judgments about the products manufactured in that country and vice versa [HAN 89], independently of the specific products' attributes [JOH 85]. Erickson et al. [ERI 84], for instance, found that when consumers rely on their perception of the general quality of a country's products, they will tend to apply those perceptions to a wide variety of goods that originate in that country, creating the halo effect.

On the other hand, when considering the country image acting as a summary [JOH 85; HAN 89], it represents the knowledge, or awareness, that consumers have of a country's products or brands. Hence, the country image summarizes consumers' beliefs about the products' attributes and affects directly the attitude toward the product (or the brand). Frequently, the summary effect occurs when the consumer uses accumulated prior experience with the country's products or brands to infer the qualities of a product. In this case, the country image affects directly consumers' attitudes towards the product.

7.2.3. The importance of the country of origin

The country of origin of a product influences consumers' perception of the product quality and impacts upon the general product evaluation [NAG 70, 77; LIL 74; BAN 78], product classes [NAG 70, 77; GAE 73; KAY 83], industrial products [CAT 82] and specific products [SCH 65]. Country of origin is, in this context, a signaling vehicle for products' attributes, although it may often be unintentionally employed.

When consumers are questioned about the importance of a product's country of origin, they may wish to seem rational and reasonable. For example, consumers may prefer to pass on the idea that their buying decisions are supported by a product's intrinsic characteristics rather than by extrinsic cues to denote an informed purchase. Nonetheless, it is possible that consumers do not look for country of origin information, but, when this information is available in a product's evaluation context, it will probably be taken into account. Papadopoulos [PAP 93] argued that, generally, the country of origin is important, even if its impact may vary from person to person. Hence, it is possible that some consumers will disregard the country of origin information; others will use it if available; and yet others may actively search for that information. This may partly explain [HON 89] the lack of conclusive evidence that a product's country of origin influences the way the rest of the product's information is interpreted and, Bilkey and Nes [BIL 82] stated that the extant research is inconclusive as to the effects of country of origin.

A country of origin effect may originate from a prior experience with a country's product, a personal experience (trip or study), an awareness about the country's culture, politic beliefs, ethnocentric trends and fear of the unknown. These experiences, acquired information and values may induce a stereotype, a bias, or an influence [AGA 99] affecting consumers' perceptions about a given country and the development of product-country images. Some known examples of country-product images – Columbian coffee, Swiss watches, Japanese electronics, French perfumes, Italian clothes and German automobiles – provide known examples of how product-country images operate. Tourism, events, participation in international conferences or study-abroad programs are examples of experiences that impact on how individuals perceive the country. Likewise, there are "word of mouth" influences whereby information and others' experiences influence consumer's perceptions.

Consumers' behavior has been shown to be related to the characteristics of the country of origin and its people [HAN 90; WAN 83]. Beyond the direct or indirect experience that an individual may have with a country's products, the individual's experience with the country itself or its inhabitants is likely to influence their perception of both the country and its products. Papadopoulos *et al.* [PAP 90], for example, noted the importance of the consumers' image of the people of a country and how a lack of familiarity with a country may lead consumers building an image based on their knowledge about the people's general ability to manufacture quality products. However, according to Hong and Wyer [HON 89], the product attributes have a substantial influence independently of whether the country of origin is familiar to the consumer at the moment attributes were described.

7.2.4. *Factors influencing the attitude towards the country of origin*

In literature on country of origin, three types of factors are usually referred to as influencing attitudes toward the country of origin: consumer-related factors, such as ethnocentrism, animosity, patriotism, nationalism and internationalism, familiarity, experience, involvement and socio-demographic characteristics; market-related factors, such as product type or attributes, market characteristics, brand image, retailer reputation, label requirements and market demand; and variables inherent in the national environment, such as presence and influence in global markets, level of economic, social, cultural and political development. Our study focuses on the latter type of factors. The social and economic development of a country seems to be an important factor affecting the perception of a product's quality and consumer behavior. Developed countries are perceived as holding advanced technology, having more product integrity and respecting environmental standards and user regulations.

There is evidence that products from more developed countries receive more positive evaluations and are perceived more favorably than products from less developed countries [WAN 83]. Products from countries perceived as industrially developed are better perceived than products from less developed countries [PAP

93]. This more positive perception seems to be due to the inherent judgment of a higher integrity of these countries' products. In fact, some countries' reputations appear to strengthen the credibility of their brands and the groups of products by which a country is known. However, products made in more developed countries are not evaluated equally [NAG 70, 77; LIL 74; BAN 78]. For instance, although France and Italy have positive country images on products and brands related to the fashion and food industries, not all these products are equally well perceived. From a similar perspective, Han [HAN 90] suggested that country image can have a greater effect on consumers' attitude towards products of a developed country than on consumers' attitude toward products of a developing country when the consumer is more familiar with the developed country's products.

Conversely, there are substantial hazards on the association of an image of "made in a developing country" [JON 94]. The poorer image of the products from developing countries probably emerges from a higher perceived risk associated with these countries, the poor technology employed in the manufacturing operations and the inability of regulatory agencies to control economic activity (eg, sanitation, public safety, food administration).

A country's national environment transcends the economic development of a country and incorporates variables such as social, cultural and political development. Such elements appear to influence people's perceptions and consumers' predispositions toward the products of a country. In this regard, Wang and Lamb [WAN 80] referred to the economic and political environment as variables that influenced consumers' willingness to buy products from foreign countries.

7.3. Research hypotheses

Our research question is straightforward as it investigates a possible relation between the conditions of a country, in particular its level of development, the attitude toward that country and the attitude toward the products originating in that country. The extant research suggests that the attitude toward products from various countries will vary from country to country because of the different countries' conditions. Indeed, studies comparing the attitudes toward different countries' products, such as Darling and Puetz [DAR 02], show that these differences exist. Specifically, this study noted that consumers perceived important differences among products based at least partially on their country of origin. Hence, our proposition, which is consistent with prior research, suggests that there are substantial differences in consumers' attitudes toward products from different countries.

Countries that are more developed economically, socially and technologically are likely to enjoy a better reputation, be more visible and act as a reference to other countries that may try to follow such countries' economic, social and technological policies. As a country's general attributes receive higher scores, the country image is highly perceived and the attitude toward the country will tend to be higher. A country's general attributes include the elements that refer to the country's state of social and economic development, as well as the perception that consumers have of the country's inhabitants [PAR 87]. The manner in which consumers perceive a country's inhabitants will incorporate and influence their image of a country. This influence is particularly evident when considering some specific sectors, such as tourism, that depend on people skills, or product categories such as the new technologies. Papadopoulos *et al.* [PAP 90] noted that the image consumers have of a country's citizens with whom they are not familiar may be based on the knowledge of those people's ability to manufacture quality products. In other words, when evaluating or demonstrating an attitude toward a non-familiar country, consumers will rely partially on the perception that they have of the country's inhabitants. Therefore, we set as hypothesis 1: *attitude towards the country is positively related to the country's general attributes.*

Some studies measured a country image and the attitude toward the country through the country's products [eg, NAG 70, 77]. In those studies, respondents were asked to evaluate or express their attitude toward products of country X and such evaluation represented the image of country X or the attitude toward country X. Other studies compared various countries' images in numerous product dimensions in an attempt to understand how consumers form evaluations of dimensions such as design, price, workmanship, or degree of innovation of the products from several countries [eg, PAP 93]. This reasoning leads us to suggest that a country's products may be used as heuristic cues to infer the country's image and may be a good indicator of consumers' attitudes toward the country. Therefore, it seems likely that a country's general attributes are positively related to the attitude toward the country. Bannister and Saunders [BAN 78] found significant differences between attitude towards the country and attitude towards specific products. These differences indicate that there are two distinct concepts; that is, the attitude towards the country and the attitude towards the country's products may be distinct, even if interdependent facets and a positive relation between the attitude towards the country and the attitude towards the country's products may be advanced. Hence, we set as hypothesis 2: *attitude towards the country is positively related to the attitude towards the country's products.*

The following model (Figure 7.1) represents the conceptual model developed in this study.

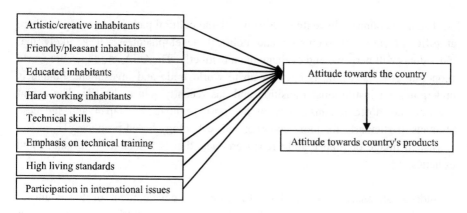

Figure 7.1. *Conceptual model*

7.4. Empirical analysis

In this section we present the empirical study. The research question requires the assessment of consumers' perceptions toward countries and products. We used a survey to assess Portuguese consumers' attitudes toward several countries and their attitudes toward the products made in each of those countries. In particular, we analyzed Portugal's conditions, from a country of origin perspective, comparing Portuguese consumers' perceptions of nine countries: China, Spain, the USA, France, the UK, Italy, Japan, Poland and Portugal. The countries were chosen using several criteria. Spain, France, the UK and Italy are the main European trading partners of Portugal and are presumably more familiar countries to Portuguese consumers. The USA, Japan and China were included because of their major relevance and presence in today's world economy. Poland, after joining the EU, has been often pointed out as one of the more direct competitors of Portugal in the context of the EU, for both manufacturing and foreign investment purposes.

The use of Portugal in country of origin research seems relevant in the present context; in particular, the complex economic and financial crisis that Portugal is facing enhances the need to understand and improve its country of origin image. In addition to the pure economic reasons, there are some social and cultural factors that justify country of origin research in Portugal, namely the overwhelming negative attitude of the Portuguese toward all that is Portuguese, which has affected national self-esteem [BAN 02].

The nine countries have diverse historical and cultural paths and heritage and are at different states of economic and political development, so it is likely that individuals will perceive and evaluate them distinctly. The USA and Japan are world economic powers. China is opening up to world trade and investment. Poland is undergoing an institutional transition and has recently joined the EU. The extant research has noted a consistency in the positive image of Japan and Japanese products, particularly for more complex and technology-based products. There is a consistent image of France and French products that is associated with status and esthetics.

Indeed, an analysis of the level of economic development of the countries included confirms wide differences between these nine countries in terms of their current state of economic and social development. Portugal had the second lowest gross domestic product (GDP) per capita (at purchasing power parity, 2004). The USA tops the list ($39,710), followed by the UK ($31,460), Japan ($30,040), France ($29,320), Italy ($27,860), Spain ($25,070), Poland ($19,250), Portugal ($12,640) and China ($5,530). The Human Development Indexes (HDI) also support wide intercountry disparities. China has made huge progress and has presented the greatest growth (0.52 in 1975 to 0.745 in 2002), but its HDI is still the lowest of the nine countries. The USA has maintained its top position (0.939 in 2002), Japan came second (0.938) and the UK third (0.936). Portugal's index has improved, but comes reasonably low among the EU member countries, rising from 0.79 in 1975 to 0.897 in 2002.

7.4.1. *Sample*

To collect data on Portuguese consumers' perceptions and attitudes toward the nine countries analyzed, we conducted an Internet-based survey. The target population of the study was composed of adult, Internet-user consumers. The survey was posted on the Internet for 30 days. Several mailing lists were used to contact our target segment encouraging their participation. In addition, any search on the Web using the terms "market study", "country of origin", "country image", "consumer behavior", or "competitiveness" (written in Portuguese) would show the Web page and invite visitors to take part.

This procedure yielded 264 questionnaires. Of these, 79 were incomplete and unusable, but the remaining ones were valid, giving a final sample of 185. The sample was equally divided between male (49.7%) and female (50.3%), was generally young (57.2% of the respondents were less than 30 years old), single (57.8% of the respondents) with a medium-high level of education (68.1% had a university degree). These characteristics are representative of Portuguese Internet users, according to a recent governmental study (study by the Unidade de Missão Inovação e Conhecimento, 2004). The sample descriptives are provided in Table 7.1.

		Frequency	%
Gender	male	92	49.7
	female	93	50.3
Age	15–19 years	1	0.5
	20–24 years	35	18.9
	25–29 years	70	37.9
	30–34 years	39	21.1
	35–39 years	24	13.0
	40–44 years	6	3.2
	45–49 years	7	3.8
	Over 50 years	3	1.6
Education	other	1	0.5
	ninth grade (legal minimum)	2	1.1
	undergraduate studies	32	17.3
	university student	24	13.0
	graduate studies	55	29.7
	master/doctoral studies	71	38.4
Occupation	unemployed/student	46	24.9
	unskilled worker	1	0.5
	skilled worker	47	25.4
	managerial/business owner	91	49.2

Table 7.1. *Sample socio-demographic profile*

7.4.2. *Instrument*

To measure the general country attributes and attitudes toward a country and a country's products, we used a self-administered consumer survey. General country attributes assess what consumers know (or think they know) about a country's production, style, design and technological innovation ability. This scale, introduced by Parameswaran and Yaprak [PAR 87] and further developed by Netemeyer *et al.* [NET 91], reflects the cognitive, affective and conative responses to the country and its people. Eight statements relative to country's inhabitants profile and perceived technical competences, living standards and participation in international issues were chosen to capture a broad image of each country. The items were rated on a five-point Likert scale, ranging from 1 – completely disagree – to 5 – completely agree. The items were "its inhabitants are friendly and pleasant", "its inhabitants are artistic and creative", "its inhabitants are well educated", "its inhabitants are hard working", "labor force technical skills are high", "its inhabitants emphasize technical training", "its inhabitants are motivated to increase the living standard" and "it is a country that participates in international issues". The Cronbach alphas were within acceptable values [see, for example, GEO 03] for all countries: 0.67 for China, 0.73 for the UK, 0.71 for France, 0.72 for Italy, 0.64 for Japan, 0.72 for Poland, 0.72 for Portugal, 0.76 for Spain and 0.74 for the USA.

Subjects were also asked to rate their attitude toward each of the countries ("please state your general attitude toward the country") on a five-point Likert scale ranging from 1 – very unfavorable – to 5 – very favorable. Finally, the attitude toward a country's products was measured in a similar manner with a single item ("please state your general attitude toward the products made in the country") on a five-point Likert scale ranging from 1 – very unfavorable – to 5 – very favorable.

7.5. Results

We established a broad proposition that consumers will form diverse perceptions and attitudes toward countries' products. In fact, the analysis of the average of our participants' perceptions of the products of each of the nine countries included in our study confirms that these differences exist. In our data, Japanese products received the higher evaluation (4.48), followed by French (3.78), Portuguese (3.73), English (3.68), Italian (3.48), Spanish (3.20), American (3.16), Chinese (2.62) and Polish products (2.39).

Moreover, using the paired samples T-tests, one can generally reject the idea that that the attitude towards a country's products is equal to the countries analyzed: China, the UK, France, Italy, Japan, Poland, Portugal, Spain and the USA. However, there are some exceptions: the pairs – Portuguese products-French products; Portuguese products-English products; USA products-Spanish products; and French products-English products – do not show a statistically significant difference. As a result, our results enable us to observe that the attitudes toward the products of the countries analyzed appear to be different, even though it is possible that Portuguese consumers perceive the Portuguese, French and British products as reasonably identical.

The first hypothesis showed a positive relation between the general country attributes and the attitude toward the country. In a first analysis, the case of Japan and the UK may be examined. Portuguese consumers perceive these countries as the best on general country attributes and the have the best attitudes toward those countries (3.85 and 3.71). Also, Portuguese consumers perceive China and Poland as the worst in terms of general country attributes and express the worst attitudes towards those countries (2.78 and 3.12). Spain (3.57), Italy (3.52) and France (3.38) are at an intermediate level. There are two exceptional cases that need to be highlighted: Portugal and the USA. Although Portuguese consumers perceive Portugal as having low general country attributes, they have a good attitude towards the country (3.44). For the USA, it is the opposite, with high scores in general country attributes and a poor attitude towards the country (3.37). Using the multiple regression technique, we found positive effects. We ran separate regressions for each of the countries to assess the impact of the country's attributes on the attitude towards that country. Table 7.2 displays the results. We may observe that the attitude towards a country is not equally influenced by all the general country characteristics considered. The "artistic and creative" characteristic is only significant for the USA and the UK; the "technical training" characteristic for France, Italy and Japan. The "friendly and pleasant" characteristic was not significant for China and Japan; the "well educated" characteristic not significant for China, Italy, Japan and Poland; the "high technical skills" characteristic for France, Italy, Poland, Spain and the UK; the "increase living standards" characteristic for France, Italy, Japan and the UK; and the "international issues" characteristic for Japan, Portugal and the USA. Hence, we confirm the first hypothesis with the data, but we caution that a more disaggregated examination of the country attributes allows greater clarification of our results.

	China	France	Italy	Japan	Poland	Portugal	Spain	UK	USA
friendly/pleasant	.037	**.229****	**.259****	.136	**.176***	**.228***	**.200****	**.133***	**.200****
artistic/creative	.075	.051	.087	-.016	.085	.051	.102	**.128***	**.188****
well educated	.152	**.264****	.076	-.059	:046	**.146***	**.188****	**.296****	**.186***
hard working	-.073	.040	.014	-.022	.058	.034	.064	-.002	.149
technical skills	**.232****	.158	.105	**.256****	.152	**.180****	.071	.115	**.224***
technical training	-.016	.171	**.157***	**.200***	.042	.006	.097	.055	-.059
increase living standards	**.144***	.096	.104	.134	**.222****	**.134***	**.318****	-.008	**.192***
international issues	**.141***	**.174***	**.193****	.124	**.177****	.114	**.148***	**.180***	.009
R^2	.258	.429	.382	.236	.308	.309	.501	.373	.364
F ratio	**7.643****	**16.548****	**13.572****	**6.810****	**9.770****	**9.841****	**22.082****	**13.112****	**12.583****

Significant findings are in bold   * $P<.05$ ** $P<.01$

Table 7.2. *Coefficients of linear regression between general country attributes and attitude toward the country*

The second hypothesis suggested a positive relationship between the attitude towards the country and the attitude towards the country's products. The results of individual analysis of variances (ANOVAs) for each country confirmed that, in fact, the attitude towards the country and the country's products are closely related (Table 7.3). The attitude towards the country affects the attitude towards the country's products. Therefore, the second hypothesis is confirmed.

	China	UK	France	Italy	Japan	Poland	Portugal	Spain	USA
Attitude towards the country's products									
F ratio									
Attitude towards country	**25.898****	**8.273****	2.412	**42.098****	**34.504****	**24.185****	**59.820****	**60.343****	**60.409****

Significant findings are in bold   * P<.05   ** P<.01

Table 7.3. *One-way ANOVA tests of the attitude toward the country
and the attitude toward the country's products*

7.6. Discussion

This chapter has addressed the issue of whether and how, the country of origin image impacts on consumers' perceptions. In particular, we sought to observe whether a possible effect would be visible for Portuguese consumers, since to the best of our knowledge no other study has yet examined the Portuguese case. First, we tested whether Portuguese consumers had different attitudes towards the products from nine different countries, namely China, the UK, France, Italy, Japan, Poland, Portugal, Spain and the USA. It is worth noting in this respect that although we found significant differences, we also observed that some pairs of countries' products were not perceived as being substantially different. We observed that Portuguese, French and British products were not perceived differently in our sample, a finding that is consistent with some previous studies [LIL 74; DAR 02], but nonetheless intriguing in the context of the low self-esteem that the Portuguese demonstrate. Indeed, the Portuguese are often rated in various studies as pessimistic and tending to underestimate the quality of Portugal's products, but in our study we found that the products from the respondents' own country (Portugal) were evaluated above the mean value and in comparison to the products from the other eight countries; only Japanese and French products were considered as better. This is *prima facie* evidence that Portuguese consumers are confident about national products. This situation was identified by some researchers as ethnocentrism (eg, [SHI 87; SHA 95]), something that would be interesting to analyze in further research. It is worth noting in this respect that Portuguese agencies long ago initiated promotional campaigns – such as *Portugal Positivo* and *Movimento 560* – to promote products "made in Portugal" to the Portuguese and the perceptions we captured may be a result of those campaigns. Moreover, national pride is on the rise after outstanding results in the most popular of sports – soccer – in the European Soccer Championship 2004 and the 2006 World Cup. Finally, it is worth pointing out that our sample is reasonably young and with an above average education and thus possibly more aware of the importance of origin. For marketers, it may be worthwhile studying whether there are differences in country effects when considering consumers with diverse levels of education or distinct ages and how consumers with such profiles may be used as opinion leaders.

In terms of the attitudes toward the products, there seems to be a hierarchy in the comparison of countries. Less developed countries received the lowest scores and more developed countries received higher scores (which is consistent with previous studies, such as [WAN 80, 83]), with two exceptional cases: Portugal and the USA. Portugal's position may be due to a nationalist or patriotic explanation, since it received a similar position in the attitudes toward its products. It would be interesting to analyze the Portuguese case and its comparison with other countries and countries' products in future research. The USA's position may be related to the attention given to the USA-Iraq conflict before and during the period of the data collection. In previous studies, the USA scored relatively higher [CAT 82], which may reinforce the previous argument or may be due to the specific sample profile. Nagashima [NAG 70] and Lillis and Narayana [LIL 74] noted that respondents from different countries show different attitudes toward the products of a country. Moreover, the previous research focused mainly on USA samples, while the present study used a Portuguese sample. This fact highlights the need for further research using distinct national samples. One other explanation may be related to Klein *et al.*'s [KLE 98] findings that consumers are able to recognize a country's product quality while expressing hostility toward the country and aversion toward its products. Hence, consumers may avoid the products of a country although they have positive perceptions toward the products or the country. We further examined how countries appear to have distinct profiles based on the perceptions of general country attributes. It is likely that the image Portuguese respondents have of some countries might be supported by their perceptions of the people of other countries. In particular, the "social" attributes ("friendly", "pleasant", "artistic", "creative", "well educated" and "participation in international issues") are highly influential as to how the Portuguese perceived other countries and products and are especially salient when evaluating Spain and the UK. However, when analyzing the "professional" or "competence" attributes of other populations, these attributes are more salient for

Japan, France and the USA. An image of technical competence associated with Japan and the USA, which was already found by other scholars (eg, [NAG 70, 77]), was also found in our study and perceived by Portuguese consumers. France, although it appeared to be less well perceived in some previous studies (eg, [LIL 74]), benefits from a positive image on the part of the Portuguese. A pattern may be drawn when comparing our results with the data from human development reports. The attitudes toward the country rank (first Japan, followed by the UK, Spain, Italy, Portugal, France, the USA, Poland and China) are similar to the human development index (the USA, Japan, the UK, France, Spain, Italy, Portugal, Poland and China) (Human Development Reports 2004), except in the case of the USA and France.

The second hypothesis suggested a positive relation between the attitude towards the country and the attitude towards the country's products. Results show that positive and significant relation. As predicted, if consumers evaluate the country positively they are more likely to consider and evaluate positively that country's products. This result is consistent with previous studies, such as [DAR 02], finding that consumers might rely on the strong reputation of Japan to estimate the quality of products designed or manufactured in Japan. According to the results of the present study and considering its limitations in terms of generality, consumers evaluated the country similarly to their country's products evaluation. It seems that, when consumers are evaluating a certain country's products, they consider the country and their perception of that country. However, the attitude toward the country's products appears to capture only a small part of consumers' attitude toward the country. The attitude toward a country's products will be also influenced by other factors, such as the type of products mentioned and the companies' actions and campaigns, among many others. The identification and intensity of such factors need further research.

Our study's results, namely the comparison of countries, seem to be very important in a context where the EU competes directly with Japan, China and the USA. The "made in the EU" concept has been increasingly used in trade worldwide. This phenomenon may be complex in terms of competitiveness since it seems complex to harmonize the image of 25 different member countries. In our study, the Portuguese consumers' perceptions of and attitude toward, the UK were positive. Likewise, the perceptions and attitudes toward Spain, France and Italy were positive, although not at the UK's level. Poland is a less well-known country, since it has only recently joined the EU. The good image of Japan, which had already been found in prior research [LIL 74], was confirmed. The USA was positively perceived in professional terms, but it did not obtain a good position in terms of the attitude toward the country. The Chinese case is peculiar since respondents admitted that

China's inhabitants are hard working, although with technical skills below average. Poland's and China's images were consistent with the low "made in a developing country" image found by [JOH 94]. In relation to Portugal, in spite of presenting below average perceptions of technical skills, technical training and standard of living, the social component appeared to compensate in the contribution to the attitude toward the country. This result may be due to a nationalist feeling.

This study has some limitations that are also opportunities for further research. First, our results may not be applicable to other countries, but known models, such as the one we applied, have already been used in other countries, as our literature review acknowledges. Our study replicates a model already applied to other countries, but applies it to a new country. The sample used captured the perceptions of a specific profile of consumers – Internet users – who represent a growing group. It would be interesting to use other samples and other countries. Moreover, the scale used to measure the dependent variables – "attitude towards the country" and "attitude towards the country's products" – are composed by a single item and future research could use multi-item scales. Nagaashima [NAG 70], Schooler [SCH 71] and Gaedeke [GAE 73] argued that, as the experience with a country's products increases, the country of origin becomes less relevant. In this regard, one other question to be raised, at a more general level, is whether, if consumers are aware that they are consuming foreign products, it affects their perceptions.

In addition to the avenues for future research already noted, other research possibilities are worth noting. Researchers may study the impact of other elements related to national culture and political, social, economic and technological development, using variables such as ethnocentrism, patriotism or internationalism to evaluate their impact on influencing consumers' perceptions. Such studies may lead to the construction of a more comprehensive framework of the factors that drive consumers' perceptions of countries and products. Moreover, it is important to fully capture the manner in which the stereotype effects vary with the type of product [NAG 77; ROT 92]. Variations in the stereotype effects by type of product provide insights on the comparative advantages that some nations have in certain products, such as is the case with French wines and perfumes that enjoy excellent worldwide reputations. Also, country of origin evaluations appear to be different when based on socio-demographic characteristics, namely age, gender or level of education [SCH 71], which is something that requires further research.

7.7. Concluding comments

As firms and countries compete in the international arena for foreign direct investment, reputation and to affirm themselves in the world markets, it is important to understand how consumers perceive and are influenced, by country of origin effects. General country attributes are one of the concepts that provide some insight about country of origin effects. The comparison of the perceptions of different countries' and the analysis of whether these perceptions are related to the attitude towards the country and towards the country's products contribute to a better knowledge of country of origin effects.

In spite of an abundant stream of research on country of origin effects in the international business and international marketing literature, we still lack a comprehensive and structured framework of how the perception, or attitude, toward a country relates to the attitude toward a country's products. Such a framework is important for academics in guiding future research for understanding how and what factors shift consumers' perceptions. It is also important for practitioners as they design marketing campaigns and decide on such factors as brand names and location decisions. For public policy makers, this framework assists in better allocating resources to promote the image of the country in foreign countries.

How can marketers and policy makers act based on our findings? For marketers, it is important to understand that part of consumers' perceptions towards a product originates in their perception of the country of origin. A well-informed marketing campaign should not overlook this dimension. This information is relevant because it is possible to act upon it, adjusting the communication and image of the product (or brand) to converge with the strengths of the country of origin image. It is also possible to deploy a global strategy of location for the activities of the value chain, in order to benefit from the idiosyncratic perceptions consumers have of each country for different activities. For policy makers, however, the task is complex because the perceptions of a country are based on a large variety of factors, some of which are related to the people, others related to the quality of the products and yet others to the level of economic development attained. Overall, the plea is for more research in order to understand in detail how consumers' perceptions and attitudes can be targeted and how firms from peripheral countries, with low levels of international experience, such as Portugal, can compete vis-a-vis with those from more developed countries.

7.8. References

[AGA 99] AGARWAL, J and *KAMAKURA*, W (1999) "Country of origin: a competitive advantage?", *International Journal of Research in Marketing*, vol 16, n. 4, pp 255–67

[BAN 78] BANNISTER, J and SAUNDERS, J (1978) "UK consumers' attitudes towards imports: the measurement of national stereotype image", *European Journal of Marketing*, vol 12, no 8, pp 562–70

[BAN 02] BANDYOPADHYAY, S, YELKUR, R, DA COSTA, M and COELHO, F (2002) "Product country of origin perceptions of Portuguese consumers", *Revista Portuguesa de Marketing*, no 12, pp 47–53

[BIL 82] BILKEY, W and NES, E (1982) "Country of origin effects on product evaluations", *Journal of International Business Studies*, vol 13, no 1, pp 89–99

[CAT 82] CATTIN, P, JOLIBERT, A and LOHNES, C (1982) "A cross-cultural study of made in concepts", *Journal of International Business Studies*, vol 13, no 3, pp 131–41

[DAR 02] DARLING, J and PUETZ, J (2002) "Analysis of changes in consumers' attitudes toward the products of England, France, Germany and the USA, 1975–2000", *European Business Review*, vol 14, no 3, pp 170–83

[ERI 84] ERICKSON, G, JOHANSSON, J and CHAO, P (1984) "Image variables in multi-attribute product evaluations: country of origin effects", *Journal of Consumer Research*, vol 11, no 2, pp 694–99

[GAE 73] GAEDEKE, R (1973) "Consumer attitudes toward products 'made in' developing countries", *Journal of Retailing*, vol 49, no 2, pp 13–24

[GEO 03] GEORGE, D and MALLERY, P (2003) "SPSS for Windows step by step: a simple guide and reference, 11.0 update", (4th edn): Allyn & Bacon

[HAN 89] HAN, C (1989) "Country image: halo or summary construct?", *Journal of Marketing Research*, vol 26, no 2, pp 222–29

[HAN 90] HAN, C (1990) "Testing the role of country image in consumer choice behaviour", *European Journal of Marketing*, vol 24, no 6, pp 24–41

[HON 89] HONG, S and WYER, R (1989) "Effects of country of origin and product-attribute information on product evaluation: an information processing perspective", *Journal of Consumer Research*, vol 16, no 2, pp 175–87

[IVE 01] IVERSEN, N and HEM, L (2001) "Country image in national umbrella branding effects of country associations on similarity judgments", *Asia Pacific Advances in Consumer Research*, vol 4, pp 140–49

[JOH 85] JOHANSSON, J, DOUGLAS, S and NONAKA, I (1985) "Assessing the impact of country of origin on product evaluations: a new methodological perspective", *Journal of Marketing Research*, vol 22, no 4, pp 388–96

[JOH 94] JOHANSSON, J, RONKAINEN, I and CZINKOTA, M (1994) "Negative country of origin effects: the case of the new Russia", *Journal of International Business Studies*, vol 25, no 1, pp 157–77

[KAY 83] KAYNAK, E and CAVUSGIL, T (1983) "Consumer attitude toward products of foreign origin: do they vary across product classes?", *International Journal of Advertising*, vol 2, no 2, pp 147–57

[KLE 98] KLEIN, J, ETTENSON, R and MORRIS, M (1998) "The animosity model of foreign product purchase: an empirical test in the People's Republic of China", *Journal of Marketing*, vol 62, no 1, pp 89–100

[KOT 93] KOTLER, P, HAIDER, D and REIN, I (1993) *Marketing Places: Attracting Investment, Industry and Tourism to Cities, States and Nations*, New York: Free Press

[LEV 83] LEVITT, T (1983) "The globalization of markets", *Harvard Business Review*, vol 61, no 3, pp 92–102

[LIL 74] LILLIS, C and NARAYANA, C (1974) "Analysis of made in product images: an exploratory study", *Journal of International Business Studies*, vol 5, no 1, pp 119–27

[MAR 93] MARTIN, I and EROGLU, S (1993) "Measuring a multi-dimensional construct: country image", *Journal of Business Research*, vol 28, no 3, pp 191–210

[NAG 70] NAGASHIMA, A (1970) "A comparison of Japanese and US attitudes toward foreign products", *Journal of Marketing*, vol 34, no 1, pp 68–74

[NAG 77] NAGASHIMA, A (1977) "A comparative made in product image survey among Japanese businessmen", *Journal of Marketing*, vol 41, no 3, pp 95–100

[NET 91] NETEMEYER, R, DURVASULA, S and LICHTENSTEIN, D (1991) "A cross-national assessment of the reliability and validity of the CETSCALE", *Journal of Marketing Research*, vol 28, no 3, pp 320–27

[PAP 90] PAPADOPOULOS, N, HESLOP, L and BAMOSSY, G (1990) "A comparative image analysis of domestic versus imported products", *International Journal of Research in Marketing*, vol 7, no 4, pp 283–94

[PAP 93] PAPADOPOULOS, N (1993) "What product and country images are and are not", in Papadopoulos, N and Heslop, L (eds), *Product-Country Images: Impact and Role in International Marketing*, New York: International Business Press, pp 3–38

[PAR 81] PARK, C and LESSIG, V (1981) "Familiarity and its impact on consumer biases and heuristics", *Journal of Consumer Research*, vol 8, no 2, pp 223–30

[PAR 87] PARAMESWARAN, R and YAPRAK, A (1987) "A cross-national comparison of consumer research measures", *Journal of International Business Studies*, vol 18, pp 35–49

[ROT 92] ROTH, M and ROMEO, J (1992) "Matching product category and country image perceptions: a framework for managing country of origin effects", *Journal of International Business Studies*, vol 23, no 3, pp 477–97

[SCH 65] SCHOOLER, R (1965) "Product bias in the Central American common market", *Journal of Marketing Research*, vol 2, no 4, pp 394–97

[SCH 71] SCHOOLER, R (1971) "Bias phenomena attendant to the marketing of foreign goods in the US", *Journal of International Business Studies*, vol 2, no 1, pp 71–80

[SHA 95] SHARMA, S, SHIMP, T and SHIN, J (1995) "Consumer ethnocentrism: a test of antecedents and moderators", *Academy of Marketing Science Journal*, vol 23, no 1, pp 26–38

[SHI 87] SHIMP, T and SHARMA, S (1987) "Consumer ethnocentrism: construction and validation of the CETSCALE", *Journal of Marketing Research*, vol 24, no 3, pp 280–89

[SHI 93] SHIMP, T, SAMIEE, S and MADDEN, T (1993) "Countries and their products: a cognitive structure perspective", *Academy of Marketing Science Journal*, vol 21, no 4, pp 323–30

[WAN 80] WANG, C and LAMB, C (1980) "Foreign environmental factors influencing American consumers' predispositions toward European products", *Journal of the Academy of Marketing Science*, vol 8, no 4, pp 345–56

[WAN 83] WANG, C and LAMB, C (1983) "The impact of selected environmental forces upon consumers' willingness to buy foreign products", *Journal of the Academy of Marketing Science*, vol 11, no 2, pp 71–84

Chapter 8

Consumer Shopping Behavior Online: The Case of Spanish Web Users

8.1. Introduction

Globalization and the ubiquitous nature of the Internet facilitate e-commerce activities across nations. As a result, companies using e-commerce and service providers recognize that a consumer focus is critical to their marketing strategies. Although some authors consider that global tastes have been homogenized [LEV 83], others have shown that there are online consumer segments with different purchase motivations [ROH 04], perceived shopping risks [BHA 04] and brand and merchant loyalties in their local environments [BRO 03]. Likewise, aspects such as consumer culture and website usability can influence the success or failure of a company's international marketing strategy in virtual environments.

Despite the growing importance of e-commerce, there are still not enough studies that provide a holistic view of factors influencing global consumer behavior in virtual environments. It is also crucial for managers to understand which aspects influence consumers' decisions to shop from international companies instead of only from domestic ones and which perceived benefits provided by e-shopping they value the most in order to assign resources effectively to obtain competitive advantages.

Chapter written by Carla RUIZ MAFE and Silvia SANZ BLAS.

Previous research into e-commerce has mainly focused on its adoption in the context of high e-commerce adoption rate regions such as North America, Denmark, UK, or Finland and, to a lesser extent, in developing regions such as Malaysia, Taiwan and Turkey. This study offers an insight into global consumer behavior in Spain, which has not previously been investigated. Distinct differences and common trends between local and global e-shoppers were observed giving a clear indication of marketing strategy that should be deployed by companies interested in implementing online international marketing.

The chapter aims to present an in-depth study of the factors influencing global consumer behavior, focusing on the purchase of electronic items. The chapter's specific goals are to:

(i) identify the types of online markets and their distinguishing characteristics;

(ii) provide a holistic view of factors influencing global consumer behavior in online environments; and

(iii) provide empirical research on the Spanish market that analyzes the influence of demographics, online experience and Internet browsing patterns in the decision to shop both on foreign and domestic company websites or only on domestic ones.

8.2. Online buyers worldwide

In this section there is a description of online buyer types worldwide, explaining the similarities and differences between markets with high (eg, the USA, Northern Europe), medium (eg, Spain, Estonia) and low (eg, Third World, deep-interior states of China) levels of e-commerce adoption.

World regions	Estimated population (2006)	Population % of World	Internet usage	Usage growth 2000–05	% population (penetration)
Africa	915,210,928	14.1%	23,649,000	423.9%	2.6%
Asia	3,667,774,066	56.4%	380,400,713	232.8%	10.4%
Europe	807,289,020	12.4%	294,101,844	179.8%	36.4%
Middle East	190,084,161	2.9%	18,203,500	454.2%	9.6%
North America	331,473,276	5.1%	227,470,713	110.4%	68.6%
Latin America	553,908,632	8.5%	79,962,809	350.5%	14.7%
Oceania	33,956,977	0.5%	17,872,707	134.6%	52.6%
WORLD TOTAL	6,499,697,060	100%	1,043,104,886	189.0%	16.0%

Source: http://www.internetworldstats.com

Table 8.1. *World Internet usage*

International markets are quite different. Some contain a fair higher concentration of prospective buyers and more fully-developed electronic marketing infaestructures than others. As Table 8.1 shows, by 2006 the online population worldwide was forecast to be over one billion, with usage growth of over 180% since 2000. The USA will continue to dominate in the overall number of Internet users, but its share will drop as Internet use rises in other regions such as Europe and Asia. It was estimated that the USA might represent as little as 20.1% of all Internet users by 2006.

Future estimates also suggest that the Asian market will grow spectacularly over the next few years, particularly in some super-populated regions, such as India, which will slowly develop a significant online presence [SIE 03]. One of the factors behind the progressive reduction in differences between the markets in the USA,

Asia and Europe is the high rate of cell phone use by citizens in Asia and Europe. Furthermore, the Internet can offer special opportunities for emerging markets as against traditional channels since in emerging markets distribution channels tend to be less developed, less direct and less efficient [QUE 96; SIM 02].

Currently, the world regions with the largest market potential for companies interested in using the Internet as a marketing tool are America, Europe and Asia. Internet use in North America is dominated by the USA and Canada. Canada is an attractive market that is smaller than the USA and has almost 70% Internet penetration. In 2000, 90% of Canadian teens went online, leading the world in music downloads [SIE 03]. Despite the fact that the Internet adoption rate in Latin America is still low, it has grown by 350% over the 2000–05 period (see Table 8.1). Brazil, Mexico and Argentina are the principal Latin American growth markets. Mexican consumers like the convenience of online shopping, but local online retailers are not delivering good customer service, prices are high and product choice is poor.

The Asian region is dominated by Japan and South Korea, although penetration is growing in China which at present is the second largest online shopping market in the world. In the last two decades, China has experienced a historical transition from central planning to reliance on market forces. Reforms and economic development have led to the adoption of modern marketing practices, the emergence of consumer societies and a growing middle class, which has favored consumption of both domestic and imported products [CHA 04; LIN 03]. Regarding Internet access, many Chinese people share the cost of Internet connection and public Internet cafés are popular log-on points. China has a young, highly-educated, urban population that is predisposed to surf the Net and purchase online. In rural areas in deep-interior states of China, however, infrastructures are lacking and consumers do not react positively to marketing campaigns by foreign companies or to new shopping channels such as the Internet. India has a population of more than one billion people and some experts predict it will overtake China as the world's population leader within the next 20 years. It has an educated workforce and a rapidly expanding information technology sector [LAF 05].

South Korea, Australia and New Zealand also are high e-commerce growth areas. All three have educated, literate consumers who are already purchasing online.

The European market is dominated by Western and Northern Europe. Northern European countries (Sweden, Norway, Denmark, Finland and Iceland) have the highest rates of Internet penetration, while Mediterranean countries (Spain, Italy) have medium adoption rates and some countries in Eastern Europe (Macedonia, Albania) have the lowest rates. Climate also appears to have particular influence on e-commerce development since the adoption rate is highest in the countries with the most extreme climates and it is much slower in countries with a Mediterranean culture where traditional commerce is more important and is favored by the urban layout.

The most basic geo-demographic division of Europe today is its division into Eastern and Western Europe ([ROJ 01]; [SIE 03]). Formation of a single market within the EU and democratization and development of a marketing economy in Eastern Europe undoubtedly enhance the standardization of marketing in the European area. This does not mean that the Western European region is culturally and economically identical or that Eastern consumers are undifferentiated. Some countries, such as Estonia, Slovenia and Hungary, have growing Internet penetration rates, due mainly to the fact that their governments encourage Internet use. Russian Internet use is rising rapidly with the Internet being used extensively in schools and at work.

Particularly significant among the areas with the lowest Internet penetration is the case of Africa which comprises over 10% of the world population, but less than 1% of the online community. The main causes for this include the lack of infrastructures and telephone lines, lack of education and the absence of liberalization in the telecommunications sector.

A country's level of development has significant influence on the degree of Internet penetration in the different markets. Citizens in more developed countries have greater purchasing power and higher educational levels and consequently more Internet penetration. The opportunity for consumers to access the Internet at school or university, combined with a decrease in the price of terminals may push up the low levels of e-commerce penetration in some countries. The rich nations may financially support those with fewer resources (through, for example, donations of obsolete computer equipment) as the nations with fewer resources are very attractive markets for the sales of the rich nations' products.

Culture is another critical factor to be taken into account by companies interested in developing an international online marketing strategy. Culture is a system of values and a set of shared norms which influence the formation of attitudes and preferences and can be seen in the daily life of consumers through non-programmed values which influence the way social interaction develops between them [HOF 80].

The influence of a culture is also reflected in how receptive its members are to innovations and the speed at which innovations such as the Internet spread. One of the dimensions of culture which influences e-commerce adoption is the degree of individualism/collectivism [VAN 02]. Individualism/collectivism refers to the form of the relationship between the individual and the collective in a given society. In individualist cultures, behavior and values are determined by personal choices, personal goals and motivation for achievement, while in collectivist cultures, the interest of the group prevails over the interest of the individual. Thus, individualist cultures value new uses and behaviors positively and their members develop a more innovative profile [HOF 80]. People from individualist cultures are more confident and perceive less risk in relations with strangers and, therefore, they develop a more positive attitude towards online shopping at the international level [VAN 02].

On the other hand, in countries where globalization has mainly been achieved through government intervention and coordination in a collectivistic manner, such as Korea and China, consumers are more likely to be ethnocentric and reject the purchase of foreign-made products than consumers in countries such as the USA, Finland or the UK who have been globalized mainly through their own experiences and self-awakening in an individualistic way ([SUH 02]; [SCH 98]).

8.3. Key drivers of global consumer shopping behavior online

This section describes the impact of demographics, Internet experience, shopping orientations and Internet browsing patterns on global consumer behavior in virtual environments.

8.3.1. Demographics

The adoption rate for online shopping is a significant variable influencing the e-shopper's profile since in countries, such as Singapore or Greece, with low Internet adoption rates, the e-shopper profile is significantly different from that of the non-shopper and is mainly a young male with a high level of education and income ([SIM 02]; [VRE 01]); in countries with a higher rate of Internet adoption, such as the USA, online shopping has increased among people with different educational and economic levels, thus assimilating both profiles [SIE 03]. In contrast with e-shoppers in the West, Chinese online shoppers are predominantly males, not necessarily young and highly educated [LAF 05].

Men and women seem to differ in their shopping orientations and shopping behavior [HOF 80]. Men are goal-oriented shoppers, while social motives are more important for women, so men value more highly the shopping benefits provided by e-shopping. Furthermore, in general, women have less online experience than men. In the newly-industrialized regions, education and work opportunities for women have been restricted and, in comparison to men, this has delayed their access to qualified jobs that provide exposure to the new technologies and, therefore, their experience of online shopping is more recent than that of men [SIE 03]. Women perceive a higher level of risk in online purchasing than men and prefer shopping on websites recommended by other consumers or which have a good reputation and therefore generate trust and credibility [BAR 99].

Since men and women differ in their shopping orientations and perceived shopping risks, it is likely that they have different shopping behavior in online environments and different attitudes towards purchasing foreign-made products.

New technological advances in some direct shopping methods, such as the Internet, need to take into account the individual's capacity to understand the changes and complexities in the new technologies. Consumer needs, interests and attitudes vary with age and younger consumers are more predisposed to adopt innovations ([AL-A 01]; [JOI 03]). The youngest consumers use the Internet from a very early age. As young people are motivated by something more than just education or work, they know many websites for the worldwide products that interest them (leisure, culture, entertainment, etc).

Previous studies focused on low e-commerce adoption rate areas report that young, highly-educated consumers on high incomes develop the most positive attitudes to e-shopping ([SIM 02]; [VRE 01]). Research done by Vrechopoulos, Siomkos and Duokidis in Greece shows that younger people shop more online and are more willing to shop online in the future than older people. Al-Ashban and Burney [AL-A 01] analyzed telebanking adoption in Saudi-Arabia and found that it is negatively associated with age and positively associated with income and educational level. High-educational level also correlates positively with online experience [LI 99]. In contrast, mature and less-educated consumers lack familiarity with the use of the Internet as a communication and shopping channel and prefer traditional shopping [TRO 00].

Age is also related to ethnocentrism. Research by Tower and Cooper [TOW 95] focused on Eastern European markets shows that younger consumers quite openly purchase goods and services from Western companies while the older ones prefer to buy products from local companies because they wish to enhance cultural integrity, belonging and security.

Given that young people have a more positive attitude toward change and innovation and a lower tendency toward ethnocentrism, it is to be expected that they will develop a greater willingness to purchase both domestic and imported products online.

8.3.2. Internet experience

The response of Internet users to marketing actions changes as their use and experience of the Internet grows ([DAH 02]; [LI 99]). Web users who spend more time surfing the Net and who have more online use experience will be more familiar with the opportunities that the Internet offers and will have more knowledge about using it as a global shopping channel [STE 00].

Research by Swaminathan, Lepkowska-White and Rao [SWA 99] shows there are different levels of experience and consequently of the perception of the usefulness of e-commerce in different scenarios of Internet use. In other words, there is a positive relation between online experience and perceived e-shopping benefits.

8.3.3. Browsing behavior

The international information which the Internet can deliver to the consumer is one of the success factors for virtual shops since it reduces the cost of the information search and increases the likelihood of finding a product which suits the consumer's needs. However, this apparent advantage may become a barrier to purchase as it can mean greater difficulty in accessing specific information worldwide and therefore can be a waste of time for the consumer. Fortunately, directories and search engines allow users to browse through comprehensive lists of vendors arranged by product and service, or to search for a vendor by name or page content all from the convenience of a home computer. They can find specific information and help the user in purchase decision-making [MON 04].

Maes *et al.* [MAE 99] suggest four functions for search engines: automatically build models of shoppers, recommend products to shoppers, negotiate on behalf of shoppers and personalise the shopping experience.

While the use of search engines has evolved quickly in countries such as Canada (85% use search engines) and the USA (73% use search engines), in Spain, use is just beginning to grow and is becoming the focus of online marketing strategies for many companies [EMA 04].

E-shoppers generally are uncertain about which website to purchase from because of variations in products offered online and to reduce this uncertainty they seek information [BHA 04]. Internet search engines allow customers to search for product characteristics from online retailers worldwide at the click of a button and to shop online. Search engines increase the quality of the decision by locating the seller offering the best conditions (price, payment terms, delivery) and considerably reducing comparison costs between different countries and currencies; hence it is expected that search engine use encourages global e-shopping behavior.

8.3.4. *Shopping orientations*

Consumers have different motivations for shopping online. We need to know what the online shopping motivations are in order to estimate future developments in global online buying.

8.3.4.1. *Convenience and time saving*

Several factors have accelerated the development and expansion of online sales in the consumer market at the international level. These include: being able to use credit cards, toll-free numbers and the fact that companies can take orders at any time of the day or night and from anywhere in the world and deliver right to the customer's home – in short, all the factors that facilitate the act of shopping.

Consumers can shop online at any time and any place. Most e-shoppers are trying to save time in order to improve their quality of life and one way of doing this is to reduce the time spent shopping [DHO 02]. Convenience and the ease of ordering from home from worldwide suppliers attracts increasing numbers of consumers who value their free time or who consider shopping from both local and foreign companies.

Store location and transportation costs are also decisive in the decision to shop online. For example, when catalogue shopping was introduced in USA, it was adopted by many families living in rural areas as they had high displacement costs. Electronic channels eliminate all displacement problems as the consumer can shop without leaving home and has the freedom and the time to choose. This is particularly positive for consumers whose age or physical disabilities prevent them from going to the sales outlet [BRO 03] and also for users with time restrictions due to work and family obligations [DHO 02].

8.3.4.2. *Access to products unavailable in the local market*

Another advantage of online buying is quick, economic and direct access to products which are not available in the local market ([ALB 97]; [PAR 03]).

The Internet eliminates the obstacles created by geography and time zones, favoring customer-business communication. Internet users benefit from, in particular, the greater quantity of products, services and information which the Internet can place at their reach. Online commercial operations can take place anywhere in the world, with the Internet acting as a market integrator [QUE 96]. For example, when certain product categories are not simultaneously available in all countries (eg, high-tech products or specialized books), they can be bought online from wherever they happen to be available.

8.3.4.3. *Variety and range of products*

Consumers can easily find a wide range and assortment of products and detailed information online. This is one of the factors behind the success of online stores [ROM 04], as international choice is an advantage for the consumer because it increases the chances of finding a product that meets his or her needs. In addition, by providing better quality information online stores can increase consumer satisfaction ([PAR 03]; [PET 97]).

Furthermore, online shopping differs significantly from traditional shopping, mainly due to the medium's highly interactive nature. In particular, the Internet can decisively affect the way consumers search for and evaluate product information [DEG 00]. The use of interactive shopping channels allows consumers to search, compare and access information worldwide much more easily and at greater depth than within the bricks-and-mortar structure. Degeratu, Rangaswamy and Wu [DEG 00] show that traditional channels provide more information on product attributes that consumers can perceive with their senses than is provided online, but information search costs are much lower in virtual environments, especially if we consider attributes other than price.

The Internet also provides an enormous amount of information, answering customer doubts, needs, or wishes, providing a very efficient information system and facilitating the purchase process by matching offer and demand more efficiently. In this sense, Peterson *et al.* [PET 97] note that when consumers decide which brand they want, they search for information on the price in different online shops, which increases competition.

8.3.4.4. *Price reductions*

A positive aspect of online shopping for the consumer is the high degree of disintermediation ([ALB 97]; [QUE 96]). This characteristic makes it more attractive than traditional shopping as the Internet eliminates any physical barrier and makes it possible to purchase goods and services from the part of the world where the cost is lower. In particular, significant discounts are available on the average price for a product or service, for better quality goods and without excessively long delivery times, an important motivation for present and potential shoppers. For some products, such as cars, the key lies in finding the areas where taxes are cheaper than in the country from where the order is being placed.

Reibstein's study [REI 02] shows that price is an important choice criteria used by most consumers in deciding where to shop online. Economically-motivated shoppers see price as an important cost component and compare prices between different alternatives. Previous research ([KOR 99]; [REI 02]) maintains that economic motivations are directly related to Internet experience, since consumers who try to obtain price reductions surf the Net for a long time in search of bargains. Therefore, there is a relation between online experience and the search for promotions.

8.3.4.5. *Adapting marketing programs*

Currently, consumers expect retailers to know who they are, what type of products they ordered in the past and how they prefer to be contacted, demanding ever more personalized attention. The key to achieving user loyalty is to be found in the company's capacity to personalize its supply, adapting it to the customer's needs. In this sense, in-home shopping systems offer companies the opportunity to establish personal contact with their customers (and thus increase loyalty) [SHA 04]. As the consumer's experience of the Internet increases, his or her involvement in the shopping process increases to include the design of the products and services. For example, Dell Computers allows consumers to produce their own personal computer. The company mass manufactures separate parts, with the subsequent scale economies and consumers personalize assembly according to their specific preferences. The Internet also allows the possibility for some products to be visualized according to where the potential client is, adapting them to local market preferences.

Many virtual establishments allow the consumer to personalize the shopping environment and thus make it easier for them to browse. Customers can generate and use personal lists of the most frequently-purchased products on previous occasions so their information search on future occasions is reduced and they can focus more on the price variable. The possibilities offered by the Internet make it more economical for companies that offer e-commerce to adapt their marketing programs to local preferences. It is worth emphasizing the fact that marketing managers can try out new products and advertising on the Internet and obtain an immediate response [QUE 96]. The Internet offers a perfect combination of standardized campaigns and personalization, with the capacity to reach thousands of consumers and give them individualized treatment, thus increasing their loyalty [SHA 04].

Undoubtedly, the different consumer motivations for shopping online will affect their global online shopping behavior.

The conceptual model of global consumer e-shopping behavior which will be contrasted in the Spanish market (see Figure 8.1) is an outcome of the literature review presented above.

Figure 8.1. *Conceptual model of global online shopping behavior*

8.4. The case of Spanish e-shoppers

The second part of the chapter presents an empirical study of the Spanish market. The use of the Internet in Spain began around 1997 with 1.6% penetration of the population. According to data from the General Mass Media Study [AIM 06], at present the Internet penetration of the population in Spain is 37.2%, far exceeding the penetration of other media such as newspapers, magazines and the cinema. If we focus on the evolution of online purchases, in recent years, Spain has seen an increase in the e-commerce adoption rate (from €0.47 million in 1997 to €2,143 million in 2005), with a third of e-shoppers purchasing from foreign company websites in 2005 [AEC 06].

The quantitative analysis provides answers to the following research questions:

– How do demographics influence the decision to purchase online from foreign companies?

– What are the main motivations for Spanish consumers to purchase online from foreign companies?

– How does Internet experience influence the local/global shopping behavior of the Spanish consumer?

– What are the effects of search engine use on global Spanish consumer behavior?

8.4.1. *Methodology*

For the quantitative research we examined secondary data set from a survey by the Spanish Association of Electronic Commerce [AEC 05]. This study collected information using the Computer Assisted Telephone Interview (CATI) method from March to April 2005. Complete responses to the questions were obtained from a random sample of 646 Internet purchasers over 14-years-old, of which 213 had purchased both on foreign and domestic company websites.

In the quantitative analysis we first tested for significant differences between the demographic and behavioral profiles of "global" shoppers (consumers who shop online from domestic and foreign companies) and "local" shoppers (consumers who only shop online on Spanish websites) using the chi-square technique. Secondly, we used logistic regression to empirically contrast the model proposed in Figure 8.1.

8.4.2. *Results*

Table 8.2 shows the description of the sample; 32.4% of Spanish consumers shop both on foreign and domestic company websites, while the rest only buy from Spanish company websites.

Characteristic		Global e-shoppers (N = 209)	Local e-shoppers (N = 437)	Total N= 646	Chi-square
Gender	female	23.9%	39.1%	34.2%	$\chi^2 = 14.527$; $p = 0.000$
	male	76.1%	60.9%	65.8%	
Age	14–19	5.7%	11.2%	9.4%	$\chi^2 = 7.142$; $p = 0.210$
	20–24	12.4%	13.5%	13.2%	
	25–34	40.2%	37.8%	38.5%	
	35–44	23.9%	21.7%	22.4%	
	45–54	14.4%	11.0%	12.1%	
	over 55	3.3%	4.8%	4.3%	
Education	primary studies	0.5%	1.4%	1.1%	$\chi^2 = 18.829$; $p = 0.004$
	school leaving certificate	2.9%	5.9%	4.8%	
	secondary education	24.4%	30.2%	28.3%	
	university graduates	72.7%	62.5%	65.8%	
Characteristic		Global e-shoppers (N = 209)	Local e-shoppers (N = 437)	Total N= 646	Chi-square
Online shopping experience	In the last 3 months	5.7%	12.8%	10.5%	$\chi^2 = 41.021$; $p = 0.000$
	2004	21.1%	37.3%	32.0%	
	2003	26.3%	22.2%	23.5%	
	2002	10.5%	10.3%	10.4%	
	more than 4 years	36.4%	17.4%	23.5%	

Internet use	everyday	78.0%	67.0%	70.6%	$\chi^2 = 8.533$; p = 0.129
	3-6 days/week	14.8%	21.7%	19.5%	
	at least once/week	4.8%	6.9%	6.2%	
	at least once/month	1.9%	3.5%	3.0%	
	less frequently	0.5%	0.9%	0.8%	
Online use experience	in past 3 months	0%	2.1%	1.4%	$\chi^2= 11.878$; p = 0.018
	2004	1.4%	3.9%	3.1%	
	2003	3.8%	5.5%	5.0%	
	2002	2.4%	5.3%	4.3%	
	more than 4 years	92.3%	83.3%	86.2%	
Use of search engines for purchasing	Yes	62.7%	57.9%	59.4%	$\chi^2 = 1.343$; p = 0.247
Shopping orientations for online shopping (multiple response)	convenience	54.1%	61.8%	59.3%	$\chi^2 = 3.489$; p = 0.062
	only channel available	16.7%	11.2%	13%	$\chi^2 = 3.827$; p = 0.053
	range of choice	23.0%	16.5%	18.6%	$\chi^2 = 3.938$; p = 0.047
	price reductions	34%	23.8%	27.1%	$\chi^2 = 7.407$; p = 0.006
	to try it out how to shop online	1.4%	4.3%	3.4%	$\chi^2 = 3.646$; p = 0.056
	speed	12.9%	9.4%	10.5%	$\chi^2 = 1.877$; p = 0.171
	ease of shopping	6.7%	5.3%	5.7%	$\chi^2 = 0.539$; p = 0.463

Shopping orientations for purchase from foreign company websites	range of assortment	35.4%	–	–	–
	unavailable local market	35.4%			
	price reductions	25.4%			
	personalized service	3.3%			
	to try out how to shop online	1.4%			
	reliability	2.4%			
Products purchased	plane/ship/coach tickets	58.9%	41.1%	30.7%	–
	accommodation	8.1%	4.6%	5.7%	
	books	19.6%	10.3%	13.3%	
	clothes	7.7%	3.4%	4.8%	
	software	6.2%	4.3%	5.0%	
	hardware	3.8%	4.6%	4.3%	
	DVDs	5.7%	3.4%	4.2%	
	music	8.1%	5.7%	3.5%	
	tickets to shows	5.7%	13.7%	11.1%	
	food	5.8%	6.8%	6.2%	
	electronic home entertainment equipment	16.3%	13.3%	14.2%	

Table 8.2. *Description of the sample*

The descriptive analysis of the sample shows that consumers who develop global shopping behavior are mainly men (76.1%), aged between 25 and 44 years old (64.1%) and highly educated (72.7% have studied at university). A high percentage of these e-shoppers access the Internet frequently (78% everyday) and have over four years of online use experience (92.3%). The data also shows that e-shopping experience is quite recent; while 36.4% have been shopping online for over four years, over 50% have done so since 2003.

Convenience (54.1%), price reductions (34%) and range of choice (23%) are the main reasons for global Spanish consumers to shop online. Furthermore, range of choice (35.4%), availability of products unavailable in the local market (35.4%) and cost (25.4%) are the main reasons why the Spanish choose to shop from foreign company websites instead of domestic ones. Search engines are a commonly used shopping tool for global e-shoppers (62.7%).

The most-purchased products by global Spanish E-shoppers are plane, ship and coach tickets (58.9%), followed by books (19.6%) and electronic home-entertainment equipment (16.3%). In general they are search goods and this result is coherent with the conclusions of the study by Girard, Silverblatt and Korgankoar [GIR 02] who state that search goods will be the most successful in non-traditional selling channels as they are those for which the perceived shopping risk is lower.

Comparison of the "global" e-shopper profile with that of the "local" e-shopper reveals significant differences with respect to gender (X2 =14.527; p =0.000), education (X2 =18.829; p =0.004), online use experience (X2 =11.878; p =0.018), online shopping experience (X2 =41.021; p =0.000) and some shopping orientations as variety/range of choice (X2 =3.938; p =0.000) and price reductions (X2 =7.407; p =0.006).

Despite the fact that the proportion of global male e-shoppers is greater than that the total of local e-shoppers, the local e-shoppers are also mainly men (60.9%) with a medium and/or medium-high educational level (92.7%) and high experience as Internet users (83.3% have over four years of online use experience). The online shopping experience of the local e-shopper is much less than that of the global e-shopper, since only 27.7% claim they have shopped online for over three years, as against 46.9% of global e-shoppers who claim they made their first purchase in 2002. In addition, the local e-shopper attaches less value than the global e-shopper to both the product variety (16.5%) and prices that can be obtained online (23.8%).

A logistical regression (N=646 Internet shoppers) was used to test the proposed model. For the regression, global e-shopping behavior was coded as a dichotomous variable including Internet users who had purchased online both from domestic and foreign company websites (n=209) against those who said they had never purchased online from foreign company websites (n=437). Independent variables included demographics (age, gender and education), Internet behavior (Internet use, online use experience and online shopping experience), Internet browsing patterns and shopping orientations (see Table 8.3).

Variable[2]	B	SE	Wald	Sig.	Exp(B)
G1	0.724	0.207	12.239	0.000	2.063
A2	-0.002	0.009	0.056	0.812	0.998
E3			11.478	0.075	
E3(1)	0.187	1.197	0.024	0.876	1.205
E3(2)	0.910	0.533	2.913	0.088	2.485
E3(3)	0.903	0.332	7.409	0.006	2.468
OSE			20.651	0.000	
OSE(1)	0.432	0.250	2.990	0.084	1.540
OSE(2)	0.703	0.321	4.796	0.029	2.019
OSE(3)	1.027	0.258	15.906	0.000	2.793
OSE(4)	1.341	0.406	10.914	0.001	3.821
IU			3.603	0.608	
IU(1)	0.360	1.186	0.092	0.762	1.433
IU(2)	0.742	1.198	0.383	0.536	2.099

2 G1 (Gender), A2 (Age), E3 (education: primary studies), E3(1) (school leaving certificate), E3(2) (secondary education), E3(3) (university graduate), OSE (Online Shopping Experience: in the last 3 months), OSE(1) (2004), OSE(2) (2003), OSE(3) (2002), OSE(4) (for over 4 years), IU (Internet Use: everyday), IU(1) (from 3 to 6 days), IU(2) (at least once a week), IU(3) (at least once a month), IU(4) (less frequently), OUE (Online Use Experience: in the last 3 months), OUE(1) (2004), OUE(2) (2003), OUE(3) (2002), OUE(4) (for over 4 years), USE (Search Engines use: yes/no), CONVENIENCE (yes/no), ONLY CHANNEL AVAILABLE (yes/no), VARIETY (yes/no), PRICE (Price Reductions: yes/no), TO TRY OUT (yes/no), SPEED (yes/no) and EASE OF SHOPPING (yes/no).

IU(3)	0.493	1.238	0.159	0.690	1.637
IU(4)	1.343	1.647	0.665	0.415	3.832
OUE			3.983	0.263	
OUE(1)	0.135	0.235	0.330	0.566	1.144
OUE(2)	0.252	0.675	0.140	0.709	1.287
OUE(3)	0.363	0.207	3.083	0.049	1.438
OUE(4)	0.678	0.379	3.195	0.044	1.969
USE	0.021	0.189	0.013	0.910	1.021
CONVENIENCE	-0.242	0.209	1.341	0.247	0.785
ONLY CHANNEL AVAILABLE	0.338	0.547	0.382	0.537	1.402
VARIETY	0.617	0.233	6.998	0.008	1.853
PRICE	0.551	0.200	7.563	0.006	1.735
TO TRY OUT HOW TO SHOP ONLINE	-0.428	0.690	0.385	0.535	0.652
SPEED	0.281	0.292	0.932	0.334	1.325
EASE OF SHOPPING	0.148	0.393	0.142	0.707	1.159
Intercept	-1.679	1.332	1.589	0.207	0.187

Table 8.3. *Logistic regression for predicting global e-shopping behavior*

Hypothesis testing of the significance of the regression coefficients (β) gave the following results (see Table 8.2):

– There are eight variables with non-significant coefficients (p>0.05) according to the Wald statistic. Therefore, the age of the interviewee together with the frequency of Internet use and online shopping search engines are variables which do not significantly influence the decision to purchase from foreign companies. Some motivations for online shopping such as convenience, channels available, trying out how to shop online and speed and ease of shopping do not appear to motivate the global online shopper.

– The results show that it is 2.063 times more likely that e-shoppers will shop on both domestic and foreign company websites if they are men and e-shoppers with high educational levels are 2.468 times more likely to do so.

– The greater the online use experience and online shopping experience, the more likely it is that global shopping behavior will develop. Global consumer behavior is 3.821 times more likely if the individual shopped online before 2001 than if he/she has recently started to purchase online (3 months ago) and it is 1.969 times more likely if the consumer's online use experience is more than 4 years than if it is less than 1 year (in the last 3 months).

– In terms of the online shopping orientation, the results show that it is 1.853 times more likely that e-shoppers will buy from both domestic and foreign company websites if they like to choose among a wide range of products and it is 1.735 times more likely if they are price-oriented shoppers.

Having checked the statistical significance of the estimated logistic regression coefficients, we proceeded to verify the overall significance of the model. The chi-square value of the empirical model shows a value of 99.220, with 29 degrees of freedom and a significance of 0.000. This value is greater than the value of the corresponding theoretical model both in level of significance of 0.05 and of 0.01 (chi-square value equals 43.77 and 50.89 respectively) and is therefore statistically significant. In addition, the value "-2LL" has reduced (-2LL0: 871.320 and -2LL1: 714.097, which verifies the fact that this model provides a better fit than the model which only contains the constant.

Given the large sample size, we have also obtained a good fit of the chi-square test with Hosmer and Lemeshow. The chi-square value is equal to 3.242, with 8 degrees of freedom (significance = 0.918), an empirical value that is below the theoretical value for a significance level of 0.05 ($X2=15.51$). It may be stated, therefore, that the model fit is good.

The predictive efficiency of the model has also been checked. The percentage of correct results was 80.9%. The results obtained suggest that this logistical regression model can be considered to be predictive.

Furthemore, the model presents very good predictive capacity: 80.9% of the cases are correctly classified, as there is a cut-off value of 0.5. To verify statistically that the overall rate of correct predictions is significant and that it differs from the expected classification only due to random effects, the Huberty Test is used and we calculate the Z^* statistic which is distributed as a normal. Since we have obtained a value of Z^* (6.29> 1.96) valid for a significance level of 0.05, this leads us to reject the zero hypothesis that the number of cases correctly classified by the model does not differ from the expected classification only due to random effects.

8.5. Conclusions and managerial implications

The main academic contribution of this chapter is that it gives insight into the different factors that influence global shopping behavior in online environments. In addition, these factors can be seen applied to the specific context of the Spanish market. Specifically, this study will improve managers' understanding of consumer demographics, online experience, Internet browsing patterns and shopping orientations and their relation to the user's willingness to shop on domestic or foreign company websites.

International markets have different e-commerce adoption rates. Currently, the regions in the world with the greatest market potential for companies interested in using the Internet as a marketing tool are the USA, Europe and Asia. The economic development of a country, the available infrastructures, the degree of liberalization in the telecommunications sector, government support for generalizing Internet use in the population, purchasing power and they level of education in society are critical factors for the introduction e-commerce. Climatic and cultural factors also influence the speed of e-commerce adoption.

The study carried out in the Spanish market has made it possible to identify two online buyer profiles: consumers who shop online from domestic and foreign companies (global e-shoppers) and consumers who only shop online from Spanish companies (local e-shoppers). The global e-shopper is quite similar to the local e-shopper in terms of age (between 25 and 44 years of age), frequency of Internet use (usually everyday), heavy use of search engines for purchasing goods or services and some motivations for e-shopping. There are, however, significant differences with respect to gender, education, online use experience, online shopping experience and shopping orientations as global e-shoppers are more price-oriented shoppers and variety seekers than local e-shoppers.

The logistic regression analysis on the set of variables analyzed has highlighted the fact that global e-shopping behavior is more likely in well-educated men, consumers who like to choose between a wide range of products and price-oriented shoppers. Internet experience is also a key driver of global e-purchase decision-making because consumers with more online use experience and those who have been shopping online for several years shop online both on local and foreign websites (global e-shopping behavior), while novice web-users prefer shopping only on Spanish websites (local e-shopping behavior). Age, frequency of Internet use and the use of search engines for purchasing have no significant influence on the decision to shop on both local and foreign company websites (global consumer behavior) rather than only on domestic ones.

The influence of gender on global online shopping behavior may be explained by the greater perceived purchase risk in women [BAR 99] and their lower level of experience as online shoppers, which may influence them to purchase products from local websites as they are more familiar with them and trust them more (either because of local communication campaigns by the companies, or recommendations from other consumers, or because these companies have a bricks and mortar establishment in Spain where the consumer can seek assistance anything goes wrong).

E-shoppers with higher education levels are more predisposed toward global shopping behavior, possibly because they have a greater need for specialized products, which are not always available in the local market (for example, foreign books or magazines), than e-shoppers with a lower level of education. Furthermore, consumers' different perceptions of the information on websites in languages other than their mother tongue, the non-adaptation of website content and design to each country's culture and the lack of information on costs, measurements and sizes are critical factors which can generate confusion and therefore lead to consumption of products/services online only from the domestic market, particularly in the case of consumers with lower education levels.

Online use experience and online shopping experience are variables with significant influence on global shopping behavior; however, frequency of Internet use is not a significantly influential variable. One explanation of this result may be that novice Internet consumers use the Internet for amusement, for domestic online shopping, for work, or to obtain information, but do not perceive the utility of making electronic transactions worldwide. In this case, it is necessary for them to assimilate the advantages offered by the Internet in the international purchasing process (ease of comparison of prices, large quantity of information on the products and services offered, etc) because this will encourage future global purchase behavior. Previous research shows that greater online experience leads to improved relations with the medium, as the individual is more familiar with it and values its benefits more ([SWA 99]; [TRO 00]).

This chapter also can help managers to develop effective strategies to attract online consumers and therefore to gain competitive advantages.

Convenience and time saving, the opportunity to acquire products/services from a part of the world where they are cheaper, access to products unavailable in the local market and access to international information are some of the benefits that companies that develop an online international marketing strategy can offer to the market niches they address. In particular, we recommend that these companies offer competitive prices and a wide assortment of goods and services. The problem of logistics (cost or delivery times) can be solved by reaching agreements with local companies or having a network of warehouses in the target markets.

Global consumer behavior is greatest among expert e-shoppers and highly-educated men, so we recommend foreign companies interested in reaching the Spanish market make this segment a priority. However, the personalization of the content of websites (language, currency, etc), including chats and forums for sharing experience with other consumers, can help companies to widen their target market to women and less well-educated e-shoppers.

A significant aspect is adapting the content and design of the website to each country's culture. For example, offering the e-shopper the opportunity to access the website in his/her mother tongue may encourage e-shoppers who speak only their mother tongue. Research by Luna et al. [LUN 02] shows that text written in Spanish connects better with consumer emotions, while technical characteristics and product specifications are better understood in English. It is also important to adapt the style of communications (formal or informal) according to the cultural characteristics of the target consumer. Adapting website design would take into account considerations such as the fact that while black as a very common background color on USA websites as it is considered attractive and mysterious, in Asia and Latin

America it has negative connotations. The problem of currency differences or size differences can be solved by including converter programs to provide information on of currency, sizing, etc, to users in different countries.

In terms of the limitations of this study, the data analyzed is based on secondary information sources and for this reason there are complementary aspects not included in the questionnaire which we think would be interesting to analyze: in particular, the influence of perceived shopping risk on consumer decision-making. Therefore, as a future line of research, we are considering complementing this study with the development and validation of a scale to measure perceived shopping risk and to propose and empirically test a general model of global consumer behavior. Given that previous research [GIR 02] suggests that not all goods will be as successful on the Internet, another possible line of study would be to analyze whether global consumer behavior online is influenced by the characteristics of the goods and services being marketed.

The consumer's cultural background is one of the aspects which can influence the creation of a favorable climate for developing and consolidating electronic transactions worldwide [VAN 02]. For this reason, we consider that another interesting line of research would be to contrast the validity of the proposed behavioral model with samples of consumers from other cultures and to compare the results obtained.

8.6. References

[AEC 05] AECE, Estudio sobre Comercio Electrónico B2C 2005, July 2005, AECE-FECEMD

[AEC 06] AECE, Estudio sobre Comercio Electrónico B2C 2006, July 2006, AECE-FECEMD

[AIM 06] AIMC, Audiencia de Internet, May 2006, AIMC

[AL-A 01] AL-ASHBAN, A and BURNEY, M (2001) "Customer adoption of tele-banking technology: the case of Saudi Arabia", *International Journal of Bank Marketing*, vol 21, no 3, pp 191–200

[ALB 97] ALBA, J, LYNCH, J, WEITZ, B, JANISZEWSKI, C, LUTZ, R, SAWYER, A and WOOD, S (1997) "Interactive home shopping: consumer, retailer and manufacturer incentives to participate in electronic marketplaces", *Journal of Marketing*, vol 61, July, pp 38–53

[BAR 99] BARTEL-SHEENAN, K (1999) "An investigation on gender differences in on-line privacy concerns and resultant behaviors", *Journal of Interactive Marketing*, vol 13, no 4, pp 24–38

[BHA 04] BHATNAGAR, A and GHOSE, S (2004) "Segmenting consumers based on the benefits and risks of Internet shopping", *Journal of Business Research,* vol 57, pp 1352–1360

[BRO 03] BROWN, M, POPE, N and VOGES, K (2003) "Buying or browsing? An exploration on shopping orientations and online purchase intention", *European Journal of Marketing*, vol 37, no 11/12, pp 1666–1684

[CHA 04] CHAN, T and CUI, G (2004) "Consumer attitudes toward marketing in a transitional economy: a replication and extension", *Journal of Consumer Marketing*, vol 21, no 1, pp 10–26

[DAH 02] DAHLEN, M (2002) "Learning the web: Internet user experience and response to Web marketing in Sweden", *Journal of Interactive Advertising*, vol 3, no 1, http://www.jiad.org/
vol3/no1/dahlen/index.html

[DEG 00] DEGERATU, A, RANGASWAMY, A and WU, J (2000) "Consumer choice behavior in online and traditional supermarkets: the effects of brand name, price and other search attributes", *International Journal of Research in Marketing*, vol 17, p 55–78

[DHO 02] DHOLAKIA, R and UUSITALO, O (2002) "Switching to electronic stores: consumer characteristics and the perception of shopping benefits", *International Journal of Retail & Distribution Management*, vol 30, no 10, pp 459–69

[EMA 04] EMARKETER (2004) "Canada presents opportunity for search engine marketing", http://www.emarketer.com/Article.aspx?1002788.

[GIR 02] GIRARD, T, SILVERBLATT, R and KORGANKOAR, P (2002) "Influence of product class on preference for shopping on the Internet", *Journal of Computer Mediated Communications*, vol 8, no 1, retrieved http://www.ascusc.org/jcmc/vol8/issue1/
girard.html

[HOF 80] HOFSTEDE, G (1980) *Culture's Consequences: International Differences in Work Related Values*, Newbury Park (CA): Sage Publications

[INT 06] INTERNETWORLDSTATS (2006) "Internet usage statistics. The big picture", 2006, http://www.internetworldstats.com

[JOI 03] JOINES, J, SCHERER, C and SCHEUFELE, D (2003) "Exploring motivations for consumer Web use and their implications for e-commerce", *Journal of Consumer Marketing*, vol 20, no 2, pp 90–108

[KOR 99] KORGAONKAR, P and WOLLIN, L (1999) "A multivariate analysis of Web usage", *Journal of Advertising Research*, vol 39, no 2, pp 53–68

[LAF 05] LAFORET, S and LI, X (2005) "Consumers' attitudes towards online and mobile banking in China", *International Journal of Bank Marketing*, vol 23, no 5, pp 362–80

[LEV 83] LEVITT, T (1983) "The globalization of markets", *Harvard Business Review*, vol 61, no 3, pp 92–102

[LI 99] LI, H, KUO, C and RUSSELL, M (1999) "The impact of perceived channel utilities, shopping orientations, and demographics on the consumer's online buying behavior", *Journal of Computer-Mediated Communications*, vol 5, no 2 http://www.ascusc.org/jcmc/vol5/issue2/hairong.html

[LIN 03] LIN, M and CHANG, L (2003) "Determinants of habitual behavior for national and leading brands in China", *Journal of Product and Brand Management*, vol 12, no 2, pp 94–107

[LUN 02] LUNA, D, PERACCHIO, L and DE JUAN, M (2002) "Cross-cultural and cognitive aspects of website navigation", *Journal of the Academy of Marketing Science*, vol 30, no 4, pp 397–410

[MAE 99] MAES, P, GUTTMAN, R. and MOUKAS, A (1999). "Agents that buy and sell: transforming commerce as we know it", *Communications of the ACM*, 42(3), 81-83

[MON 04] MONTGOMERY, A, HOSANAGAR, K, KRISHNAN, R and CLAY, K (2004) "Designing a better shopbot", *Management Science*, vol 50, no 2, pp 189–206

[PAR 03] PARK, C and KIM, Y (2003) "Identifying key factors affecting consumer purchase behavior in an online shopping context", *International Journal of Retail and Distribution Management*, vol 31, no 1, pp 16–29

[PET 97] PETERSON, R, BALASUBRAMANIAN, S and BRONNENBERG, B (1997) "Exploring the implications on the Internet for consumer marketing", *Journal of the Academy of Marketing Science*, vol 25, no 4, pp 329–46

[QUE 96] QUELCH, J and KLEIN, L (1996) "The Internet and international marketing", *Sloan Management Review*, pp 60–75

[REI 02] REIBSTEIN, D (2002) "What attracts customers to online stores and what keeps them coming back?", *Journal of the Academy of Marketing Science*, vol 30, no 4, 2002, pp 465–73

[ROH 04] ROHM, A and SWAMINATHAN, V (2004) "A typology of online shoppers based on shopping motivations", *Journal of Business Research*, vol 57, pp 748–57

[ROJ 01] ROJSEK, I (2001) "A comparison of the purchasing and consumption behavior of Slovenian and other Eastern European consumers", *International Marketing Review*, vol 18, no 5, pp 509–20

[SCH 98] SCHÜTTE, H and CIARLANTE, D (1998) *Consumer Behavior in Asia*, New York: New York University Press

[SHA 04] SHARMA, A and SHETH, J (2004) "Web-based marketing. The coming revolution in marketing thought and strategy", *Journal of Business Research*, vol 57, pp 696–702

[SIE 03] SIEGEL, C (2003) *Internet Marketing: Foundations and Applications*, Boston: Houghton Mifflin Company

[SIM 02] SIM, L and KOI, S (2002) "Singapore's Internet shoppers and their impact on traditional shopping patterns", *Journal of Retailing and Consumer Services*, vol 9, no 2, pp 115–24

[STE 00] STECKEL, J (2000) "On-line shopping: how many will come to the party? And when they will get there?", working paper, Stern School of Business, New York University.

[SUH 02] SHU, T and KWON, I (2002) "Globalization and reluctant buyers", *International Marketing Review*, vol 19, no 6, pp 663–80

[SWA 99] SWAMINATHAN, V, LEPKOWSKA-WHITE, E and RAO, B (1999) "Browsers or buyers in cyberspace? An investigation of factors influencing electronic exchange", *Journal of Computer-Mediated Communications*, vol 5, no 2, http://www.ascusc.org/jcmc/vol5/issue2/swaminathan.html

[TOW 95] TOWER, R and COOPER, P (1995) "Beyond post-Perestroika Russia and post-Communism Eastern Europe: the impact of individualism and collectivism on attitudes to work, relationship and consumer choice", Towards a Market Economy: Beyond the Point of No Return, Second East and Central European Conference ESOMAR, Warsaw, pp 121–42

[TRO 00] TROCCHIA, P and JANDA, S (2000) "A phenomenological investigation of Internet usage among older individuals", *Journal of Consumer Marketing*, vol 17, no 7, pp 605–16

[VAN 02] VAN BIRGELEN, M, DE RUYTER, K, DE JONG, A and WETZELS, M (2002) "Customer evaluations of alter-sales service contact modes: An empirical analysis of national culture's consequences", *International Journal of Research in Marketing*, vol 19, pp 43–64

[VRE 01] VRECHOPOULOS, A, SIOMKOS, G and DOUKIDIS, G (2001) "Internet shopping adoption by Greek consumers", *European Journal of Innovation Management*, vol 4, no 3, pp 142–52

Chapter 9

The New, Improved, Indian Consumer

9.1. Understanding the billion minds

Understanding "the billion minds" that constitute the entity known as the Indian consumer is slowly becoming more complex. Underlying this is the theory that managers can and ought to be able to direct and manage marketing outcomes; that is to say, predict them, plan them, moderate them, or make them happen. Also underlying this thought is the belief that what we need is the exact location, scale and scope of the consumer market in terms of purchasing power. We should then be able to pick the sectors of it that we consider profitable to address and, like a skilful shot, pick them off one by one. It is, of course, true that no manager has the power, the ability, or the knowledge to measure and tweak everything he does in order to make the consumer dance to his tunes, yet this is something that the average manager finds difficult to admit. One should at least be aware of this control trap.

Even though we cannot know everything that is to be known, we do need some in-depth knowledge about the consumer, starting with who he/she is. Is there a real Indian consumer or is there a set of stereotypes? All conventional wisdom in market research tends to favor the view that there are distinct types; we need to isolate them according to certain parameters and then label them. The general tendency has been to develop classifications and analytical partitioning of a product's target consumer group, either according to their sociodemographic types or according to

Chapter written by Partho GANGULY.

psychological typing; for instance, the pleasure seekers, the value seekers, the novelty seekers, the bargain hunters or whoever. This method is one of division and hinges mainly on finding the most appropriate basis for dividing up the mass of customers and sorting them into more manageable groups. Yet, how useful is it to have such a structural knowledge of the market? How do we move from there to a strategic phase of brand building if it is not supported by an understanding of the behavioral processes that the consumer (or customer) undergoes in coming to the purchase, use and post-purchase follow-up relating to any category?

In the ultimate analysis, the marketing profession seems to be agreed on one basic desirable goal, namely that of creating a lasting, or at least a strong, preference amongst selected consumers and moving them to some action. Of course, to think of marketing as the task of finding consumers and doing something to them is the height of managerial attitude and corporate arrogance and yet another mental trap. It is by no means enough to impinge upon the perceptions of the consumer through powerful persuasion and high-tech communication. In order to participate with consumers in a co-evolution of the product – to use the more current thinking on the subject – there is a need to bridge the current chasm or disconnect that exists between management understanding or mental models and consequent actions.

Recent thinking and research into this area has reached the view that such a mental picture, however rough, is a necessary first step for any marketer. In the absence of such a working hypothesis or theory, however tentative and subject to modification, it is difficult to justify the steady growth of spending of marketing funds year after year. Nor is it possible to bring anything like the degree of precision and accuracy we are used to in other functions into the marketing discipline. So this step is essential, at least from a productivity point of view. How do we acquire a more fundamental understanding of why the pie (or pyramid) is shaped the way it is – in other words, why do consumers in any specific category behave the way that they do? What is their stance or mental attitude toward the category itself? What motivations, expectations and behaviors are seen, in particular with respect to the category (soap, cars, diapers, chocolates or razor blades) by the relevant subgroups?

It has always been difficult to second guess the Indian consumer. Just when we believed that consumer spending was firmly on a high growth trajectory – based on the wonder years of 1993–98 – it spluttered and slowed to a crawl. The fast-moving consumer goods (FMCG) sector had a difficult time as some product categories actually shrank in size, while consumer-durables manufacturers struggled to reconcile capacity with demand. There was a fast-growing yet minuscule population of the very rich that continued to lap up everything from plasma TVs to Mercedes cars – but that was cold comfort for the majority of the marketers.

The growth spurt of those years was attributed to a confluence of events – a release of pent-up demand of the rich who always had money, but nothing much to buy; a television boom that fueled aspirations; a distribution boom that brought products and services within easier reach; the discovery of the sachet strategy that made everything affordable to more people; and, finally, a string of heavy monsoons.

They also shelved the idea of the huge, homogenous, mass market made up of the Indian middle class, which would be a tireless engine of growth and, having come to terms with the new reality of the market, marketers worked hard on tactical actions to stimulate growth even while turning their gaze inwards, focusing on operational performance improvement and financial restructuring to keep the bottom line growing.

Meanwhile, many little changes were taking place in the market. It is a market whose potential and desire to consume has perhaps moved ahead of the marketer's mental model of it. It continues to be a multi-tiered market, with the bicycle and the business class co-existing. It continues to require a portfolio of price/performance points, but it is a market that is now unified by certain common demographic characteristics and consumption desires. The question is: are there enough relevant products and services available to take advantage of this? In short, it does appear that the Great Indian Consuming Class has arrived and is waiting to be served.

PROFILING THE CONSUMER CLASSES OF INDIA

% of Households	30-50%	51-70%	>70%
Samriddha I	Flat TV, AC, fabric bleaches	PC, deodarant,	Four wheeler, ketchup, camera
Samriddha II	Four-wheeler,PC	Camera, milk food, drinks, ketchup, instant noodles	Washing machine floor cleaner, ghee
Sampanna	Deodrant, honey CD player, jam, ketchup, camera	Washing machine, floor cleaner	Mosquito repellent, toilet cleaner, rubs & balms, music system,telephone, motorised transport
Siddha	Instant noodles, motorcycles, milk food, drinks, floor cleaner	Vanaspati, toilet cleaner, telephone, motorised transport	Refrigerator, bank account, fabric whitener
Unmukh	Toilet ceaner, telephone, motorised transport, refrigerator	Mosquito repellent, ghee music system	Bank account, pressure cooker, utensil cleaner, talcum powder,
Saamaanya	Mosquito repellent, ghee	Bank acc., Utensil cleaner Rubs & Balms, P. cooker	Shampoo, toothpaste, TV
Sangarshi	Music system, pressure cooker, rubs & balms, Bank a/c	Shampoo, talcum powder toothpaste, TV fabric Whitener,	Biscuits, fresh milk
Nirdhan	Vanaspati, shampoo, toothpowder	Fresh milk, biscuits	Detergent cake/bar, washing powder, Tea, edible oil, toilet soap, hair oil

Source: 'Guide to Indian Markets, 2006

Table 9.1. *Profile of the consumer classes of India*

9.1.1. *Income growth*

Between 1996–97 and 2000–01, per capita income on an aggregate basis grew by a compounded annual rate of 3.2%. However, high-income households grew much, much faster – by about 20% year after year – between 1995–96 and 1998–99, according to the National Council for Applied Economic Research (NCAER). Upper-middle-income households grew by 10% on a compounded annual growth basis during the same period. In urban India, the trend is even more pronounced.

9.1.2. *Affordability growth*

Supply-side changes also shape a market's buying power and there have been a host of them: falling interest rates, easier consumer credit, increase in variety and quality of products and services at every price point, etc.

The liberalization-generation children (born from 1984 onwards) grow up: the post-liberalization generation is coming of age. Rural India is moving beyond and has reduced its dependence on agriculture. NCAER occupation data show a decline in people who work the land and there is evidence of households in rural India. Add to this the exposure levels of the top end of rural society through television and the rural market is becoming closer in its mindset to the urban market. Note also the rise of the self-employed: rural India has always been largely self-employed. The proportion of self-employed in urban India has risen to above 40%, replacing the employed salary earner as the new "mainstream market". A Hansa Research Group (HRG) study shows that even in the "creamy layer", which is the top of two social classes living in towns represent 1 million of population in urban India, 40% of the main wage earners of households are shop owners, small traders, businessmen and self-employed professionals.

Unlike the salary earner, the self-employed use products to signal success and are also fast adopters of productivity tools, such as cell phones and two-wheelers, which can help them earn more.

Environmental changes drive aspiration: better connectivity and communication and the leap in literacy levels are together increasing the aspiration of the Indian consumers at every level. The reason why these changes drive aspiration is lucidly explained by the well-known anthropologist, Arjun Appadurai, of Yale University: "Imagination is not about individual escape. It is a collective social activity. Informational resources are needed for people to even imagine a possible life, weave a story and a script around themselves and place products in emerging sequences."

The Indian consumer now has enough information resources to imagine a better life. Plurality of income, singular mindset: when marketers were waiting for the great, Indian, middle-class boom, its key trigger was expected to be a significant number of households above a certain level of income, which would become the critical mass of consumption. Striving: most Indian consumers, whether rich or poor, want to get ahead in a hurry. From being destiny-driven and resigned, they are now destination-driven and strive to grasp opportunities to earn more in order to construct a better life for themselves and their children. If one were to segment the country into "the arriving", "the striving" and "the resigned", the proportion of the resigned has definitely decreased and become geographically concentrated, rather than well-dispersed, as it was earlier.

"I can": the rise of the self-employed and the service economy, which requires less capital and more effort, has changed the mindset of the Indian consumers from one of demanding social justice to one of grabbing economic opportunity.

Not so much from earning the second income (a mere 23% of Indian households have working wives and that proportion decreases as incomes increase).

9.1.3. *Obsession of education- and health-consciousness advances*

Indian consumers are obsessed with giving their children the education and skills that will provide the foundation to move to a higher station in life – and they have seen enough evidence of this to know that it is possible. Health is the other obsession – probably because ill health adversely impacts earning ability. A study conducted by HRG in 2003 for the Media Research Users Council (MRUC) – of 2,000 households in Mumbai – shows interesting differences in household expenditure between the top social class (SEC A) and the lowest social classes (SEC D/E).

Education and clothing attract the same proportions of expenditure in both the income groups, but the poor probably spend a bit more (proportionately) on medical expenses than the rich. Pragmatism in consumption and the preference for "real value" products and services: in the past, marketers assumed that progress and evolution of a market meant the adoption of "feel good" products, a susceptibility to razzle-dazzle branding, a Westernized self-image and identity and bountiful days for FMCG categories. However, the latest trends show that consumers are going more for "quality of life" improvement products and services.

The Indian consumer wants a visibly better quality of life for themselves and their children, where that life is described in terms of durables that make life better: education, healthcare, transportation and communication. (NSS data show that these are the three big growth areas in consumption expenditure.) Pragmatism and functionality are the hallmarks of their consumption expenditure. The threshold of their expectations of how this functionality is delivered is high: for example, low-priced motorcycles must look like motorcycles and deliver enough power. Basic cell phones must be small, even if they are not feature-rich; and low-priced garments and footwear cannot have antiquated styles.

9.1.4. *Entertainment*

Entertainment is becoming a big feature. The country has traditionally been starved of family entertainment, with the only options being to watch television or to go to places of religious worship. However, family entertainment is becoming a big issue for consumers as they try to find avenues of bonding in an era of nuclear families.

Comfort with borrowing to fund future consumption: being in debt used to be an area of high discomfort for everybody, except the very poor who had no other choice but to borrow for survival. Now, however, the concept of EMI (equalized monthly installments) is legitimizing borrowing in other social groups, especially for the funding of future consumption.

Comfort with consumption

Economists talk about the wealth effect, wherein it takes time before consumption decreases in response to decreasing income. Equally, it takes a while for comfort with consumption to happen and consumption typically lags behind income increases. One reason for this could be that the country has celebrated abstemiousness for so long that it takes a supply explosion to spark desire and then translate that desire into actual consumption. However, that has now happened.

Comfort with technology

Information technology (IT) awareness, whether it is IT power (what a computer can do to solve problems or improve life) or IT-driven employment opportunities, has arrived in the lowest social classes and in much of the rural population. One example of IT-awareness is the "Cyber-grandmas" from upper-middle and upper classes, who have become e-mail literate to communicate with their scattered flock.

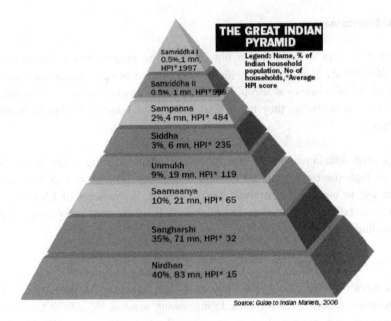

Figure 9.1.

9.2. A springboard for more consumption

Current levels of penetration influence the pace of future penetration. Penetration increases are not linear; instead they accelerate as base penetration increases till a point where saturation sets in. If only one out of 20 households in a given affluence grade have a washing machine or a two-wheeler, adoption will be slow, but when one out of every 10 has it, it becomes something that gets on the radar screen of aspiration for the rest. When it gets to one in five families, it serves to rapidly penetrate the remaining households because it now becomes a "must have now" product for them.

For consumer durables, the top (in terms of affluence grades) 40 million households in India – 24 million in urban India and 17 million in rural India – based on their penetration levels would constitute the core consuming class. The magic number of 200 million consumers (assuming five members to a household) has arrived at last!

Within rural India, there are two different grades of overall affluence, which we can call the developed and the developing states. The developed states comprise

Punjab, Haryana, Gujarat, Maharashtra, Karnataka and Kerala. They account for about one-third of the rural population and have shown higher penetration in most categories.

The market has enough scale to offer and enough desire to consume. The consumer is ready and waiting to be served. The new Consumer India will pose a huge challenge to marketers because it offers a difficult revenue model of large but not enormous volumes, modest prices and high benefit expectations. It will reward real innovators and ignore marketing hype. Most of all, it will continue to comprise many markets at different stages of evolution, demanding a complexity of strategy that is far in excess of its worth. And yes, it will continue to throw up unexpected answers to the arithmetic of (medium penetration) x (large size of consumer base) x (low price-willing to pay) x (modest per capita consumption).

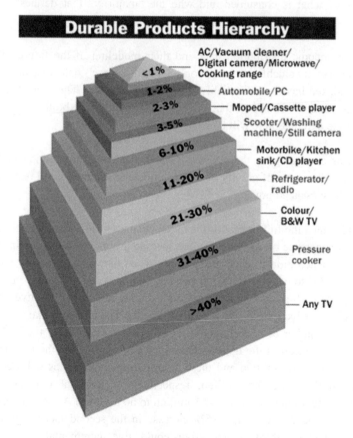

Figure 9.2.

For FMCG, penetration is certainly not an issue. NCAER data shows that for 1998–99, the basket of 22 FMCG products that it tracks cost a total of over Rs 91,500 crore. Of this, 37% was spent by the two lowest-income groups in rural India and only about 20% by the top two income groups in urban areas.

9.3. A new consumption push for 2006–07

Why does the changing shape of income distribution herald a change in consumption behavior? A traditional bottom-heavy triangle, with most people in the lower income group and a few in the top, indicates that the centre of gravity of market consumption and of the reference group, which defines aspirations, is very low. As the shape of income distribution starts bulging in the centre, both the centre of gravity of what is consumed and who the "majority" that defines aspirations should be, shifts.

NCAER income distribution data and their modeling of the future of income distribution are invaluable. It is the only "single source" data that also looks at inflation-indexed income and reliably shows shifts in shape. The projected shape of urban India in 2006-07 shows that the centre of gravity will be the upper-middle-income group and that there will be a large consumption push.

Taken as an aggregate, the projected shape of income distribution in 2006–07 suggests that the centre of gravity of consumption and aspiration will rest with those who have "just escaped poverty".

To understand the full impact of the urban change, it is necessary to compute the arithmetic of increase or decrease in each income group as well as the increase (or decrease) in penetration in each group. Only when viewed together do we get the full picture. In some categories, depending on supplier strategies and starkly lowering price-performance points, the results could be counter-intuitive. However, for the rest, this is likely to be the typical arithmetic. The tale goes like this. NCAER estimates the number of households to increase by 8.6 million in the high-income group and 7.3 million in the upper-middle-income group, while the middle-income number grows by 4.3 million and the bottom two income groups will decrease by about 2.3 million and 7.5 million, respectively. (The total number of urban households is set to increase from 49.1 million to 60 million.) A 10% increase in the top income group penetration, a 15% increase in the second income group and a 10% increase in the third income group could give incremental volumes of 7.5 million in the highest income group, 5 million in the next income group and a mere

2.7 million in the third income group. The urban market is indeed on the periphery of a huge consumption push.

Rural India will have two points of significant household increases – 4.6 million high-income households and 13 million middle-income households will be added by 2006-07 (the total number of rural households will increase from 122.8 million to 139 million). Let me present a sampler of the same typical arithmetic for a well-penetrated category, which has 45% penetration in the high-income group, 25% penetration in the upper-middle-income group and 10% penetration in the middle-income group. By 2006-07, a reasonable estimate, given the current penetration base and past patterns from urban areas, is that it would increase to 60%, 30% and just 13%. Therefore, the incremental volumes would be 3.3 million from the upper-income group and 2.3 million from the middle-income group. Given the increasing urban exposure of rural India, the urban and the rural upper-income groups can form an interesting continuum market, giving it a scale of 23 million households, or 115 million population. In 2006-07, the consuming class, as we defined it earlier, would be about 60 million households, or 300 million consumers. However, a state-wise look at rural income shapes show a totally different pattern. It shows that in states that account for about half the rural GDP of the country (as defined by the Crisil Centre for Economic Research Analysis), the center of gravity of consumption and aspiration has already moved towards the middle/upper-middle-income classes, again suggesting that there is another inflection point of consumption that is about to happen, and that perhaps these states are far more ready for sophisticated consumption than we imagine them to be.

Fired by buoyant markets and high economic growth rates, China and India topped ACNielsen's latest Consumer Confidence Study. While China ranked as the most optimistic among all markets surveyed, with 78% of consumers looking forward to further economic improvement over the coming year, following closely behind were India (77%) and Indonesia (76%). Completing the top 10 spots were the USA, ranking ninth (43%), followed by Norway at 10th (42%). Of the top 10 countries in the world that are most optimistic about the next 12 months, eight are from the Asia-Pacific region.

Conducted over the Internet last November, ACNielsen's Consumer Confidence Study was expanded this time to cover 28 markets across Asia-Pacific, Europe and the USA, interviewing 14,134 consumers.

This robust degree of consumer confidence among Asian markets such as India, China and Indonesia has contributed to the Asia-Pacific region's overwhelming optimism compared with Europe and the USA. This bodes well for the outlook of global investors, who have pinned their hopes on the Asian economies. Looking at the countries where consumers have the highest penchant to save money, the top nine were from the Asia-Pacific region – led by Indonesia (59%), Malaysia (58%) and Thailand (57%), with the Netherlands the only market outside the Asia-Pacific making it into the top 10.

For the Asia-Pacific region as a whole, 40% of consumers surveyed thought their country's economy had improved over the previous six months and 53% expected it to improve further over the next year. However, 43% of Americans remained positive about the year ahead and optimistic their economy would improve and, while 31% of Europeans were of a like mind, a further 35% expected the situation to deteriorate over the coming year.

A sizable 48% of Americans and 40% of Europeans thought their economies had deteriorated over the previous six months. Consumers surveyed in the USA perceived that their economy had not improved in the last six months, but were more optimistic of a turnaround in the year ahead, with 43% expecting an improvement. The Europeans, however, were split in their opinion: about a third each felt the outlook would improve, remain the same or deteriorate over the next 12 months.

In the portion of the survey on "How We Spend Our Spare Cash", in India and across the world, during good times and bad, consumers appear to respond differently when it comes to how they spend their spare cash. For Indians, buying new clothes, short, local vacations, home improvements and investing in shares and mutual funds seems to be a greater priority than consumers in other parts of the Asia-Pacific region. For 50% of Indians, saving money is also a priority, like most other countries in Asia.

In the Asia-Pacific region, when asked how they use spare cash once they have covered their living expenses, nearly half said they put it in savings or deposit accounts. The second-most-mentioned was out-of-home entertainment (32%), followed by paying off credit-card debts or loans (29%).

In the USA, however, the top three priorities were reversed, with 33% claiming they were paying off credit-card debts or loans, followed by out-of-home entertainment (29%) and savings and deposits (23%). This compared with 37% of

Europeans spending on out-of-home entertainment, followed by savings or deposits (34%) and new clothes and home improvements each coming in at 33%.

It has been predicted that the Asian economies of China and India will be the main vehicles of growth for the world economy, making up the engines of a new world economic order. This point was highlighted recently at the World Economic Forum at Davos, Switzerland, where "India Everywhere" was the theme. This was reflected in the words of the Confederation of Indian Industry chairman YC Deveshwar, who said he detected a certain sense of insecurity among Western governments and corporations as they were getting increasingly uneasy over the prospect of being bought out by Indian or Chinese multinationals.

Professor Jagdish Bhagwati also pointed out that the West was imposing its own labor standards and other social-justice norms on emerging economies. In fact, the key to the fresh and vibrant business optimism in "Chindia" (as the Asian growth phenomenon is being called) is the rise of the middle classes.

The rising middle class in China and India

Propelling China's growth is a steady stream of foreign investment attracted by the country's seemingly inexhaustible pool of workers and its growing body of consumers. Economists note that even if only 8% of Chinese make a middle-income salary, that would still amount to 100 million people – a base of consumers almost as big as the entire USA middle class. In 2003, foreigners invested US$60 billion in the Chinese mainland and more than $30 billion in Hong Kong. It was the second year in a row that mainland China displaced the USA as the world's most popular investment locale.

The impact of that investment was magnified by the artificially low value of China's currency. Economists estimate that one Chinese yuan can buy as much in China as $4.60 can buy in the USA, so $60 billion worth of investments there has the same impact as $276 billion in the USA. Since China opened its economy to international trade in 1978, foreign investments have totaled more than half a trillion dollars, helping fuel one of the greatest industrial expansions the world has ever seen.

Similarly, in India, the middle class forms 20-25% of the total population (200 million to 250 million people) and is driving demand in the economy. Increased spending by India's middle class is estimated to be more than $300 million. The lifestyle orientation of people is changing: the super-rich class of 17 million will increase to 35 million in five years. More than 40 million in India already have the same purchasing power as Americans. Overall consumer spending grew at a pace of 6% per year in past 10 years. In addition, about 75% of population in India is under 40 years of age.

India is marketing itself as the world's fastest-growing free-market democracy. This time, it is hitting the right chords with foreign investors who are otherwise wary of the two Asian giants teaming up (*Asia Times Online*, February 8, 2006).

9.3.1. *The rising middle class in India*

In India, the middle class forms 20-25% of the total population (200 million to 250 million people) and is driving demand in the economy. Increased spending by India's middle class is estimated to be more than $300 million. The lifestyle orientation of people is changing: the super-rich class of 17 million will increase to 35 million in five years. More than 40 million in India already have the same purchasing power as Americans. Overall consumer spending grew at a pace of 6% per year in past 10 years. In addition, about 75% of population in India is under 40 years of age.

9.4. Impact on marketing

It has been said earlier that there is a new Consumer India waiting to be served with relevant products and services.

9.4.1. *Required: mature market strategies*

Mature market strategies. Two-wheelers have penetrated about 12% of all households. By this metric, it is clearly an underdeveloped market that should grow from first-time buyers and should not be lapping up (or even accepting) higher-level features. Yet, half the sales in a year are from repeat buyers and half from first-time buyers, and about half from small markets (with populations below 1 lakh). In many categories, consumers exhibit plus one level up behaviour – whatever you think they should be buying given their affluence and the state of market development, they buy one level better than that. Outdated technology, low performance and plain looks are rejected, no matter how attractively priced. The answer to this puzzle is in the differential levels of penetration. Urban penetration is about 24%, but in the top

30 million households by affluence, penetration is 52%. Moreover, the trend of two-wheelers giving way to cars in this top urban affluence grade is expected to be picked up by the second affluence grade as prices of small cars drop further.

In the case of refrigerators, the overall penetration is 10.4%, suggesting an underdeveloped market. Maturing supply shifts the basis of competition and, hence, drivers of brand choice. Improved supply, "performance, features and quality" parity of all major brands and the near price-parity between them shift the basis of competition to the augmented product from the basic product. Add-on services (like removing pain points and not piped music in showrooms) and buying experience will be the driver of brand choice. Can the air-conditioner be fixed without the usual hassle of chipped paint five different contractors, broken walls, etc, in just a day? Does your cell phone company view your bills online when you call them so that it can advise you on what is the best tariff plan? Can the family be given 12 lessons at home after the personal computer arrives? These will be the issues based on which choices will be made. Changing markets need new bases of segmentation. As the market matures and is subjected to multiple changes at the macro level and in related categories, segmentation has to go beyond the product-centric paradigm. Instead of looking at "Premium, popular, discount" price-performance bands, it is time to look at consumer groups, how they view the market and what drives their choices. The question to ask of research is not "how is the market segmented?" (the answer to that is that it is segmented the way marketers have segmented it so far), but what is the new way in which to cut it up so customers can be served better? Take refrigerators. The context in which the category exists has changed. There is more eating out, more phone call deliveries of food and groceries; women are changing and reorganizing their time and their household chores, etc. Clearly, there are segments beyond the modern mum and the good health-conscious housewife, which need to be identified (again on a functional usage and attitude basis rather than on whether she wears her hair short or gives parties – the lifestyle kind of variables).

There is more eating out, more ordering of food and groceries by phone, women are changing and reorganizing their time and their household chores, etc. Clearly there are segments beyond the modern mother and the good health-conscious housewife which need to be identified (again on a functional usage and attitude basis rather than on whether she wears her hair short or gives parties – the lifestyle variables).

Usage patterns are now so different that they form a good basis for segmentation, product design, pricing and service design. From a psychographic point of view,

Young and Rubicam, in a cross-cultural study done years ago, identified groups that we see in Consumer India, and which could form a useful basis for segmenting the market.

The "mainstreamers", "succeeders' and "aspirers" are correlated by occupation, age, stage of life and geography. Qualitative researchers say that cities can be characterized this way too; hence, they show different consumption quantities and character even for a given income distribution.

The only question that rises from this is what is happening in Consumer India. Are values in India changing? The answer: some changes, mostly morphing change, "this as well as that" compromises, new ways of doing old things; let us not confuse changes in ritual with changes in religion.

India is forging ahead on the consumption track, with all lights at green and no stop signs visible, but though full throttle, it was a large mass moving at a modest speed with modest and modestly increasing acceleration; rich getting richer and increasing in numbers, many poor becoming gaining some bit of affluence. However, market researchers totally disagree with this characterization of upwardly creeping, slow burn consumption. They feel that there was going to be a huge consumption explosion just around the corner. It is concerning that maybe the insidious Indian consumer market sneakily changed when I wasn't looking, as he/she is wont to do.

But having looked at all the numbers, some perspective is required. We are getting carried away with the tip of the ice berg looking better and larger than before – forgetting that it is just the tip of the iceberg and that the rest of the ice berg does not look like the tip. Sure, the tip of a large iceberg is large. The top 10% of India is a little over a 100 million people and that is three times the size of Canada, five times Australia, a little less than double of France, etc. Mostly urban, they harbor approximately 40% of the total income. Again, blurring the precision a bit of the income metric a little, this lot having a per capita GNP of 60% of Malaysia and 80% of Brazil (with a population equivalence of about 60% of Brazil). But then we all know that India is a land of conflicting truths. Yes, all of Consumer India is unified in its deep desire to consume and information about what to consume, but the actual quantum of consumption is limited by income and availability of appropriate price-performance products. For higher-end, more sophisticated durables and consumer product categories, the A and B socio-economic classes of urban India (the SEC classification of the Indian market, used by most consumer businesses, is based on the occupation x the education of the chief wage earner) is a very ripe target. This group of about 15 million households, a bit less than 10% of all Indian households, is a high education and exposure group, an explosive growth consumption machine, ready to snap up whatever sensible price-value equation is available. Their general orientation is to pay more to obtain greater benefits, rather than to pay less for fewer benefits. For this group, the share of the premium segment (higher levels of benefit and price than the category average) to total product category purchases is already high, ranging from 35 to 50% for most categories, and is rising, fueled by more frequent upgrading replacement. By the sheer statistics of what happens to the rich tail when the mean of an income distribution improves, we will see premium products and consumption of more "mainstream" international norm products grow very fast. A lot of talk focuses on the BPO Employees fueling consumption and the number is expected to touch 1 million in 2006. That is still quite a small number and while it is an interesting youth-market niche in an otherwise ageing world, it is not "Youth India" – just a tiny fragment of it.

Durables such as cell phones, two-wheelers and color TVs, which have managed the transition in peoples minds from "nice to have" to "necessary to have", whether for emotional or functional reasons, have already achieved substantial penetration in lower SECs. For such products, the target market is larger, comprising SEC A, B and C as well as rural RI (marketers classify rural SEC as R1 to R4 based on the type of house and the education of the chief wage earner). This consumer segment is composed of about 30 million households and is growing in number and income. That is the good news. The bad news is that this target market is still under 20% of Indian households. The consuming upper and upper-middle classes of India have arrived and are igniting consumption – but it is a poorer class of consumers than in most other countries, as suggested by the Living Standards Measurement Survey scale developed by the World Bank.

What will cause a discontinuous growth in consumption across the entire iceberg? Availability of affordably priced, adequately performing products and services. Whenever any such offering has happened, be it in healthcare, televisions, retail formats, financial services, cell phones or apparel, the market has always discontinuously grown. This does not mean that Consumer India has suddenly got discontinuously rich. It just means that some smart suppliers have got their consumer value equations right and have a cost base that enables them to still make a profit.

9.5. Conclusion

So, overall, how does the future look? Optimistic or pessimistic? Let us be realistic. Let us celebrate the opportunity of a growing "Rich India". But let us not make the mistake of extrapolating its growth in size, affluence and consumption habits to the rest of India, because then we would have a repeat of the "great Indian middle-class muddle" all over again.

9.6. References

SEC

The socio-economic classification (SEC) groups urban Indian households on the basis of education and occupation of the chief wage earner (CWE: the person who contributes the most to the household expenses) of the household into five segments (SEC A, SEC B, SEC C, SEC D and SEC E households in that order). This classification is more stable than one based on income alone and being reflective of lifestyle is more relevant to the examination of consumption behaviour. In this article "high" socioeconomic classes refers to SEC A&B, "mid" socioeconomic class refers to SEC C and 'low' socioeconomic classes refers to SEC D&E. Data sourced from Indian Readership Survey (*IRS 1998-1999) gives the education and occupation profile of the chief wage earner of households.

BPO (Business Process Outsourcing Industry)

Bibliography

1. The Kaleidoscope Of Consumer Demand, Rama BijaPurkar, *The Economic Times* – May 2000

2. The Real Ice Phenomenon, Rama Bijapurkar, *The Economic Times* – Jan 2001

3. Connecting With the Future Consumer India, Rama Bijapurkar, *The Economic Times* – May 2003

4. But are Marketers Ready?, asks Rama Bijapurkar, *The Business World* – Dec 28, 2003

5. Cut the Fluff: Basics of Consumer Spending in India, by Rama Bija Purkar, *The Economic Times* – September 25, 2006

6. The Shining, Growing Tip of the Iceberg, by Rama Bijapurkar, *The Economic Times* – Nov 21, 2005.

7. China, India Lead Consumer Confidence Survey, by Shehla Raza Hasan, *The Asia Times Online*, Feb 8, 2006

8. Indian Consumers and the Market, *The Business World* – May 2006

9. http://www.ramabijapurkar.com

Chapter 10

Globalization and Consumer Behavior: A Case Study of Cell Phone Owners in India

10.1. Introduction

The developments in telecommunication have played a significant role in the applications and uses of information and communication technologies (ICTs). With the capability of linking together the various elements of ICTs, regardless of geographical distance and locations, a telecommunication infrastructure is the crucial factor contributing to the convergence of the ICT elements in general. This in turn has widened the scope of development of human activities in socio-economic and geographical spheres. During the globalization era, ICTs have dramatically influenced consumer behavior in terms of commodity and services awareness, searching, evaluation, purchasing and use. It enables consumers to order from home, online or by telephones or cell phone. Thus, the development of communication technology has brought about a drastic change in consumers' behavior, lives and habits, business organization and the telecommunication industry itself, due to the transition from landlines to cell phones.

Cell phones are an important element of ICT. Cell phones are a popular means of communication in both the social and the work spheres. Compared to personal computers and net technologies, cell phones are used by a larger section of the world population. Cell phones have a greater effect on social life and, hence, people are

Chapter written by Velan NIRMALA and U. DEVASENADHIPATHI.

willing to spend more on the mass-produced, less expensive cell phones and pay cell phone bills rather than pay for internet services [GES 2004]. This is because the cell phone technology has the capacity to connect even the less privileged and less educated population in less developed countries (LDCs), as compared to the computer technology [TOW 00; ITU 02]. Cell phone technology has been very successful in developed countries and is emerging as a great communication infrastructure in the developing countries. As a consequence, in 2001, the total number of phones in the world surpassed the number of television sets for the first time [KAT 02]. An International Telecommunication Union study revealed that the cell phone has narrowed the gap in telephone use between developed and developing countries. In 2001, more than 100 countries had more cell phones than landline telephones [ITU 02].

Cell phones offer mobility to people so that they can work or interact with others from anywhere. Ling and Yttri [LIN 99, 02] identified the use of cell phones for three purposes: i) micro-coordination, ii) hyper-coordination and iii) safety and security. Micro-coordination refers to use for logistical purposes in day-to-day personal life and work, such as arranging the time and place of a meeting. Hyper-coordination refers to its use for the purpose of social interaction, personal expression and self-presentation, such as the choice one makes as to physical model of the phone. The purpose of use for safety and security is the use of the phone in emergencies. At work, it provides three inter-related mobilities: i) locational mobility, ie, geographical movement of the workers, ii) operational mobility, ie, the ability to be flexible in business activities and the ability to give independence and iii) interactional mobility, ie, capability of interacting freely with a large number of people from anywhere [KAK 03; HUR 05].

Cell phones are becoming a social and cultural phenomenon, providing an opportunity to express personal emotions and the advantage of communicating with anyone anywhere. Through its varied functionalities, it also ensures non-intrusion by restricting the people who can access the owner as the owner can decide to whom the cell phone number may be given and when to switch it on or off, by giving the owner the ability to manipulate the ringing and voice volumes, to view the caller's number and thus filter out unwelcome callers. It also makes it possible to divert calls to other routes, such a voice message box or a Short Message Service (SMS), thus giving the owner the choice of whether or not to respond to the caller. Cell phones are also empowering in the sense that they help to control actions and thus assume personal responsibility of situations, from a distance. For instance, women generally keep cell phones for social purposes, such as contacting children, family or friends, as well as using it as a means of personal security [PUR 02]. Hence, the cell phone has metamorphosed into an "umbilical cord" as a woman can be in touch with her family, whether she is at home or at work. In addition, a worker can communicate with their employer or vice versa, ensuring accessibility and continuity in work, thus resulting in greater productivity. Cell phones also reduce formal meetings – both official and informal. Therefore, while being advantageous to the business fraternity, cell phones represent a means of greater productivity, interaction and efficiency. They enhance social relationships through SMS and voice contacts. As a result, cell phones are fast replacing personal computers, with their enlarged facilities which make them a multimedia device for text messages, e-mailing, photography, music, radio, movies, software programs and everything that is digitally coded. As cell phones' multimedia accessories are light-weight, handy, user-friendly and available at prices that are affordable, they are accessible to all sections and all ages of the population (children or elderly people, male or female, disabled or illiterate people and even those with a low income) [GES 04]. Thus, there are more cell phone owners worldwide today than there are computer or even television owners.

Since the 1990s, the number of cell phone subscribers has risen from zero to about half a billion worldwide [ITU 02]. Although India has made remarkable achievements in network expansion in the telecommunication industry, the tele-density is low compared to other geographically smaller nations. This is attributable to the country's large population size and income gaps. Nevertheless, the total tele-density world ranking in terms of total telephone subscribers and cell phone subscribers per 100 inhabitants improved from 160 in 1990 to 145 in 2000 and further to 111 in 2004. During 2004 the total telephone subscribers per 100 inhabitants was 8.44 and the cell phone subscribers per 100 inhabitants was 4.37. However, the subscribers are far below the numbers in China, which were 49.74 and 25.76 respectively. The percentage of total cellular mobile subscribers to total telephone subscribers was 51.8 for both countries. The compound growth rate of cell phone subscribers in India from 1999–2004 was reported to be 90.5% [ITU 04]. The Cellular Operators' Association of India reports the current number of cell phone owners in the country to be more than 110 million [SCH 06]. In addition, the Telecom Regulatory Authority of India (TRAI) reports the cell phone tele-density to be growing at a rate of 60 to 65% a year. However, the rural tele-density has remained stagnant at 2% since independence (1947), reflecting serious regional imbalance. Nevertheless, the TRAI promises to overcome this gap within six to eight months through the Universal Service Organization (USO) fund which is being allocated for cellular telephony. In addition, new technologies, such as Wi-Fi and

Wi-Max, will be taken to rural areas, which will connect them with cell phone networks faster than landline telephones [SIN 06].

In recent years, there has been a growth in research on mobile communications worldwide. Besides examining social networks, literature also focuses on the uses and varied perceptions of cell phones. For instance, Ling [LIN 96] found that many cell phone users perceived their instruments "as a means of personal display". Alexander [ALE 00], Hulme and Peters [HUL 01] and Green [GRE 03] observed that adolescent cell phone users, in particular, used the instrument as a fashion symbol. Studies by Gant and Kiesler [GAN 2001] indicated that some cell phone users considered the instrument as an extension of themselves. Studies by Taylor, Alexander and Harper [TAY 01] and Green [GRE 03] also revealed that to some users a cell phone was a symbol of social status.

Research also reveals that the Social Influence (SI) model of technology use provides a useful framework for explaining some of the perceptions and uses of the communication media in an organization [CAM 03]. The SI model states that "Media perceptions are, in part, subjective and socially constructed" [FUL 90, 93, 95]. According to the SI model, "contextual social factors influence the development of perceptions and use of communication technologies". In other words, the behavior, statements and attitudes of those in close contact play an important role in determining how communication media are perceived and used [CAM 03].

The usage pattern of cell phones has also been examined in terms of: i) usage intensity (amount of usage, regardless of the nature of use); ii) usage breadth (number of people called and received calls from) and iii) usage variety (the different purposes for which the phone is used, regardless of the frequency of use) [RAM 90; GES 04]. The ongoing review of literature, however, shows that there are very few studies that focus on the socio-economic and cultural factors that determine the ownership of cell phones.

Given the noticeable change in cell phone ownership in Indian households, this chapter attempts to examine some of the aforementioned issues in the context of the Pondicherry region of the Union Territory of Pondicherry (UTP) in south India, which shares a similar cell phone scenario to the rest of India. It attempts to gauge the popularity of the media in the study area, in terms of usage intensity (ie, time spent on making and receiving calls) and variety intensity (ie, the purpose for which the phone is used, regardless of the frequency of calls) [RAM 90; GES 04]. Further, given the low penetration rate and socio-economic constraints at work in India, it has been deemed important to examine the factors that influence the probability of the households in the Pondicherry region owning a cell phone. The study also attempts to verify the hypothesis of whether perceptions and uses of cell phones are socially constructed in the study area, ie, whether friends and family influenced the purchase of cell phones, or whether the cell phones were handed down from other family members.

Thus, the objectives of the study are: 1) to analyze the determinants of the probability of cell phone ownership among the sample households in the Pondicherry region; 2) to examine the cell phone usage intensity and usage variety among the sample households during the survey and 3) to verify the relevance of SI hypothesis among those households.

The chapter is organized as follows. Section 10.1 of the chapter introduces the problem, followed by the description of data and methodology used in section 10.2. The empirical results of the study are discussed in section 10.3 and the final section, 10.4, gives the conclusions drawn from the results.

10.2. Data and methodology

The UTP in south India has a cell phone density similar to that of rest of the states and the country in general. A case study of the consumer behavior of cell-phone-owning households has been conducted in the Pondicherry region of UTP. The study focuses on the cell-phone-owning and non-owning households in the region, so as to analyze the socio-economic factors contributing to cell phone ownership in the study area. Using a random sampling survey method, with no specific focus on classifications by socio-economic characteristics, 350 households were interviewed using a pre-tested schedule during March–June 2006. Out of the total sample households, 264 (75.43%) owned cell phones and the rest (24.57%) did not. Among the former category, 67.05% of the households also possessed landline phones, while in the latter group 81.40% had landlines. The chapter attempts to analyze the probability of cell phone ownership and intensity of its usage by the sample households in the study area. The objectives of the present study have been pursued using simple averages, percentages, descriptive statistics, the Garret ranking technique [GAR 69] and multiple and simple logistic regressions.

A logistic regression has been adopted to examine the factors determining the probability of cell phone ownership by the sample households. The estimated regression equation is:

$$MOBD = b_0 + b_1REGN + b_2SLIS + b_3SOCL + b_4INCM + b_5SEMP + u$$

where:

MOBD = probability of cell phone ownership dummy, taking value one if owned and zero otherwise;

REGN = region dummy, taking value one for urban area and zero otherwise;

INCM = monthly household income in Rupees;

SLIS = standard of living index score (for calculation and for SLI categorization, see Appendix);

SOCL = social influence dummy, taking value one if purchase was influenced by others and zero otherwise;

SEMP = number of self-employed in the household; and

U = error term.

The regression was initially estimated by including more independent variables, such as age and education of the household head and age of the teenage children in family who influence such purchases. However, they had to be dropped under the step-by-step procedure of analysis employed because of their poor influence on the dependent variable. The purpose of using the step-by-step procedure was to overcome the emergence of multi-collinearity problems, if any, in the estimation of the logit regression. The theoretically expected *a priori* association between the dependent and independent variables will be briefly discussed here.

As the diffusion of cell phones is more rapid in urban society, moving from rural to urban areas is hypothesized to have a positive effect on cell phone ownership by the household, due to greater awareness, exposure and availability of the product in the region.

Monthly income includes the incomes earned by all members of the household, while the standard of living index represents all the comfort and luxury items possessed by the household and the values of any house and landed property owned.

The two variables are also expected to lead to the ownership of cell phones, owing to better economic conditions.

The social influence dummy is also hypothesized to be positively associated with the probability of cell phone ownership, owing to the pressure from neighbors, friends, or relatives to own one, in addition to the bandwagon or demonstration effect.

The number of self-employed in the household is again expected to be positively associated with the dependent variable, due to the need for continuous communications for business activities.

Furthermore, simple logistic regressions have been estimated in order to analyze the direct effects of economic factors and social influence on the probability of cell phone ownership by the sample households. The estimated equation is:

$$MOBD = a + a1Xi + u$$

where:

X_i = i) INCM;

    ii) SLIS;

    iii) INST (mobile instrument price in Rupees);

    iv) MBIL (monthly mobile services use bill in Rupees); and

    v) SOCL.

Following Ram and Jung [RAM 90], the study examines the usage pattern of cell phones in terms of usage intensity and usage variety. The study ignores usage breadth, as the details of the calls made and received were not clearly maintained by the respondents. The usage intensity is measured in terms of usage of mobile phones, regardless of the nature of use, on the basis of the time and amount spent per week and the number of household members using the phone. Usage variety is examined on the basis of the different purposes for which the phone has been used, regardless of the frequency of use.

The Garret ranking technique [GAR 69] has been employed to examine the significance attributed to reasons for the choice of the cell phone brand purchased, type of connection used and usage variety by the sample households. During the interview, the respondents were asked to assign ranks to each reason on the basis of priority. The reasons ranked were then converted into percentage position by adopting the Garret ranking technique. The formula used was:

$$\text{Percentage position} = \frac{100(R_{ij} - 0.5)}{N_j[1]}$$

where:

- R_{ij} = rank assigned to the ith factor by the jth individual; and

- N_j = total number of factors ranked by the jth individual.

The percentage position thus obtained for each rank was further converted into scores by using the Garret's rank table. The scores of all respondents for each factor were then added together and divided by the total number of respondents who had responded, so as to calculate the mean scores for each factor. These mean scores were then arranged in a descending order and ranks were allotted.

10.3. Empirical results and discussions

This section discusses the empirical results of the analyses conducted to pursue the objectives of the study. Since the focus of the chapter is to analyze the probability of cell phone ownership by the sample households, the analyses largely focus on the consumer behavior of cell-phone-owning households.

Table 10.1 gives the descriptive statistics on the socio-economic features of the cell-phone-owning (75.43%) and non-owning (24.57%) sample households during the survey. The age and education pertain to the household head, as they are generally the decision makers in the Indian family and they are the ones who pay for the purchase and use of cell phones.

Sl. No.	Variables	Owner		Non-owner	
		Mean	SD	Mean	SD
1.	AGER	46.83	15.92	43.77	18.39
2.	EDCN	0.61	0.49	0.42	0.50
3.	SEMP	0.08	0.27	0.07	0.26
3.	INCM	16,612.47	20,507.65	12,601.80	10,447.09
4.	SLIS	35.17	8.80	27.81	7.97
5.	REGN	0.96	0.20	0.87	0.34
6.	SOCL	0.56	0.50	–	–
7.	MBIL	440.12	325.72	–	–

Note: SD = standard deviation; US $1 = Rs. 44 at the time of survey.

Table 10.1. *Descriptive statistics*

The table shows the mean age of the household head (AGEH) to be around 47 years for the cell phone owners and 44 years for the non-owners. As regards the education of the household head (EDCN), more owners (61%) than non-owners (42%) have completed secondary school education and higher education. This could be because the more-educated are more likely to rely on ICTs.

The economic status reveals that 8% of owner and 7% of non-owner sample households have members who are self-employed. The average total household income per month was also comparatively larger for the former (Rs. 16,612.47) than for the latter (Rs. 12,601.80). Likewise, the standard of living index also shows that for the former the living standards were better than that of the latter during the survey. This indicates that better economic conditions increased cell phone ownership in the study area. Furthermore, the area of residence shows that more owner (96%) than non-owner households (87%) reside in the urban areas, which provide greater exposure to cell phones and greater opportunities to own cell phones.

In the case of cell phone owners, the average monthly expenditure on services use (MBIL) was Rs. 440. The survey also reveals that about 56% of the sample of cell phone owners was influenced by others (neighbors, friends, or relatives) to purchase the instrument.

Table 10.2 gives the estimated logit regression results of the factors determining the probability of cell phone ownership among the sample households in the Pondicherry region.

The results show that living in urban areas of the Pondicherry region did not positively or significantly influence the decision of sample households to own a cell phone. This is attributable to the fact that in urban Pondicherry, there are several other alternative means of communications, such as landline telephone, Internet and Net phone, which means that cell phone ownership is not indispensable.

The family's standard of living and monthly income both have a positive effect on the decision of whether or not to own a cell phone. However, the impact is significant only in the case of standard of living and not monthly income.

Sl. No.	Variables	Coefficients
1.	Constant	-3.145 (25.18)*
2.	REGN	-0.732 (1.68)
3.	SLIS	0.108 (29.87)*
4.	SOCL	2.525 (39.76)*
5.	INCM	0.000 (0.01)
6.	SEMP	0.343 (1.83)
	Log likelihood ratio	277.65

Note: Brackets show t–value; and * indicates statistical significance at 1% level.

Table 10.2. *Logistic regression: cell phone ownership function*

The effect of the social influence dummy on cell phone ownership emerges as positive and highly significant, thus strongly supporting the validity of SI hypothesis in the context of the Pondicherry region.

As regards the number of self-employed members in the household, their larger number also has a positive influence on cell phone ownership. However, the impact is insignificant because the number of households with self-employed members in the sample is negligible. Further, the self-employed are engaged in traditional business activities only, where the role of cell phone communication is highly limited.

In sum, standard of living and social influence emerge as the significant factors determining the probability of cell phone ownership in the study area.

Table 10.3 gives details on the cell phone instrument and services used by the owner households.

Sl. no.	Details	Number	%
A.	Brand:		
	i) Nokia	147	55.7
	ii) Samsung	55	20.8
	iii) LG	36	13.6
	iv) Sony	18	6.8
	v) Motorola	8	3.1
	Total	264	100.0
B.	Amount spent on instrument (Rs.):		
	i) Less than 2,000	33	12.5
	ii) 2,000–4,000	138	52.3
	iii) 4,000–6,000	59	22.3
	iv) 6,000–8,000	18	6.8
	v) 8,000 and above	16	6.1
	Total	264	100.0
C.	Type of service used:		
	i) GSM	233	88.3
	ii) Airtel	142	53.8
	iii) CellOne	53	20.1
	iv) Aircell	21	8.0
	v) Hutch	17	6.4
	vi) CDMA (Reliance)	31	11.7
	Total	264	100.0

Note: US $1 = Rs. 44 at the time of survey; GSM = global systems for mobile communication; CDMA = code division multiple access.

Table 10.3. *Mobile instrument details*

During the survey, more than half the sample households owned Nokia cell phones, followed by Samsung (20.8%) and LG (13.6%). The percentage ownership of Sony (6.8%) and Motorola (3%) brands was quite low.

As regards the cost of the instrument, more than half the sample households (52.3%) spent between Rs. 2,000 and 4,000 on cell phones. About 22% spent between Rs. 4,000 and 6,000, and 12.5% spent less than Rs. 2,000. Around 6% spent Rs. 6,000 to 8,000 and another 6% spent Rs. 8,000 and above.

The types of services used in the Pondicherry region are GSM and CDMA. Only Reliance comes under the latter, with 11.7% households using it. In the case of GSM (88.3%), Airtel service was the most popular due to its attractive pioneering special service offers, like free SMS and incoming calls, etc. About 53.8% of the respondent households opted for it. It was followed by CellOne (20.1%), Aircell (8%) and Hutch (6.4%).

Thus, while Nokia is the most popular instrument, Airtel is the most desired for its services among the sample households in Pondicherry region.

Table 10.4 contains the ranked reasons for the brand purchased and type of connection used in terms of post-paid (where usage bills are paid at the end of the month) or pre-paid (where cards are paid for usage beforehand for specific amounts according to the customer's conveniences).

Sl. no	Particulars	Total score	Mean score	Rank	Number responded
A.	Brand purchased:				
1.	instrument cost	9,691	51.55	2	188
2.	instrument design	9,511	48.77	3	195
3.	ease of operation	10,806	48.24	4	224
4.	functionality	9,140	51.93	1	176
5.	advertisement influence	5,877	45.91	7	128
6.	social influence	7,045	47.6	6	148
7.	gift	762	47.63	5	16
B.	Nature of connection:				
a.	Post-paid connection:				36 (13.64%)
i)	unlimited use	1,424	45.94	2	31
ii)	enhanced facilities	817	58.36	1	14
b.	Pre-paid connection:				228 (86.36%)
1.	No post usage bill payments	9,902	57.70	1	172
2.	limits expenditure	9,753	43.74	2	223

Table 10.4. *Reasons for choice of brand purchased and type of connection*

Among the stated seven reasons for the brand of mobile phone purchased, instrument-related functionality, its cost, design and ease of operation were the top four priorities respectively, whereas factors such as the phone having been a gift, social influence and advertisement influence were assigned the subsequent ranks by the sample households.

The reasons for the nature of connection chosen, in terms of pre and post-paid connections, have also been examined. Pre-paid cell phone connections are found to be more popular among cell phone owners (86.36%) than post-paid connections (13.64%). As regards the main benefits of pre-paid connections, no post usage bill payment hassles and the limitation of expenditure to the value of the card purchased were quoted as the major benefits. The post-paid connection users ranked other facilities, for example, lower cost of calls, cheaper SMS and longer distance accessibility at lower costs, followed by unlimited use, as the major benefits.

Table 10.5 gives details on cell phone usage intensity among the sample owner households. The usage intensity is measured in terms of the amount spent per month on cell phone use, the number of family members using the services and the number of hours that the cell phone is used per week.

Sl. No	Details	Number	%
A.	Amount spent/month (Rs.):		
	i) less than 200	45	17
	ii) 200–400	128	48.5
	iii) 400–600	58	22.0
	iv) 600–800	7	2.7
	v) 800–1000	23	8.7
	vi) 1,000 and above	3	1.1
	Total	264	100.0
B.	Number of cell phone users:		
	i) 1	188	71.21
	ii) 2	62	23.48
	iii) 3	12	4.55
	iv) 4	2	0.76
	Total	264	100.0
C.	Hours spent/week:		
	i) less than 5	25	9.5
	ii) 5–10	124	47.0
	iii) 10–15	56	21.2
	iv) 15–20	12	4.5
	v) 20–25	17	6.4
	vi) 25–30	7	2.7
	vii) 30 and above	23	8.7
	Total	264	100.0

US $1 = Rs. 44.

Table 10.5. *Cell phone usage intensity*

The expenditure on monthly bills for cell phone service use shows that nearly half the sample households (48.5%) spend between Rs. 200 and 400, followed by 22% who spend between Rs. 400 and 600 and 8.7% who spend between Rs. 800 and 1,000. Less than 3% spend between Rs. 600 and 800 (2.7%) and only 1.1% spend Rs. 1,000 and above.

As regards the number of cell phone users per household, more than two-thirds of households were single-user households (71.21%), while less than a quarter (23.48%) had two users (23.48%). In less than 5% of households there were three users (4.55%), while only about 1% of households had four users (0.76%).

The number of hours of cell phone use reveals that more than two-thirds of households used it for 5 to 15 hours per week, 47% for 5 to 10 hours a week and 21% for 10–15 hours per week. Only 8.7% of the households used cell phones for 25–30 hours per week, while the remaining 13.6% used it for 15–30 hours per week. About 9.5% of households used cell phones for less than 5 hours per week.

Thus, the usage intensity shows that the average monthly bill of the sample cell phone user household was quite low and the hours of its use per week ranged between 5 and 15 hours for the majority of them. Besides, the number of users were largely one or two per household.

Table 10.6 shows the ranked reasons cell phone usage variety among the sample owner households.

Sl. No.	Particulars	Total score	Mean score	Rank	Number responded
1.	To maintain personal contact	7,114	58.8	1	121
2.	Oral communication	4,770	54.2	2	88
3.	SMS	9,257	47.0	4	197
4.	Business	5,659	50.1	3	113
5.	Other services	7,542	46.7	5	155

Table 10.6. *Reasons for cell phone usage*

As regards the types of usage, the sample households quoted to maintain personal contact as the first reason, while the second most important reason was for oral communication and the third was for business communication. SMS and other services (such as entertainment) were ranked fourth and fifth respectively.

Table 10.7 shows the direct effects of income, price and social influence on the household's decision to own a cell phone.

Sl. No.	Variable	Coefficient
1.	INCM	0.000 (4.59)*
2.	SLIS	0.101 (35.90)*
3.	INST	0.030 (0.001)
4.	MBIL	0.583 (0.0004)
5.	SOCL	2.406 (41.48)*

Note: The figures in the parentheses are t–values; * indicates statistical significance at 1% level.

Table 10.7. *Direct effects on cell phone ownership*

The table reveals the effect that income elasticity and standard of living have on cell phone ownership to be positive and significant. It indicates that a rise in income and standard of living encourages a household to own a cell phone. The price elasticity of the instrument and user bills is also positive, but not significant. This implies that an increase in instrument price or cell phone usage bills does not significantly influence the decision to own a cell phone. This could be because the benefits of cell phone ownership are far greater in comparison to the costs and expenses of owning the phone.

In addition, the effect of social influence of neighbors, friends, or relatives on cell phone ownership emerges as positive and highly significant, thus confirming the validity of the SI hypothesis in the context of the study area.

10.4. Conclusion

In the wake of growing consumerism in the globalization era, this chapter attempts to identify the factors influencing the probability of cell phone ownership among Indian households. In this context, a case study of the Pondicherry region in South India was conducted by interviewing a random sample of 350 households during March–June 2006. The study also examined the cell phone usage intensity and types of usage among cell phone users (264), as well as verifying the relevance of the social influence model to the study area. The objectives of the chapter have been analyzed using simple averages, percentages, Garret ranking techniques and simple and multiple logistic regressions.

Although there are not many variations in the socio-economic characteristic features of the cell-phone-owning and non-owning households, the empirical results of the study revealed the probability of cell phone ownership to be positively and significantly influenced by both economic (standard of living) and social influence factors. In addition, the majority of the cell phone owners possessed Nokia instruments brand and preferred less expensive instruments. Further, pre-paid connections were more popular, owing to reasons such as no post-bill payments and limited bill expenses.

Usage intensity revealed that for the majority of cell phone owners, phone bills were quite low, the phone was used for an average of 5–15 hours per week and the phones were largely used by one or two members of the household. Usage variety indicated that the phones were mostly used for maintaining personal contacts, for oral communication, business communication and SMS.

Income elasticity and the effects of living standards and social influence were revealed to be the strongest factors among the sample households that encouraged the decisions to own cell phones. Thus, the study validates the social influence hypothesis in the context of the study area.

Cell phones are a cheaper, more user-friendly, economic, efficient and convenient means of communication and are used for micro-coordination and partial hyper-coordination by the sample households in the Pondicherry region. The consumer behavior with respect to cell phone ownership is largely influenced by the economic status of the household and social influence.

10.5. References

[ALE 00] ALEXANDER, PS (2000), "Teens and mobile phones growing-up together: Understanding the reciprocal influences on the development of identity", paper presented at the Wireless World Workshop, University of Surrey, Surrey.

[BHA 03] BHATTACHARYA, M (2003), "Telecom sector in India: Vision 2020", background paper submitted to the committee on India: Vision 2020, Planning Commission, Government of India, New Delhi.

[CAL 04] CALLEGARO, M and TERESIO, POGGIO (2004), "Where can I call you? The mobile (phone) revolution and its impact on survey research and coverage error: A discussion of the Italian case", in Proceedings ISARC 33 VI International Conference on Logic and Methodology: Recent Development and Application in Social Research Methodology, Amsterdam.

[CAM 03] CAMPBELL, SW and RUSSO, TC (2003), "The social construction of mobile telephony: an application of the social influence model to perceptions and uses of mobile phones within personal communication networks", *Communication Monographs*, vol 70, no 4, December, pp 317–34.

[FUL 90] FULK, J, SCHMITZ, J and STEINFIELD, CW (1990), "A social influence model of technology use", in Fulk, J and Steinfield, CW (eds), *Organizations and Communication Technology*, Newbury Park, CA: Sage, pp 117–39.

[FUL 93] FULK, J (1993) "Social construction of communication technology", *Academy of Management Journal*, vol. 36, pp 921–50.

[FUL 95] FULK, J, SCHMITZ, J and RYU, D (1995), "Cognitive elements in the social construction of technology", *Management Communication Quarterly*, vol 8, pp 259–88.

[GAN 01] GANT, D and KIESLER, S (2001), "Blurring the boundaries: cell phones, mobility and the line between work and personal life", in Brown, B, Green, N and Harper, R (eds), *Wireless World: Social and International Aspects of the Mobile Age*, London: Springer, pp 121–32.

[GAR 69] GARRET, HE and WOODWORTH, RS (1969), *Statistics in Psychology and Education*, Bombay: Vakils, Feffer and Simons Private Ltd.

[GES 04] GESER, H (2004), "Towards a sociological theory of the mobile phone", University of Zurich, May, http://Socio.ch/mobile/t-geser1.pdf, accessed on 25 June 2006.

[GOI 02] GOVERNMENT OF INDIA (2002), *Annual Report 2001–2002*, New Delhi: Ministry of Communications and Information Technology, Department of Telecommunications.

[GRE 03] GREEN, N (2003), "Outwardly mobile: Young people and mobile technologies", in Katz, JE (ed.), *Machines that Become Us: The Social Context of Communication Technology*, New Brunswick, New Jersey: Transaction Publishers, pp 210–18.

[HUL 01] HULME, M and PETERS, S (2001), "Me, my phone and I: The role of the mobile phone", CHI 2001 Workshop: Mobile Communication: Understanding Users, Adoption and Design, Seattle, http://www/cs/colorodo.edu/paten/chi_workshop

[HUR 05] HURME, P (2005), "Mobile communication and work practices in knowledge-based organisations", *Human Technology*, vol 1, no 1, April, pp 101–08.

[ITU 02] International Telecommunication Union (2002), *World Communication Development Report* 2002, Geneva.

[ITU 04] International Telecommunication Union (2004), "World Telecommunication Indicators", *World Telecommunication Development Report* 2004, Geneva.

[JAN 06] Jan Samachar: Multilingual News and Feature Agency Devoted to Rural Issues (2006), "Telecommunication in India: A Review", New Delhi.

[KAK 03] KAKIHARA, M (2003), "Emerging work practices of ICT – enabled mobile professionals", unpublished doctoral dissertation, London School of Economics and Political Science, University of London, retrieved from www.Kakihara.org on 10 April 2006.

[KAT 02] KATZ, JE and AAKHUS, MA (2002), "Introduction: framing the issues", in Katz, JE and Aakhus, MA (eds), *Perpetual Contact Mobile Communication, Private Talk, Public Performance*, Cambridge: Cambridge University Press, pp 1–14.

[KOP 00] KOPOMAA, T (2000), *The City in Your Pocket: Birth of the Mobile Information Society*, Helsinki: University Press.

[LIN 96] LING, R (1996), "One can talk about common manners! The use of mobile telephones in inappropriate situations", Report No 32/96, Kjeller, Norway: Technor Research and Development.

[LIN 99] LING, R and YTTRI, B (1999), "Nobody sits at home and waits for the telephone to ring: Micro and hyper coordination through the use of the mobile phone", Report No. 30/99, Kjeller, Norway: Technor Research and Development.

[LIN 02] LING, R and YTTRI, B (2002), "Hyper coordination via mobile phones in Norway", in Katz, JE and Aakhus, M (eds) *Perpetual Contact: Mobile Communication, Private Talk, Public Performance*, Cambridge: Cambridge University Press, pp 139–69.

[MAS 04] MASSINI, S (2004), "The diffusion of mobile telephony in Italy and the UK: an empirical investigation", *Economics of Innovation and New Technology*, vol 13, no 3, April, pp 251–77.

[PAL 00] PALEN, L, SALZMAN, M and YOUNGS, E (2000), "Going wireless: behavior and practice of new mobile phone users", ACM CSCW 2000 Conference on Computer Supported Cooperative Work Proceedings, Philadelphia, P.A., New York: Association of Computing Machinery Inc, pp 201–10.

[PUR 02] PURO, J-P (2002), "Finland: a mobile culture", in Katz, JE and Aakhus, MA (eds), *Perpetual Contact: Mobile Communication, Private Talk, Pubic Performance*, Cambridge: Cambridge University Press, pp 19–29.

[RAM 90] RAM, S and HYUNG-SHIK, J (1990), "The conceptualization and measurement of product usage", *Journal of the Academy of Marketing Science*, vol 18, Winter, pp 67–76.

[ROY 99] ROY, TK, JAYACHANDRAN, V, SUSHANTA, K and FEE, B (1999), "Economic condition and fertility: is there a relationship?", *Economic and Political Weekly*, vol 34, nos. 42 and 43, 1999, 16–23 October, pp 3041–3046.

[SCH 06] SCHNEIDER, M (2006), "Updates", *View Journal*, 5 September, p 1.

[SIN 06] SINGH, P (2006), "India cell phone story has a long way to go", *New Indian Express*, 20 September, p 10.

[TAY 01] TAYLOR, AS and HARPER, R (2001), *The Gift of the Gab?: A Design Oriented Sociology of Young People's Use of "mobilZe!"*, Guildford Publications, England.

[TOW 00] TOWNSEND, AM (2000), "Life in the real-time city: mobile telephone and urban metabolism", *Journal of Urban Technology*, vol 7, no 2, pp 85–104.

10.6. Appendix

Scores for the variables used in the calculation of Standard of Living Index

Sl. No.	Variables		Scores
A.	Household Amenities:		
1.	Separate room for cooking	Yes	1
		No	0
2.	Type of house	concrete	2
		tiled	1
		thatched	0
3.	Source of lightning	electricity	2
		kerosene or gas or oil	1
		others	0
4.	Fuel for cooking	electricity or gas	2
		kerosene or coal	1
		others	0
5.	Source of drinking water	own well or pipe or hand pump	2
		public well or pipe or hand pump	1
		others	0

6.	Toilet facility	own pit toilet	3
		public toilet, shared pit toilet	2
		others	0

7.	Ownership of goods	television	3
		radio and transistor	1
		refrigerator	3
		two-wheeler	3
		phone	2
		cell phone	3
		video/compact disk player	3
		bicycle	2

B.   Standard of Living Index score range: 0 – 36

C   **1.**

2. CATEGORIES OF SLI:

Low SLI –	0 – 9
Medium –	10 – 19
High SLI –	20 and above

Source: [ROY 99] ROY, TK, JAYACHANDRAN, V, SUSHANTA, K and FEE, B (1999), "Economic condition and fertility: is there a relationship?", *Economic and Political Weekly*, vol 34, nos 42 and 43, 1999, 16–23 October, pp 3041–046.

Chapter 11

Factors Affecting Technology Adoption in India: A Consumer-Based View

11.1. Introduction

Many researchers who worked on technology said that technology is a universal, uniform and consistent factor across national and cultural boundaries [KEE 01]. They have argued that there are no cultural boundaries limiting the application of technology. Once a technology is developed, it immediately becomes available everywhere in the world. If a company knows how to manage a technology in one country, it has experience that is relevant for the rest of the world.

Researchers who advocate such thought assume that the diffusion process of any innovation is not based upon cultural dissimilarities. They argue that mass media has a very strong and direct effect on a mass audience and diffusion occurs through several promotional activities of mass media. Another body of literature ([ROG 95]; [BAS 69]) advocates that opinion leaders, who have similar cultural, social and economic background, such as innovators, take a leading role in the diffusion process. They influence the prospective adopters to take a positive attitude toward an innovation. However, the rate of adoption varies depending on economic and sociological structure of the country.

Chapter written by Atanu ADHIKARI and A.K. RAO.

11.2. History of diffusion of innovation

The origin of research in diffusion of innovation dates back to the work of Gabriel Trade in the early 1900s. Trade is called the father of the concept of diffusion. He identified certain common characteristics in several legal cases and societal trends and called them the "laws of imitation". Trade observed that diffusion of innovations follows a generalized path.

In the 1920s, anthropological research spent a good deal of time on diffusion research. That research continued up to the early 1950s when Bryce Ryan and his professor, Neal Gross, worked on diffusion through their research on hybrid seed corn. An explosion of diffusion research took place in Latin America and Africa and the leader of that research was Evett Rogers.

Technology diffusion theory helps to explain the process of adoption of an innovation. The societal process and its change across countries at large and population segments in particular is the main center of diffusion theory. Technological innovation can be in the form of an idea, practice (intangible) or object (tangible). The perceived benefit of technological innovation, its convenience and adopters' positive attitudes determine the reaction towards any innovation. Innovators take a leading role in communicating such advantages through specific channels over a period of time to the prospective adopters in a social system.

Since the adoption process starts with a small number of innovators, the rate of growth of cumulative adopters is very slow. This is because the social groups who advocate in favor of technology diffusion constitute a small percentage of the population (approximately 2.5%). As the number of adopters increases, the rate of adoption also increases due to the increasing influence of the adopters on the prospective adopters. This process continues for a considerable time depending on the nature of the technological innovation as well as the cultural, social and economic background of the adopters; however, the rate of adoption increases exponentially. Once a considerable proportion of prospective adopters adopt the innovation, the rate of adoption slowly decreases as there is a very small proportion of prospective adopters left to adopt. This entire phenomenon follows an S-shaped curve. The first part of the curve shows a very slow rate of adoption, then it increases with a faster rate and finally increases with a decreasing rate. Frank Bass [BAS 69] modeled such phenomena mathematically through logistic curves and showed that the probability of adoption of a technological innovation depends on coefficient of innovation, as well as on the coefficient of imitation.

Naturally, the number of adopters at any point in time follows a bell-shaped (normal) curve. Rogers [ROG 62] divided the normal curve into five segments. The relative advantage of the innovation is identified through a risk-return analysis by 2.5% of individuals. The risk adversity of this segment is very low and they are prone to explore new ideas, products or services. They believe that innovation gives them a relative advantage in their daily lives. While this segment of adopters perceives the benefit of technological innovation, their sources of information about such benefit is often different.

The next group of people is averagely risk averse and is positively influenced by the innovators over a period of time. Bass [BAS 69] called them "imitators". There are four groups of people who are imitators: early adopters, early majority, late majority and laggards.

Both lateral and longitudinal diffusion occurs in the innovation process. Lateral diffusion takes place when technology connects business processes of one area with the other. For example, Net-banking systems, centralized reservations or connecting downstream production with upstream production show horizontal diffusion. Longitudinal diffusion takes place when technological knowledge is transferred in a vertical direction from an idea to an application through some process. Any diffusion process requires a channel through which technology will transfer from one point to another. Innovators and early adopters work as such a channel, helping technology to diffuse. Another important channel is mass media. Media plays a significant role in increasing the probability of adoption of particular technology. While the amount of information transmitted through the media is same for all prospective adopters, the degree of personal influence varies, based on the number of people who have already adopted the technology. Hence, the probability of adoption at any point "t" follows a linear model with an intercept of probability of innovation (through mass media) and a gradient of probability of imitation (the influence of people who have already adopted). The ultimate objective is to increase the amount and quality of technology transfer in a unit of time.

Technological innovation in Web-based channels, especially the Internet, has been of interest to researchers for a long time. In general terms, the various pieces of research on technology adoption have explained that the diffusion of the Internet plays an essential role in product growth and the inclination of consumers to use it. Opinion leaders and followers are two vital players in diffusion process. Technological difference between opinion leaders and followers can be introduced where information flows from leaders to followers to increase their propensity to adopt innovative technology. Therefore, there is more potential growth for the follower as compared to the leader. In this way and from the point of view of Internet policies, it would be advisable to make the process of Internet diffusion easier by eliminating obstacles to the effective technological catch-up process among leaders and followers, otherwise the growth of adoption by poor consumers and convergence among other consumers, would stop.

In a divergent and developing country like India, technology adoption in the form of the Internet is critical as well as complicated. This is because India is in a developing stage and both personal computer and Internet penetration is reasonably low. Technology gap theory, while it allows for the important public good aspect of technology, may not be suitable for some of the technology-based services in other developing countries. The main reason behind such delay in adoption is that the adoption process of technology-enabled services in such developing countries depends on some motivators as well as many inhibitors.

Technology is the key concept for success in today's business world. The banking sector is one of the largest business sectors that use information technology (IT). Although technology is an immense benefit to the banking sector throughout the world in general and in India in particular, the role played by IT in the consumer interface is not important enough to be examined here. Traditionally, technology has provided support and solutions to banks to enable them to take care of their customers' accounts and back-office requirements. This has subsequently given way to a large-scale implementation of services aimed at the bank's customers, for example Automated Teller Machines (ATM), centralized database solutions and payment and settlement systems, etc. Another huge area that Indian bankers are targeting is Net banking.

The emphasis of electronic banking is on providing effective front-line systems to render customer contacts user-friendly. This is made easier because the physical presence of the customer is not required. However, the relevant enabling technology and systems should be accessible to customers. Most banks import the new technology for this very purpose. Another advantage of Internet banking is that it increases revenues (eg, through the ease of informing customers about products and the ease of proactive cross-selling). It also represents a competitive advantage through differentiation of banking services and image improvement. Finally, Internet banking allows a modular approach for cost-effective development and is of course an inexpensive option when compared with doing business in bank branches.

All these perceived advantages forced banks to import technology from foreign countries.

The next part of this chapter attempts to find out the factors that influence adoption of electronic banking technology in India. A literature review shows that the acceptance of technology by any country, in order to reduce a technology gap, primarily depends on the attitude toward adoption. In this chapter, the authors have identified the main dimensions that play a major role in the adoption of technology-based banking services in India which is an industrially- and economically-developing country.

11.3. A theoretical framework

A conceptual model of consumers' technology adoption is developed on the basis that consumer adoption of technology-based services depends on individuals' inclinations toward technology-based services. Consumers' adoption of technology-centric products, processes or services mainly depends on three dimensions: access to technology, individual characteristics and product or process characteristics. Limited or no access to the Internet is a major inhibitor to consumer-adoption of technological innovations, especially in the case of new innovations [ZEI 87]. Access to the Internet depends on availability or access to the Internet at home or at the office. The individual characteristics dimension is, mainly, the individual's technology inclination [ADH 05a] which consists of push factors and pull factors. Product and process characteristics deal with the tangible and intangible features of the product or process. Our research is on individual, as well as product and process, characteristics.

11.4. Adoption of electronic banking service innovations

Product and process characteristics and socio-economic characteristics have been proposed as determinants of consumer-adoptions of technological innovations [GAT 85]. Perceptions of technology-based services innovations includes *perceived benefits of technology* [LEE 02], *security* [PAR 00], *complexity* [ROG 95), *need for human interaction* [CRO 90], *triability* [ROG 95] and *observability* [ROG 95].

Davis [DAV 89] suggested that the choice to use a new technology is determined by the extent to which the consumer believes that it adds value to the cost that he pays compared to the current method, or traditional methods, of executing transactions. Tornatzky and Klein [TOR 82] argued that consumers adopt technology when they perceive significant benefits in technology, otherwise consumers continue with their traditional way of doing things.

Reliability of a new technology refers to the degree to which a consumer believes that the electronic banking service will function without failures. Research identified [MOH 92] that perceived reliability has a positive effect on consumer adoption of technology-based innovations. The likelihood of consumer adoption increases as the reliability of a technology-based service increases.

Security concerns may be one of the major inhibitors for consumers who are considering whether to use an electronic banking service. Apprehension about transaction security, such as cyber-crime or errors in transactions, can act as an inhibitor in the adoption of technology-centric services. Often consumers are reluctant to give information electronically due to their security concerns [PAR 00]. Hence, perceived security concerns have a negative effect on consumer adoption of electronic banking services.

Complexity is the consumer's perception of the level of difficulty in learning and adopting electronic banking services. Rogers [ROG 95] suggested that the complexity of the innovation, as perceived by potential adopters, is negatively related to the adoption of the technology innovation.

Trialability is another factor that influences adoption and is the chance given to the customer to try technology-enabled services before they actually adopt them [ROG 95]. An innovation that can be test run by consumers (high trialability) is more likely to be adopted than an innovation that can not be tried before adoption. Lee, Lee and Eastwood [LEE 03] showed that consumers with access to electronic banking will try to use electronic banking.

Research identified that a consumer has a strong desire to interact with other humans. Crosby et al. [CRO 90] show that consumers have different tolerance levels for automated services. If a consumer has a strong preference for person-to-person interaction, the increased benefits of adopting technology are overshadowed by the loss of human contact.

11.5. Data

The primary survey was conducted by questionnaire in five Indian cities, namely Hyderabad, Kolkata, Chennai, Pune and Delhi. Information from a sample of 309 individuals was collected from these five cities through a non-probabilistic procedure. Considering the similarity of the consumer base for electronic banking services in other Indian cities, responses from these five cities will give a reasonable overview. Lowley and Maxwell [LOW 71] suggested that interdependent multivariate tests, such as factor analysis, are appropriate if the sample contains at least 51 more cases than the number of variables under consideration, that is, $N - k - 1 > 50$, where N is the sample size and k is the number of variables. Another rule of thumb is that the minimum sample size should be more than four times the number of variables that the researcher considers. The sample size of this research fulfills both requirements. The measurement of sample adequacy (MSA) for individual variables was also checked in this research during factor analysis. This ranged from 0.62 to 0.88. The Kaiser-Meyer-Olkin (KMO) measure was 0.856 which is above the acceptable limit and confirms that correlations of pairs of variables are comparatively much higher than their partial correlations.

11.5.1. *Measures and scaling*

Factors affecting the adoption of electronic banking services are measured through 19 variables, which are given in the appendix to this chapter. Survey questions were phrased in terms of electronic banking which was explicitly defined by the interviewer as computer banking, direct bill payment and transfer of funds. Responses were collected in a 5-point Likert scale. The Likert scale is a widely-used rating scale in this kind of research. Categories assigned to the negative statement by the respondents are scored by reversing the scale. Rogers [ROG 62] divided the normal curve into five segments. The relative negative statement reflects an unfavorable response, whereas an agreement with a positive statement reflects a positive response. The reliability of the scale measured through its internal consistency is tested by calculating Cronbach's alpha. The alpha is 0.847.

11.5.2. *Analysis*

The data collected was analyzed using factor analysis to identify the underlying factors of the consumers' perceptions about electronic banking services. Independent variables in the questionnaire are used to capture the innovation adoption of the consumer. Since these variables measure one attribute, the responses seem to curve. Rogers [ROG 62] divided the normal curve into five segments. The relative is correlated. As a result assuming the factors to be orthogonal may not be justified. We avoided factor analysis with varimax rotation and oblimin rotation was applied. In order to identify the latent factors, principal component analysis with varimax rotation and oblimin rotation was applied and it is found that factors derived from oblimin rotation are more clearly associated.

11.5.3. *Factor analysis*

Bartlett's Test of Sphericity [BAR 50] tests the zero hypothesis that the correlation matrix is an identity matrix (ie, there is no relationship among the variables). A larger value of Bartlett's test indicates a greater likelihood that the correlation matrix is not an identity matrix. The zero hypothesis is rejected at 0.000 level of significance with a very high χ^2 value is observed. The KMO test is a measure of sampling adequacy that compares the magnitudes of calculated correlation coefficients [KAI 74] and has a "meritorious" value (>0.8).

Principle component analysis (PCA) was carried out to find out the underlying factors among 19 variables. PCA is especially useful when the researcher wants to summarize the relationships among a large number of variables with a smaller number of components [TAB 01]. To determine the number of initial factors, those factors for which the eigenvalues are greater than 1.00 are selected. This would mean that these factors would account for more than their share of the total variance of the variables [GUT 54]. Comrey and Lee [COM 92] caution that the eigenvalue > 1 criterion should only be used when 1.0s are inserted on the diagonal as the initial communality values (eg, PCA), which is advice that was followed in this research.

Five factors have emerged (Table 11.1) for the computer-banking adoption model. The bold face indicates large factor loading scores. These five factors appear as an adequate curve. Rogers [ROG 62] divided the normal curve into five segments. The relatively reflect respective underlying dimensions and explain 72.5% of the total variance. The eigenvalues ranged from 1.028 to 7.851. These five factors are perceived benefit, security, complexity, human contact and reliability.

11.6. Discussion and conclusion

The successful diffusion of technological innovation is contingent upon consumer acceptance ([MAH 90], [ROG 95]). This research has tried to ascertain the factors affecting consumers' adoption of electronic banking in developing countries such as India.

The results provide some valuable insight for Indian banks and financial institutions that have imported electronic banking services technology into India. To enhance the customer's likelihood of adopting technology-based electronic banking services, banks and financial institutions should design and implement effective communications that promote the benefits and other positive features of such services. The promotion also should address those aspects that eradicate the consumer's perceived security concerns. This will increase the use of technology-based services that involve online transactions. Communication of the reliability of technology-based banking services will also increase adoption their adoption.

Priorities must include the successful importation of foreign technology and its implementation, customer access to the innovative technology and an overall reorientation of the enterprise targeting their customers are two essential requirement for effective technology adoption. Banks must defend and reinforce their technological identities and cater for an e-customer base that will judge an institution by the performance of its technology as well as by how well it delivers its primary commercial functions. E-banking is new and evolving fast, hence the Indian banks and financial institutions must remain open to new technologies and newly-evolved best-practice models. Therefore, the baseline objective of any e-banking strategy should be to convey a package to the customer where the package presents core values in easily-accessible, user-friendly electronic formats.

11.7. References

[ADH 05] ADHIKARI, A and RAO, AK (2005), "Segmentation of Indian consumers based on their technology inclination", *Conference Proceedings of INT*, Evry, France

[ADH 05a] ADHIKARI, A (2005) "Technology inclination of Indian consumers and organizations' strategy – a research perspective" *The ICFAI Journal of Service Marketing,* vol III, no 1, pp 26–33

[ADH 05b] ADHIKARI, A (2005) "Technology inclination of Indian consumers – a taxonomy", in Conference Proceedings of the Paper Presented at the International Conference on Service Marketing, pp 942 –46

[BAR 50] BARTLET, MS (1950) "Tests of significance in factor analysis", *British Journal of Psychology*, vol 3, pp 77–85

[BAS 69] *Management Science*, 15 (January), 215-227.

[BIT 00] BITNER, MJ, BROWN, WB and MEUTER, ML (2000) "Technology infusion in service economics", *Journal of the Academy of Marketing Science*, vol 28, no 1, pp 138–49

[BUR 90] BURNETT, J (1990) "Adult single: an untapped market", *International Journal of Bank Marketing*, vol 8, no 4, pp 10–16

[COM 92] COMREY, AL and LEE, HB (1992) *A First Course in Factor Analysis*, Hillsdale, NJ: Lawrence Erlbaum.

[CRO 90] CROSBY, LA, EVANS, KR and COWELS, D (1990) "Relationship quality in service selling: an interpersonal influence perspective", *Journal of Marketing*, vol 54 (July), pp 68–81

[DAV 89] DAVIS, FD (1989) "Perceived usefulness, perceived ease of use and user acceptance of information technology", *MIS Quarterly*, vol 13, no 3, pp 319–39

[FAI 97] FAIN, D and ROBERTS, M L (1997) "Technology vs consumer behavior: the battle of the financial services customer", *Journal of Direct Marketing*, vol 11, no 1, pp 44–55

[FRA 98] FRAMBACH, RT, BARKEMA, HG, NOOTEBOOM, B and WEDEL, M (1998) "Adoption of service innovation in business market: an empirical test for supply-side variables", *Journal of Business Research*, vol 4, no 2, pp 161–74

[GAT 85] GATINGNON, H and ROBERTSON, TR (1985) "A propositional inventory for new diffusion research", *Journal of Consumer Research*, vol 11 (March), pp 849–67

[GUT 54] GUTTMAN, L (1954) "Some necessary conditions for common factor analysis", *Psychometrika*, vol 19, pp 149–61

[HAI 03] HAIR, JF, ANDERSON, RE, TATHAM, RL and BLACK, WC 2003) *Multivariate Data Analysis*, (1st edn), New Delhi: Pearson Education Inc

[HET 87] HETTER, TJ (1987) "Go with those you know: sell to existing customers", *Bottomline*, vol 4, no 11, pp 15–20

[KAI 58] KAISER, HF (1958) "An index of factorial simplicity", *Psychometrika*, vol 39, pp 31–36

[KAI 65] KAISER, HF and CAFFREY, J (1965) "Alpha factor analysis", *Psychometrika*, vol 30, pp 1-14

[KEE 01] KEEGAN, W (2001) *Global Marketing Management*, (5th edn), New Delhi: Prentice Hall of India

[KIM 78a] KIM, JO and MULLER, CW (1978) *Introduction to Factor Analysis: What It Is and How to Do It*, (1st edn), California: Sage Publications

[KIM 78b] KIM JO and MULLER, CW (1978) *Factor Analysis: Statistical Methods and Practical Issues*, (1st edn), California: Sage Publications

[LAW 71] LAWLEY, N. R. and MAXWELL, A. E. (1971), *Factor Analysis as a Statistical Method*, 2nd ed., Butterworths, London.

[LEE 02] LEE E.J, JINKOK L. and SCHUMANN D. (2002), "The influence of communication source and modality of consumer adoption of technological innovations", *Journal of Consumer Affairs*, Vol 36, No 1, pp 1-27

[LEE 03] LEE, E.J. JINKOOK LEE, DAVID EASTWOOD (2003), "A two-step estimation of consumer adoption of technology-based service innovations", *Journal of Consumer Affairs*, Vol 37 No 2, pp 256–282

[LEV 83] LEVITT, T (1983) "The globalization of markets", *HBR* (May-June), p 92

[MAH 90] MAHAJAN, V, MULLER, E and BASS, FM (1990), "New product diffusion model in marketing, a review and direction for research", *Journal of Marketing*, Vol 54 (January), pp 1-26

[MOH 92] MOHAMED, Z (1992) "Measuring success in ATM implementation using customer-supplied interaction criteria", *International Journal of Operation and Production Management*, vol 12, no 10, pp 34–55

[MUR 86] MURPHY, NH and ROGERS, RC (1986) "Life cycle and the adoption of consumer financial innovation: An empirical analysis of the adoption process", *Journal of Bank Marketing*, vol 17, no 1, pp 3–8

[PAR 00] PARASURAMAN, A (2000) "Technology readiness index (TRI): a multiple item scale to measure readiness to embrace new technologies", *Journal of Service Research*, vol 2, no 4, pp 307–20

[PED 91] PEDHAZUR, EJ and SCHMELIN, LP (1991) *Measurement, Design and Analysis: An Integrated Approach*, Hillsdale, NJ: Lawrence Erlbaum

[ROG 95] ROGERS, EE (1995) *Diffusion of Innovation*, (4th edn), New York: The Free Press

[TAB 01] TABACHNIK, BG and FIDEL, LS (2001) *Using Multivariate Statistics*, (4th edn), Boston: Allyn & Bacon

[TOR 82] TORNATZKYL, K and KLEIN, KJ (1982) "Innovation characteristics and innovation adoption implementation: a meta-analysis of findings", *IEEE Transactions on Engineering Management*, vol 29, pp 28–45

[ZEI 87] ZEITHMAL, V and GILLYM, MC (1987) "Characteristics affecting the acceptance of retailing technology: a comparison between elderly and non-elderly consumers", *Journal of Retailing*, vol 63, no 1, pp 49–68

11.8. Appendix

Age in years		Frequency	%	Valid %	Cumulative %
Valid	18–24	14	12.8	13	13
	25–34	40	36.7	37	50
	34–44	8	7.3	7.4	57.4
	45–54	23	21.1	21.3	78.7
	55–64	19	17.4	17.6	96.3
	>64	4	3.7	3.7	100
	Total	108	99	100	

Table 11.1. *Age*

	Frequency	%	Valid %	Cumulative %
Valid Not adopted	46	42.2	42.6	42.6
Adopted	62	56.9	57.4	100
Total	108	99.1	100	

Table 11.2. *Adoption*

	Frequency	%	Valid %	Cumulative %
Valid Do not have access	32	29.4	29.6	29.6
Has access	76	69.7	70.4	100
Total	108	99.1	100	

Table 11.3. *Access*

Kaiser-Meyer-Olkin Measure of Sampling Adequacy		.856
	Approx Chi-Square	1,287.832
Bartlett's Test of Sphericity	df	171
	Sig.	.000

Table 11.4. *KMO and Bartlett's test*

	Component				
	1	2	3	4	5
convenient	**.820**				
better	**.864**				
save_tim	**.800**				
advantag		**.660**			
mstk_cor			**.902**		
mstk_occ			**.810**		
useful		**-.609**			
efficient	**-.886**				
safe		**.811**			
cmft_pin		**.761**			
difficult			**-.817**		
can_try	-.367		**.712**		
seen_oth	-.337		**.631**		
man_touc				**.957**	
crdt_car					**.957**
atm					**.715**
mobile					**.773**
ph_banki	**.422**		.388		
e_bankin	**.684**		.397		

Extraction method: PCA
Rotation method: Oblimin with Kaiser normalization
A Rotation converged in 7 iterations

Table 11.5. *Pattern matrix (a)*

Electronic-banking technology-adoption survey

Research is being conducted for academic purposes by doctoral fellows of IIMT, IBS, Hyderabad. Your response to this questionnaire is highly appreciated and will go a long way to achieving an educational purpose. The questionnaire consists of 19 statements to give an overall idea about your perception of electronic banking. Electronic banking is, broadly, Net banking, direct bill payment, transfer of funds, asking for financial instruments, and all other work relating to the bank using your computer. Read all the statements and indicate your choice in a 5-point rating scale – 1 being strongly disagree and 5 being strongly agree – by **darkening** the corresponding digit.

(In this case **[4]** is darkened)

       [1] – Strongly disagree
       [2] – Disagree
       [3] – Neither agree nor disagree
       [4] – Agree
       [5] – Strongly agree

1. Electronic banking is convenient to use (convenient):

   [1]   [2]   [3]   [4]   [5]

2 Electronic banking helps me to manage my personal finances in a better way (better):

   [1]   [2]   [3]   [4]   [5]

3. I think that using electronic banking saves time in my financial activities compared to doing it in traditional ways (save_tim):

   [1]   [2]   [3]   [4]   [5]

4. I believe that electronic banking is very advantageous to use (advantag):

   [1]   [2]   [3]   [4]   [5]

5. It is more difficult to have mistakes corrected in electronic banking than in traditional banking (mstk_cor):

   [1]   [2]   [3]   [4]   [5]

6. Mistakes are more likely to occur in electronic banking than in traditional banking (mstk_occ):

   [1]   [2]   [3]   [4]   [5]

7. Electronic banking is useful as it can be done 24 hours a day (useful):

   [1]   [2]   [3]   [4]   [5]

8. Electronic banking is an efficient way of doing financial activities (efficient):

[1]   [2]   [3]   [4]   [5]

9. When I use electronic banking, my money is as safe as it is when I use other services (safe):

[1]   [2]   [3]   [4]   [5]

10. I feel comfortable giving my Personal Identification Number in the electronic banking system (cmft_pin):

[1]   [2]   [3]   [4]   [5]

11. Electronic banking is difficult to use (difficult):

[1]   [2]   [3]   [4]   [5]

12. I have the opportunity to try various electronic banking services (can_try):

[1]   [2]   [3]   [4]   [5]

13. I have seen how others use electronic banking (seen_oth):

[1]   [2]   [3]   [4]   [5]

14. It bothers me to use a machine for banking transactions when I can talk with a person instead (man_touc):

[1]   [2]   [3]   [4]   [5]

Please give your response in a 5 point scale – [1] being "Never use" and [5] being "Always use".

15. I use credit cards to purchase of goods and services (crdt_car):

[1]   [2]   [3]   [4]   [5]

16. I use ATMs for my regular bank transactions (atm):

[1]   [2]   [3]   [4]   [5]

17. I use a cell phone for telephonic communication (mobile):

[1]   [2]   [3]   [4]   [5]

18. I use phone banking to ascertain all my account details whenever I require them (ph_banki):

[1]   [2]   [3]   [4]   [5]

19. I use electronic banking services (e_bankin):

[1]   [2]   [3]   [4]   [5]

Do you think that you can do electronic banking from a cyber-café?

[Y]   [N]

Do you think that you can do electronic banking from your office?

[Y]   [N]

I have a computer *in my home*

[Y]   [N]

I have my own PC *at the office*

[Y]   [N]

Demographic data:

Age: 18–24 yrs [1]; 25–34 yrs [2]; 35–44 yrs [3]; 45–54 yrs [4]; 55–64 yrs [5]; > 64 yrs [6]

Gender: Male [ ]   Female [ ]

Monthly Income: <10,000 [1]; 10,000–15,000 [2]; 15,000–17,500 [3]; 17,500–20,000 [4]; 20,000–25,000 [5]; 25,000–30,000 [6]; > 30;000 [7]

Education level: No formal education [1]; Up to High School. [2]; Graduate [3]; Post-graduate [4]; Doctorate and post-doctorate [5]

Chapter 12

Chinese Culture and
Chinese Consumer Behavior

12.1. Introduction

China is a fascinating place. It is China's turn to reclaim its place in world history. It is playing an increasingly important role in the world's economy. Its emergence as the world's most rapidly-growing industrial economy is continuing to transform the international economic and financial landscape. It is the single largest destination for foreign direct investment (FDI) and its economy will grow by as much as 10% per annum, resulting in a huge increase in the number of middle-class consumers. This enormous Chinese consumer market offers potential opportunities; however, certain important challenges also exist.

Some statistics give a clear overview:

– In the past 25 years, China has moved 300 million people out of poverty and quadrupled the average person's income.

– China will be the country with the second-largest economy in the world in 2021.

– China is now the world's largest producer of coal, steel and cement, the second largest consumer of energy and the third largest importer of oil.

Chapter written by Lei TANG.

– China manufactures two-thirds of the world's photocopiers, microwave ovens, DVD players and shoes.

– In 2006, there are now 123 million Internet users and close to 400 million cell-phone users in China.

With this background, the period 2005–07 could be an important turning point for China's consumer market. Several things will or may happen that would hasten the further development of this huge market: increased interest, on the part of foreign retailers, in China's retail sector; possible revaluation of the Chinese currency; efforts by the Chinese government to shift the sources of economic growth away from investment and exports and toward consumer spending; and accelerated reform of China's banking system resulting in a bigger and more efficient market for consumer credit.

However, very little thought has been given to rethinking the theories, underlying models, concepts and views of Chinese culture and to the motives of Chinese consumers and how they behave.

In China, consumption currently makes up just 50% of its gross domestic product (GDP), which is well below the 65% norm of most major economies. Putting it another way, 20% of the world's population accounts for only about 3% of total global consumption. The potential of the Chinese consumer could well be one of the greatest opportunities for the global economy in the 21st century.

The purpose of this chapter is to identify the cultural differences between the West and China and their measurements; and to give an overview of Chinese traditional culture and its main aspects. Through an in-depth of analysis of three doctrines of Chinese cultural systems, this chapter assesses and identifies the role of culture in influencing Chinese consumer behavior in Chinese business operations. In the discussion afterwards, the author integrates relevant concepts and managerial implications for Chinese consumers, brand management and marketing strategy in China.

On the basis of the growth of business in China and the distinct lack of attention paid to the influence of Chinese traditional culture on Chinese consumer behavior in the past, the results of the analysis will be useful to practitioners and managers in assisting them to decide on appropriate marketing strategies and tactics.

12.2. The cultural difference between China and the West

Based on preliminary cross-cultural studies, Hofstede [HOF 87, 91] explained that culturally-based value systems comprise four dimensions: power distance, individualism/collectivism, masculinity/femininity and uncertainty avoidance. Further research by Michael Bond [BON 89] identified a fifth "Eastern" dimension called long-term/short-term orientation.

By comparing some Western countries and China along these five dimensions according to their cultural dimension scores [HOF 91], some tentative conclusions are as follows:

– First, Western countries seem to be generally lower (United States of America (USA) 40, Canada 39, United Kingdom 35, Germany 35 and France 68) than China (80) in power distance.

– Secondly, in terms of individualism, Western countries are generally much higher (USA 91, Canada 80, United Kingdom 89, Germany 67 and France 71) than China (20).

– Thirdly, Western countries seem to have short-term orientation, while China is considered to be long-term oriented.

– Therefore, a comparison between the West and China seems to help clarify the cultural differences and related cross-cultural challenges.

Cultural dimensions	Western culture	Chinese culture
Individualism/collectivism	Strong individualism	Strong collectivism
Power distance	Medium	Centralized, tendency towards democracy
Uncertainty avoidance	Risk-taking	Risk-avoiding
Masculinity/femininity	Medium masculinity	Medium femininity
Long/short-term orientation	Short-term orientation	Long-term orientation

Table 12.1. *Cultural differences between the West and China*

China and Western countries differ greatly with regard to their economic systems, political systems, social values and laws, despite the substantial changes that have occurred in China during recent years [HOF 93]. First, in terms of power distance, the scores of China are more higher than those of the West (80–60), which indicates that China is centralized (though it has shown some tendency toward decentralized power), while the West is relatively decentralized. Secondly, the West ranks first in individualism (strong individualism), while China is low in individualism (strong collectivism). Thirdly, the West puts higher value than China on masculinity, which indicates that the West has medium masculinity, while China has medium femininity. Fourthly, China has higher values for uncertainty avoidance than the West, which shows that the Chinese are relatively risk-avoiding, while the West is relatively risk-taking. Finally, the West has a short-term orientation, while China has a long-term orientation.

To measure Chinese traditional culture, several models have been developed in the US and Europe. Basing it on the Kluckhohn and Strodtbeck [KLU 61] value orientation model, Yau [YAU 94] developed a Chinese-values research framework embedded within the five major elements: ideal life orientation, man-nature orientation, relational orientation, behavioral orientation and time orientation. A more direct indicator designed to measure the unique aspects of Chinese traditional values was also developed by Yau [YAU 94] and included: (1)hierarchical nature; (2) the importance of face and guanxi ((traditional Chinese: 關係 ; simplified Chinese: 关系 ; pinyin: gūanxi) describes the basic dynamic in personalized networks of influence; the pinyin is becoming more widely used instead of the two common translations – "connections" and "relationships"); (3) clan-based structure; and (4) long-term orientation. The introduction of altruism and personal ideology (humanism) provide the final links designed to capture Chinese traditional values.

Another measure representing cultural effects was derived from the literature in the preceding section and the instrument known as the Chinese Value Survey (CVS) which was developed by the Chinese Culture Connection [CHI 87]. The CVS instrument groups Chinese cultural values into four dimensions:

– Integration: representing integrative social stability which is crucial for maintaining harmonious relationships with other people.

– Confucian work dynamism: characterized by social hierarchy, personal virtue, reciprocation, respect for tradition and saving one's face.

– Human-feeling: referring to the attitude toward interpersonal relationships and the manner of dealing with others, whether the interaction with others is business-oriented or relationship-oriented.

– Moral discipline: referring to the perceived need and the ability of self-control.

Another model, the CVS, was suggested as more appropriate: first, this culture measurement tool is comparable to the well-received, Western-based instrument developed by Hofstede [HOF 84] as three of the CVS dimensions – integration, feeling and moral discipline – are highly correlated with Hostede's four dimensions [CHI 87]. Secondly, the issue of how to put into operation the culture concept to develop theoretical structures for explaining cross-cultural difference in human behavior is essential to the validity of cross-cultural research [FOS 79]. In this regard, several researchers [ALD 89] have warned that researchers cannot overlook the limitations of extending Western-based constructs and measurement tools to non-Western countries. Hofstede's culture measurement tool is limited to capturing the features of Chinese culture based on Confucian dynamism. The CVS has been proved to tap into concerns fundamental to the Chinese worldview. It has been used to investigate Chinese cultural impact on the buying behavior of the middle classes [CHA 95] and the findings show good reliability.

12.3. Chinese traditional culture and its values

Culture is of critical relevance to marketers in China because successful strategies cannot be developed without taking into account the specific features of Chinese culture. Relationships and group orientation are deeply rooted in the culture that permeates all aspects of Chinese society. Chinese traditional cultures have been shaped by Confucianism, Taoism and Buddhism as the three doctrines values [ZHE 97]. These three doctrines were an important part of daily life in old China and remain so.

12.3.1. *Confucianism and core beliefs*

Confucianism was the most influential Chinese religion. It was founded by Confucius or Kung-fu-tzu. Confucianism was the state religion from the establishment of the Han Dynasty in 202 BC to the end of the imperial epoch in 1911. Confucius was a Chinese scholar and statesman who lived during feudal times (over 2,000 years ago). He established an ethical and moral system that governs all relationships: father and son, ruler and ruled, husband and wife, elder brother and younger brother and among friends.

Confucianism views the family as the basic unit of society. Certain reciprocal relationships and responsibilities must be observed to preserve harmony. A specific hierarchy is pragmatic and places the greatest importance on rank and age in all interactions. Saving face and not causing shame to another are important. Since the family is the core unit, all the actions of an individual reflect on the family when the virtues of kindness, righteousness, propriety, intelligence and faithfulness are practiced.

Confucian doctrine	Essential beliefs
Five ethical elements	The relationships between father and son, ruler and ruled, husband and wife, elder brother and younger brother and among friends.
Six virtues of humanity	*Li*: includes ritual, propriety, etiquette, etc *Xiao*: love within the family: love of parents for their children and of children for their parents *Yi*: righteousness *Xin*: honesty and trustworthiness *Ren*: benevolence, humaneness toward others – the highest Confucian virtue *Cheng*: loyalty to the state, etc
Sacred texts	The *Si Shu* or Four Books The *Wu Jing* or Five Classics

Table 12.2. *Confucianism and core beliefs*

Confucianism is a philosophy of living rather than a religion and may guide one's life while one practices other religions, such as Taoism and Buddhism, without contradiction.

12.3.2. *Taoism*

Taoism is the most important strain of Chinese thought through the ages. It is almost entirely different from Confucianism, but is not contradictory. The Tao has no concern for affairs of the state, for mundane or quotidian matters of administration, or for elaborate ritual; rather, Taoism encourages avoiding public duty in order to search for a vision of the transcendental of world of the spirit.

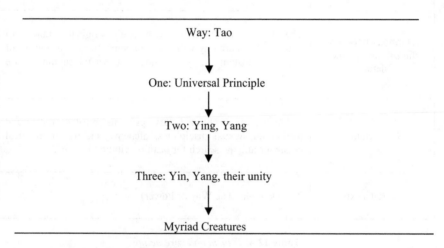

Table 12.3. *The way of Taoism*

Taoism is based on the idea that behind all material things and all the change in the world lies one fundamental, universal principle: the way of Tao, the interplay among five elements (ie, metal, wood, water, fire and earth) and the interdependence between the macrocosm and the microcosm (eg, man's relation to the universe). This principle gives rise to all existence and governs everything, all change and all life. The purpose of human life is then to live life according to the Tao, which requires passivity, calmness and non-strivingness, known by Taoists as "Wu Wei".

Taoism doctrine	Core beliefs
Eternality	The ineffable, eternal, creative reality is the source and end of all things.
Principle of *Wu Wei*	The Taoist prefers a life of total inactivity. It is rather a life of no purposeful action (*wu wei*).
Moral wisdom	"Manifest the simple", "embrace the primitive, reduce selfishness, have few desires".
Harmony between human beings and nature	The Tao is in harmony with one's original nature. An individual in harmony with the Tao comprehends the course of Nature's constant change and does not fear the rhythm of life and death.
Immortality	Achieving immortality: dietary regimens, breathe control and meditation, sexual disciplines, alchemy, the use of magical talismans and the search for healthy, vitality, long life, etc.
Sacred Texts	*Tao-De-Ging* (The Way of Power)

Table 12.4. *Taoism and core beliefs*

When Yin and Yang embrace each other, they reveal that they are not a world that can be divided into black and white, but black-in-white and white-in-black, forming a unity.

Figure 12.1. *Yin: (eg, dark, moist, feminine) and Yang: (eg, bright, dry, masculine)*

Taoism is not a religion. Taoism is a philosophy, a way of looking at life and a way of thinking about things. Taoists believe that if you look at life and think about things in the right way, then you will be much happier.

12.3.3. *Buddhism*

Buddhism was introduced to China from India between 58 and 76 AD, but only began to flourish in the 3rd century. It was founded by Siddharta Gautama, or Buddha, a contemporary of Confucius. Buddhism believes that desire is the source of all pain and that pain can be overcome by suppressing desire through meditation.

The major Buddhist values are: love, wisdom, goodness, calmness and self-control. Buddhists believe that people should try to end suffering; all things should be seen as having no self or essential nature. Put somewhat differently, nothing should be seen as literally existing or "standing apart" from all other things in self-sustained independence. On the contrary, all things should be seen as arising interdependently and as ultimately empty of any permanently abiding essence. In ancient China, people thought of Buddhism as a chart of behavior that they could follow to lead them to Nirvana.

Buddhism doctrine	Core beliefs
Three Trainings or Practices	Virtue, good conduct, morality. This is based on two fundamental principles: – the principle of equality – the principle of reciprocity: This is the "Golden Rule" in Christianity Concentration, meditation, mental development. Discernment, insight, wisdom, enlightenment. This is the real heart of Buddhism.
Four Noble Truths	Suffering exists: loss, sickness, pain, failure, the impermanence of pleasure. There is a cause for suffering: it is the desire to have and control things. It can take many forms: craving of sensual pleasures; the desire for fame; the desire to avoid unpleasant sensations, such as fear, anger or jealousy. There is an end to suffering: suffering ceases with the final liberation of Nirvana. The mind experiences complete freedom, liberation and non-attachment. It lets go of any desire or craving. In order to end suffering, you must follow the Eightfold Path.
Five Precepts	Do not kill: "not harming" or an absence of violence. Do not steal: the avoidance of fraud and economic exploitation. Do not lie: this is sometimes interpreted as including name-calling, gossip, etc. Do not misuse sex: for the laity, adultery is forbidden, along with any sexual harassment or exploitation, including that within marriage. Do not consume alcohol or other drugs: the main concern here is that intoxicants cloud the mind, as do such things as movies, television, etc.
Eightfold Path	Right understanding, right thinking, right speech, right conduct, right livelihood, right effort, right mindfulness and right concentration.

Table 12.5. *Buddhism and core beliefs*

To conclude these three doctrines of Chinese culture: Confucianism is concerned with human society and the social responsibilities; Taoism emphasizes nature and what is natural and spontaneous in man; and the contribution of Buddhism is particularly noticeable in developing conceptions of the afterlife.

12.4. Some essential aspects of Chinese culture

12.4.1. *Group orientation*

Chinese culture "regards people as members of colonies, not as individuals". This concept is reinforced by Confucian doctrines that emphasize ties of kinship and close personal relationships [XIN 95]. The need to exist in groups is emphasized; the relationships among group members and correspondingly some ethical and moral standards to regulate their interactions are thereby defined. One important rule is that group members "should adopt group goals and opinions in exchange for reciprocal care and protection" [XIN 95].

Respect your family's elders

Within the family, the rule was "filial piety", which is the household equivalent of having to respect those who are superior in society. The widespread Chinese respect for age and seniority comes from Confucian values: an older person is often seen as more experienced, wiser and, in some not clearly-defined way, superior to those younger.

The family comes first, but the group matters

It often helps if you consider a Chinese person as being part of his or her family and group, rather than as a single individual. Major personal decisions, such as a suitable career that in the West would be made by the individual, are often made on a family basis. The group is seen as a source of strength and comfort and business decisions are generally made on a consensus basis, within the framework dictated by the top person, whether the owner of the firm or the entrepreneur.

Respect authorities

The importance of belonging to and identifying with a group has a strong impact on the tolerance of humor and criticism. The Chinese do not find jokes about their country's political leaders or policy funny; indeed such irreverence shocks them. The visitor should make a point of not making jokes about these things, or even about their own government or its policies, which in Chinese eyes would demean both the visitor and their family/group.

In Confucian China, people were educated and trained to know their place and to be content with it; deviations, criticism and rebellious behavior were not to be tolerated.

12.4.2. *Guanxi is one of the secrets to success in China*

Guanxi, based on personal connections, is an important factor in Chinese culture; it is an implication of the above-mentioned collectivism.

Good *Guanxi* can affect other situations, such as business connections. "Good exchange within a *Guanxi* network can be anything as long as it is of value to parties concerned, be it legal or illegal, corruptive or non-corruptive" [WU 94]. Hence, *Guanxi* cannot be limited only to some aspects of a relationship, but instead in any situation can affect all other situations.

Guanxi involves reciprocal obligation [LEU 93]. If a person has received a favor, she or he is obliged to return the favor when requested. With favors you can also strengthen your *Guanxi*. When giving favors, one should consider the cost of the favor, the effective component, the probability of reciprocation of the favor from the receiver and reaction from the social network of persons involved [BON 87].

Guanxi not only involves favors between two persons, but also extends obligations to entire *Guanxi* networks [LEU 93]. Building up *Guanxi* includes building immediate trust through common connections (ie, friends, relatives, classmates). Thus, mutual trust in a *Guanxi* relationship can be established immediately through common connections without any exchanges between the actors and the exchanges do not have to be institutionalized in order to gain trust in a relationship. This differs from a normal relationship because it exists between two parties without any previous direction connections between these parties.

Hence, *Guanxi* is a social resource, which exists at the varying levels of sentimental depth. Emotionally, the deepest relations occur in primary groups, such as family; in the other extreme situation, they occur in relationships with relatives, neighbors, classmates, colleagues and people from the same region and so on. These relationships may be intimate between close or first-tier friends, or *Renqing* relationships tied with an emotional bond between good or second-tier friends [JOY

01]. *Renqing* translates into English as human sentiment or human emotion (*ren* refers to human being, *qing* refers to sentiment, emotion, favor, kindness, relationship). In Chinese philosophy, *renqing* denotes a human being's common emotional response, although it implies an obligatory affective component which serves to define the responsibility one has towards the other [CHA 91].

Face-work

A way of strengthening *Guanxi* is through what is known as "face-work". The Chinese language and culture distinguish two kinds of face: *lian* and *mianzi*. Building up *Guanxi* at any level of human behavior involves both *lian* and *mianzi*. Face-work is an important way of asking for and giving favors. Favors must be requested and rejected in a way that saves face for both partners [BON 87]. For this reason a negative answer from a person in a Chinese culture is less direct than a negative answer in a Western context.

The habit of giving gifts is connected to favors and has its roots in the history of tributes to the imperial court. A weaker member, for example, with a lower hierarchical status in Cardinal Relations in the *Guanxi* network can pull *Guanxi* by, for instance, giving gifts to the stronger member. The stronger member is obliged to do the requested favor if they have accepted the gift. Both parties have gained benefits: the weaker the desired favor and the stronger *mianzi* face through the achieved reputation in the *Guanxi* network [HAR 94]. By receiving a gift, one becomes indebted to the donor of the gift and similarly one can give a gift, so placing the receiver in debt. Face-work through giving and receiving favors in a *Guanxi* relationship does not need immediate "equal reciprocation" from the partners involved. Years may pass before the gift giver requests a favor from the gift receiver. The importance of reciprocity depends also on the depth or type of a relationship [JOY 01]. Hence, classy, expensive and prestigious gifts are exchanged by the Chinese. Furthermore, luxury clothing and choice of restaurant are considered to enhance one's status. Conspicuous consumption is a way to show off one's position in the network of one's social circle [SCH 95].

Behavior in Chinese society is based on the individual's tendency to act according to external expectations or social norms. The objective is to maintain harmony in a group and maintain face. However, it should be noted that collectivism does not mean a homogenous society. Collectivism works within small social contexts like family and clan and the nation is constituted from these smaller units.

As for this behavior, frequent contact with group members and reliance on informal channels as well as the speed-of-message transference points to the significance of word-of-mouth communication in China [YAU 88].

12.4.3. *The Chinese are superstitious*

Most Chinese are superstitious and even well-educated, apparently totally Westernized people may cling to traditional beliefs. Many superstitions exist and they vary in different parts of China so that it is not easy to know what a particular person will believe in. Numbers have a special significance to Chinese people. Most Cantonese believe that numbers 4, 44, 444 and so on are very bad luck, as they are a homonym for death in Chinese language; they would not buy a motor car with such a license plate or stay in a hotel room with such a number. Eight is however seen as good luck and the more eights the better. Nine is an extremely lucky number.

Colors play an important part in superstition too with different meanings in different circumstances.

Other factors relating to cultural values, which may have an impact on Chinese consumer behavior, are the Chinese beliefs in modesty and self-effacement as well as their situational orientation and pragmatism [YAU 88], which will affect their purchasing attitudes.

12.5. Who are the major customers in China?

China is not yet a single market. Together with differences in revenue, consumption, power, education, personal habits and tastes, these disparities characterize China as one nation, but certainly not one national market. Where is the challenge?

In mainland China, a rough segmentation can be made of rural and urban populations. The rural and urban populations differ in their purchasing power and consumption habits; for instance, rural consumers buy more domestic products and have less trust in advertising than their urban counterparts [LI 95].

Schütte and Ciarlante [SCH 98] have suggested that Chinese consumers could be divided into different consumption generations according to their historical, political and economic experience. Those born before 1945 have seen China's transformation to a socialist society and have been called "a socialist generation". This group is austere in its consumption and has a negative attitude towards consumer society. The following generation (born in 1945–60) is called "the lost generation" since they experienced the Great Cultural Revolution. Many of them lack education and have struggled to meet the requirements of China after Deng Xiaoping's reforms. The last generation born after the 1960s, "the lifestyle generation", is the first group that has had a true chance to adopt the values of a consumer society. Their consumption is modern and differentiated [SCH 98].

The most affluent population lives in eastern areas of the country and the poorest in the west. [CUI 00] have divided urban China into "growth markets" in the south, "emerging markets" in the center and "untapped markets" in the north.

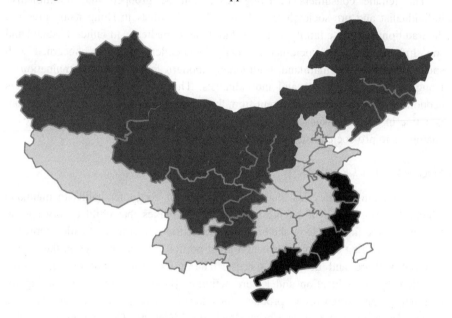

Figure 12.2. *Chinese consumer market [CUI 00]*

Generation X and Y

Generation X – people currently in their late 20s and 30s – and Generation Y – people in their late teens and early 20s – are very different to Generations X and Y in Europe, the US, or in Latin American, where this age group is often viewed as a generation of slackers. Chinese Generations X and Y have increasing drive, aspirations and demands; it is a highly literate and information-savvy group that refuses to be taken for granted. These young adults, who are generally the first generations of the one-child policy, are open to Western ideas and products, yet still proudly supportive of their own culture and they are looking for more ways to express their individualism through fashion, the media, technology and art.

Chinese women hold up half of the sky

As Chinese women's education and their participation in the workforce grow, their status improves. They are becoming increasingly sophisticated and demand higher-quality products with diversified designs. Younger women, in particular, are very fashion-conscious and are able to indulge in costly foreign brands.

The female consumers in Hong Kong can be grouped into traditionalist, individualist and pro-societalists [SIN 01]. Traditionalists in Hong Kong preserve the traditional Chinese family values of family and obedience to father, husband and son. Individualists are socio-economically independent and less concerned with social issues. On the mainland, traditionally modern females are a combination of Hong Kong traditionalists and individualists. The last group, pro-societalists, is economically independent, different from the traditional Chinese role of women, but is active in societal issues. The mainland segment of educated/working females is analogous to pro-societalists in Hong Kong.

Single-child market

The one-child policy has many implications for consumer habits in mainland China. The possibility of having only one child makes that child a very special treasure for the family. He or she becomes the "Little Emperor" or "Little Empress". Parents are willing and able to spend a great portion of their income on the child's material welfare and academic success. The investment is put on the child's nutrition, health, education and leisure activities [DAV 00]; when purchasing for children, parents often prefer products for educational purposes and buy toys as a reward for good grades or as a prize [DAV 00; MCN 99]. Children do get "gifts" from their parents, grandparents, uncles and aunts during the Spring Festival, but these "gifts" are usually *hong bao*, ie, small, red envelopes filled with money [MCN 99].

For children, the most important source of information about new products is television, followed by their parents and store visits [MCN 99]. Store visits seem to be an even more important information source where small purchases, such as snacks, are concerned.

Chinese ethnic minorities

From the hinterlands of the north to the lush jungles in the south, from the mountains of Taiwan in the east to the top of the world in the west, China serves as home to 56 official ethnic groups. The largest group, the Han, make up over 92% of China's vast population and it is the element of Han civilization that the world considers "Chinese culture". Yet, the 55 ethnic minorities, nestled away on China's vast frontiers, maintain their own rich traditions and customs and all are part of Chinese culture.

12.6. Brand effect on Chinese consumer behavior

Studies show that Chinese consumption is unique in some dimensions. The social dimension in consumption is important [SCH 98]. Brands are used to distinguish oneself from the social group one does not belong to and brands communicate the membership of one's own group [TSE 96].

Today, Chinese consumers are looking for esthetic and social value instead of just focusing on the basic needs of warmth and the protective function of products. Chinese consumers' willingness to purchase is highly brand-conscious. The reputation and track records of the brand will usually act as the criterion by which the quality of the product will be judged.

Chinese consumers rely on price as a mark of quality and brands accounted for one-third to one-half of all consumers' expressions of intent to purchase, because a successful brand is thought to be the indicator of a popular product with good style, high quality and so on; thus, the status of the brand is crucial.

Chinese consumers need more product information, rather than elaborate product presentation in stores. Strong brand information makes the stores effective channels in attracting early adopters and the Chinese consumer will look for the product if they have heard about it. As they want to see complete information and even specification details, they read product information carefully to improve their understanding and to gain a feeling of security about the product. Therefore, a brand can only attract consumers to buy it if it can really provide enough information to influence their decision making.

12.7. Managerial implications and suggestions

The three doctrines of traditional Chinese culture define the three types of seeking consumer.

Based on Confucian dynamism, the consumption-oriented are *Prestige Seeking Consumers*. Face-work, showing their social status with luxury products, has an impact on Confucian consumers.

The collective nature of the society also affects the degree of involvement in purchasing situations, particularly through giving and receiving favors, which like gifts, are for social purposes but for which the degree of involvement is much higher. [SCH 98]. A product bought for social purposes is important because it signals the factors that give face for both receiver and giver. Such factors are price, brand name, prestige and packaging [SCH 95].

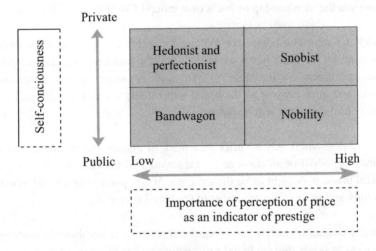

Table 12.6. *Interpersonal effects of Prestige Seeking Consumer behavior (created by Lei TANG based on [VIG 99])*

Taoism defines the consumption-oriented *Health Seeking Consumer*, which balances between the Yin and Yang forces of the universe. The traditional formulation of this group is based on naturalistic and rationalistic principles. So, due to their perception of the emergence of nature, health products will be considered. Images of natural forms are highly attractive to the Chinese consumer as a brand; peaceful images such as lakes, mountains and forests are therefore popular in advertisements as they are all considered to be tranquil and calm. They can also be found in brand names and trade marks.

Buddhism influences, the *Utility Seeking Consumer*. Buddhist values provide "Buddhist economics": real happiness does not come from acquiring or consuming material things. Happiness is essentially a state of mind and mind is distinct from matter. Thus, Buddhism considers the path of mental or spiritual development superior to that of material development. What really matters is to psychologically detach oneself from matter and strive for liberation and enlightenment, which is considered the ultimate state of happiness and fulfillment. This is achieved by the cultivation of values within one's mind, such as insight, compassion, tolerance and detachment. Only this will bring true happiness, both for the individual and society. Hence, simple, low-quality, inexpensive products will appeal to this target group:

– Among modern Chinese women, both the traditionalist and the independent professional, the demand for high-quality – luxury – clothing and cosmetics is increasing. Similarly, convenient home-commodities such as fast food, kitchen appliances and luxury cell phones are in demand.

– As the cost of education and health care increases, the larger portion of household income will go to these expenses, at the same time creating a market for education and health services.

– Chinese consumers like to shop in a free environment without interference. If a sales assistant in a retail store is too eager to help and approaches a consumer who has not decided what to buy, the consumer will feel uneasy and go away. The proper way is to keep a certain distance from the consumer, but at the same time let the consumer know that the sales assistant is always ready to help.

– There is evidence that people do not express their dissatisfaction as directly as those accustomed to Western cultures. However, this does not mean that Chinese consumers do not complain at all; they may just not complain directly at the point of sale. This can be disastrous if consumers are not satisfied with what they have bought.

The nature of segmentation

For a marketer of branded and foreign products, the most lucrative segments are "yuppies", entrepreneurs, "little rich", even "salaried class" and the "lifestyle generation". Many of them live in eastern and southern China. Competition for these consumers is already tough and the competitive advantage of a marketer should reach beyond quality products and price. Half of China's population is aged between

15 and 39 years and the top pastime activity for them is window-shopping [TAM 97]. Although they may not be immediate buyers, it is likely they are seeking market information about products to help them to make purchasing decisions later.

– Initiate a brand-building process to enable marketers to systematically identify and align their core brand values to manage the performance of their brands.

Preparatory work	Analyzing consumer behavior, decision making process	Define of brand drivers	Analyzing strengths and weaknesses	Definition brand strategies
Understand the brand value and potential impact on market share	Evaluate the need of the consumer	Determine the principal drivers in the process	Identify the strengths and weakness compared to the competitors	Model the marketing mix to determine the brand strategies

Table 12.7. *Brand-building process created by Lei Tang*

This brand building process may help companies to improve their branding strategy in China.

12.8. Discussion and limitations

The increasing trend towards globalization of business activities provides a strong reason for understanding the cultural context of consumer behavior [MAH 00]. The marketing strategies in international ventures need to be particularly sensitive to the cultural diversity of their customer base.

Chinese consumers are becoming more and more sophisticated, mainly due to advances in technology and education throughout the country. New technology, such as computers, satellite television and the Internet, provides consumers with information that they could not access in the past. The new technologies also help consumers to exchange ideas and experiences with others in different markets.

Future studies on Chinese consumer behavior should provide qualitative research and quantitative research, taking into account market structure and cultural differences. Regional differences within the market are quite common in China and the applicability of the results to the different cities is needed.

The use of a quasi-experimental design will help to isolate and control for the impact of other variables such as the micro or macro-cultural context, which might confound findings. The research design of a longitudinal study is likely to be desirable.

12.9. Conclusion

Despite the current market, there is still great potential for growth. Consumption levels are still low and are likely to rise in the future. A company can only be successful by gaining an in-depth understanding of the local culture and consumers' attitudes and being prepared to cope with unexpected changes in the marketplace.

The Chinese market is changing all the time and firms need to understand the market and serve the consumer better than their competitors. Putting marketing efforts into a complex cultural context is the key to future success in the Chinese market.

In China, the consumer's expectations of product quality in general have been steadily rising, owing to the increase in income and sociological forces which have prompted high expectations of a better lifestyle. The challenge will be to navigate the risks and obstacles of operating in the Chinese market while taking full advantage of the opportunity that rapid growth is creating. This will entail exploiting a company's best features while adapting to Chinese culture and Chinese consumers and it will extend a company's culture to a new environment by integrating local culture.

12.10. References

[ALD 89] ALDER, N, CAMPBELL, N and LAURENT (1989) "In search of appropriate methodology: from outside the people of China looking in", *Journal of International Business Studies*, (Spring 1989), pp 61–74

[BIA 94] BIAN, Y (1994) "*Guanxi* and the allocation of urban jobs in China", *The China Quarterly* 140, pp 971–99

[BON 88] BON, M (1988), "Finding universal dimensions of individual variation in multicultural studies of values: the Rokeach and Chinese Value Surveys", *Journal of Personality and Social Psychology* 55, pp 1009-1015

[BON 03] BOND, SA and HWANG, S (2003), "A measure of fundamental volatility in the commercial property market", *Real Estate Economics* 31(4), pp 577-600

[BUT 96] BUTTERY, FA and LEUNG, K (1996) "The difference between Chinese and Western negotiations", *European Journal of Marketing* 32(3/4), pp 374–89

[BUT 99] BUTTERY, FA and WONG, YH (1999) "The development of a *guanxi* framework", *Marketing Intelligence and Planning* 17(3), pp 147–54

[CHA 91] CHANG, HC and HOLT, GR (1991) "More than relationship: Chinese and the principle of kuan-his", *Communication Quarterly* 39, pp 251–71

[CHA 95] CHANG, K and DING, C (1995) "The influence of culture on industrial buying selection criteria in Taiwan and mainland China", *Industrial Marketing Management* 24(4), pp 277-284

[CHE 91] CHENG, S (1991) "Comparing Eastern and Western ways of thinking", *Migration Monitor* 21–22, pp 6–11

[CHE 96] CHEN, ZL and JIA, RG (1996) Beijing: l'école du Ru, *Maison d'édition de la culture et de la religion*

[CHI 87] CHINESE CULTURE CONNECTION (1987) "Chinese values and the search for culture-free dimensions of culture", *Journal of Cross-Cultural Psychology* 18 (June 1987), pp 143–67

[CUI 00] CUI, G and LIU, Q (2000) "Regional market segments of China: opportunities and barriers in a big emerging market", *Journal of Consumer Marketing* 17(1), pp 55-72

[DAV 00] DAVIS, DS and SENSENBRENNER, JS (2000) "Commercializing childhood, parental purchases for Shanghai's only child", in *The Consumer Revolution in Urban China*, ed Davis DS, Berkeley: University of California Press, pp 54-79

[DUN 01] DUNFEE, TW and WARREN, DE (2001) "Is *guanxi* ethical? A normative analysis of doing business in China", *Journal of Business Ethics* 32(3), pp 191–204

[FOS 79] FOSCHI, M and HALES, WH (1979) "The theoretical role of cross-cultural comparisons in experimental social psychology", in Eckensberger, LH, Lonner, WJ and Proortinga, YJ (eds), *Crosscultural Contributions to Psychology,* Lisse: Swets and Zeitlinger, pp 244-254

[FUN 48] FUNG, YL (1948) *A Short History of Chinese Philosophy*, New York: Macmillan

[GUD 92] GUDYKUNST, WB, GAO, G, SCHMIDT, KL, NISHID, T, BOND, MH, LEUNG, K, WANG, G and BARRACLOUGH, R (1992) "The influence of individualism-collectivism on communication in ingroup and outgroup relationships", *Journal of Cross-Cultural Psychology* 23, pp 196–213

[HAB 96] HABER, D and MANDELBAUM, J (1996) *La revanche du monde Chinois*, Paris: Economica

[HAR 94] HARRIS, P and YAU KWOK, K (1994), "Understanding Chinese buying behavior: a cross-cultural interaction model", *paper presented in International Conference On Management Issues For China In the 1990s*, Cambridge, March 23-25

[HOF 01] HOFSTEDE, G (2001) *Culture's Consequence*, 2nd edition, Beverley Hills: Sage Publications

[HOF 80] HOFSTEDE, G (1980) *Culture's Consequences, Beverly Hills, CA: Sage Publications*

[HOF 84] HOFSTEDE, G and BOND, MH (1984) "Hofstede's culture dimensions: an independent validation using Rokeach's value survey", *Journal of Cross-Cultural Psychology* 15, pp 417–33

[HOF 84] HOFSTEDE, G (1984) "Culture's consequences: international differences in work-related values", Berverly Hills: Sage Publications

[HOF 88] HOFSTEDE, G and BOND, MH (1988), "The Confucius connection: from cultural roots to economic growth", *Organisational Dynamics* 16(4), pp 4-21

[HOF 94] HOFSTEDE, G 1991) *Cultures and Organizations: Software of the Mind*, McGraw-Hill

[HOF 94] HOFSTEDE, G (1994), Vivre dans un monde multiculturel; comprendre nos programme mentales, *Paris: Les Editions d'Organisations*

[HOF 94] HOFSTEDE, G (1994), Value Survey Module, 1994, The Netherlands, Tiburg University

[HON 01] HONG, YY and CHIU, CY (2001) "Toward a paradigm shift: from cross-cultural differences in social cognition to social cognitive mediation of culture differences", *Social Cognition* 19, pp 181–96

[HOO 69] HOOKHAM, H (1969) *A Short History of China*, New York: New American Library

[HU 44] HU, H (1944) "The Chinese concept of face", *American Anthropologist* 46 (January/March), pp 45–64

[HWA 87] HWANG, K (1987) "Face and favour: the Chinese power game", *American Journal of Sociology* 92, pp 33–41

[IMI 03] IMI (2003) *Consumer Behaviours & Life Styles Yearbook,* 2003

[JOY 01] JOY, A (2001) "Gift giving in Hong Kong and the continuum of social ties", *Journal of Consumer Research* 28, pp 239-256

[KLU 61] KLUCKHORNl, F and STRODTBECK, FL (1961) *Variations in Value Orientation*, Evanston, Illinois: Row, Peterson

[LAO] Laozi (5th century BC), Dao De Jing

[LEU 93] LEUNG, T, WONG, S and WONG, YH (1993), "Hong Kong businessmen's perceptions of *guanxi* in the People's Republic of China", *paper presented in the Academy of International Business Conference*, Hong Kong 23-25 June

[LIA 63] LIANG, S (1963) *The Essential Features of Chinese Culture*, Hong Kong: Jicheng Book Co

[LID 95] LI, D and GALLUP, AM (1995) "In search of the Chinese consumer", *The China Business Review* 22(5), pp 19-22

[MAH 00] MAHESWARAN, D and SHAVITT, S (2000) "Issues and new directions in global consumer psychology", *Journal of Consumer Psychology* 9(2), pp 59-66

[MAR 95] MARKETING GUIDE MAGAZINE (1995) "Features and trends", *Characteristics and Prospects of Consumption Market in China*, Feb (in Chinese)

[MCN 99] MCNEAL, JU and JI, MF (1999), "Chinese children as consumers: an analysis of their new product information sources", *Journal of Consumer Marketing* 16(4), pp 345-364

[MOR 98] MORRE, M (1998) *Les religions et les philosophies d'Asie,* Paris La Tableronde

[POL 98] POLSA, P (1998) "Distribution of consumer goods in the People's Republic of China: an empirical study of packaged food products", no 43, licentiate thesis, Helsinki: Swedish School of Economics and Business Administration

[ROB91] ROBINET, I (1991) *Histoire du Taoïsme des origines au XIVe siècle*, Paris: Cerf

[SCH 95] SCHUTTE, H and VANIER, V (1995) "Consumer behavior in Asia", Euro-Asia Center Research Series, INSEAD Euro-Asia Center

[SCH 98] SCHUTTE H and CIARLANTE, D (1998), *Consumer Behavior in Asia*, New York: New York University Press

[SIN 01] SIN, LYM, SO, SLM, YAU, OHM and KWONG, K (2001), "Chinese women at the crossroads: an empirical study on their role orientations and consumption values in Chinese society", *Journal of Consumer Marketing* 18(4),pp 348-367

[SOU 95] SOUTIF, M (1995) *L'Asie, source de sciences et de techniques*, Grenoble, Edition PUG

[TAM 98] TAM, JLM and TAI, SHC (1997) "A lifestyle analysis of female consumers in greater China", *Psychology and Marketing* (14)3 , pp 287-307

[TRI 89] TRIANDIS, HC (1989) "Cross-cultural studies of individualism and collectivism", *Nebraska Symposium on Motivation: Cross-cultural Perspectives*, Lincoln: University of Nebraska Press, pp 41-133

[TRI 95] TRIANDIS, HC (1995) *Individualism and Collectivism*, Boulder, San Francisco: Westview Press

[TRI 97] TRIANDIS, HC and BHAWUK, DPS (1997) "Culture theory and the meaning of relatedness" in Earley, PC and Erez, M (eds) *New Perspectives on International Industrial/Organizational Psychology*, San Francisco: The New Lexington Press

[TRI 98] TRIANDIS, HC and GELFAND, MJ (1998) "Converging measurement of horizontal and vertical individualism and collectivism", *Journal of Personality and Social Psychology* 74(1), pp 118–28

[TSE 96] TSE, DK (1996), "Understanding Chinese people as consumers: past findings and future propositions", in *The Handbook of Chinese Psychology*, ed Bond, MH, Hong Kong: Oxford University Press

[VIG 99] VIGNERON, F and JOHNSON, LW (1999) "A review and a conceptual framework of prestige-seeking consumer behavior", http://www.amsreview/org/amsrev/theory/vigneron01-99.html

[WAN 86] WANG, H (1986) "Traditional culture and modernisation – a review of general situation of cultural studies in China in recent years", *Social Science in China* (Winter 1986), pp 9–30

[WEB 68] WEBER, M (1968) *The Religion of China*, New York: The Free Press

[XIN 95] XING, F (1995) "The Chinese culture system: implications for cross-cultural management", *Advance Management Journal* 17, pp 14–20

[YAN 57] YANG, LS (1957) "The concept of Tao as a basis for social relations in China", in Fairbank, JK (ed), *Chinese Thought and Institutions*, Chicago, IL, University of Chicago Press, pp 291–309

[YAU 88] YAU, O (1988) "Chinese cultural values: their dimensions and marketing implications", *European Journal of Marketing* 22, pp 44–57

[YAU 94] YAU, OHM (1994) *Consumer Behaviour in China: Customer Satisfaction and Cultural Values*, Routledge: London

[YU 96] YU, A-B (1996) "Ultimate life concerns, self and Chinese achievement motivation", in Bond, MH (ed), *The Handbook of Chinese Psychology*, Hong Kong: Oxford University Press, pp 227–46

[ZHE 97] ZHENG, Y (ed) (1997) *The Compilation of Three Religions: Confucianism, Taoism and Buddhism, Taibei*, Taiwan: Zheng Yishan Press (in Chinese)

[ZHU] ZHUANGZI (3rd century BC), ZhuangZi 600

Chapter 13

Modeling the Indicators of Purchasing Behavior Toward Counterfeits: An Exploratory Study in China

13.1. Introduction

Brands represent the most valuable assets that firms possess, yet many brands are increasingly threatened by the worldwide phenomenon of product counterfeiting [SIL 05; GRE 02; DEL 00; SIM 99; GRO 88]. Counterfeiting involves an attempt to misrepresent an authentic good by creating a fake good of a lower quality that appears in all respects identical to the authentic one, including using the same trade address and in some cases including the name and address of the original manufacturer [CHO 00]. In less than 10 years, losses to legitimate businesses have tripled in magnitude, yielding serious economic damage [DEL 00]. By 2002, sales of counterfeit products have risen to 9% of overall world merchandise [TRO 02].

Although much attention as been given to the economic effect of counterfeits, little attention has been placed on the consumption side of this problem. Only a few researchers have done empirical research on the purchasing behavior area [CHA 06; BLO 93; ANG 01]. First, it has been found that if a consumer's attitude toward counterfeiting is favorable, it is highly likely that he or she would consider the purchase of a counterfeit product [WEE 95]. Secondly, evidence suggests that consumers are willing to pay more for counterfeits than for generic products of

Chapter written by Sindy CHAPA and Monica D. HERNANDEZ.

similar quality because of the value of the prestige related to the brand name trademark [GRO 88]. Thirdly, the literature suggests that consumers buy counterfeits only for certain product types [BLO 93; CHA 06]. Chapa *et al.* [CHA 06] found that consumer responses toward counterfeits were more favorable for products used in public compared to those consumed in private. This study also suggested that the country of origin influences the consumption preference for counterfeits. Evidence suggests that Chinese counterfeits are preferred over counterfeit products "made in" other countries. Finally, it has been implied that better-educated consumers might be less attracted to counterfeits than less educated consumers [CHA 06].

Despite recent efforts to study counterfeit purchase behavior, there are still important research questions with regard to the consumption demand. For example, what types of traits identify those counterfeits' potential consumers? This investigation intended to answer this question by modeling those variables identified in the marketing literature as significant as related to traditional purchase behavior.

China, as the world's largest source of counterfeit products, has the highest number of people involved in the production, selling and consumption of counterfeits [MOG 02; KAP 06]. China is considered to be the world's largest source of counterfeit products where counterfeits make up between 15% and 20% of all products, accounting for about 8% of the country's GDP [MOG 02]. Therefore, the purpose of this exploratory study was to develop a model testing the traits that might perform as indicators of Chinese purchasing behavior toward counterfeits.

13.2. Hypotheses development

13.2.1. *Risk perception*

It has been found that risk perceptions affect consumers' attitudes toward counterfeits [BLO 93; WEE 95; NIA 00]. The literature suggests that regardless of the type of risk (social, financial, physical, temporal, or performance), consumers only buy counterfeits of those products where risks are perceived to be low. In China, counterfeit products can be found openly displayed in many street markets as well as in small- and medium-sized businesses. Consumers of counterfeits face the possibility of being arrested on charges of criminal activity. However, enforcement of China's anti-counterfeit laws is still a concern for local and global brand owners [CHO 00]. By extension, consumers who have a weak perception of being caught and charged will exhibit more positive attitudes toward the purchase of these products. The level of perceived risk is a function of the consumer's perception of what is at stake and his or her certainty that the consequences will be favorable or unfavorable [CLO 96]. Therefore, the following hypothesis is proposed:

> **H1:** There is a positive relationship between low-risk perception towards counterfeits and a positive attitude towards counterfeits.

13.2.2. Brand parity

Brand parity is defined as the "overall perception held by the consumer that the differences between the major brand alternatives in a product category are small" [MUN 96: 411]. In other words, brand parity determines how similar, or different, various brands in the same category are perceived to be. Brand parity varies widely from one category to another. For example, in the banking industry, brand parity is high as most customers do not see much difference between brands within this category and yet for perfume, brand parity is quite low. In addition, it has been found that when two brands appear similar, positive word-of-mouth recommendations concerning the follower brand increases the likelihood of consideration while it decreases the choice probabilities of the early brand [GRE 03]. In China, since counterfeiting consumption is a common practice which is viewed as normal [MOG 02; KAP 06], we expected that Chinese consumers would perceive a high brand parity between the real brand and the fake one within a product category. Therefore, in our proposed model, we expected that when consumers viewed a brand and its counterfeit as similar, parity would be high and so the attitude toward counterfeits would be high as well. Therefore, our next hypothesis claims:

> **H2:** There is a positive relationship between brand parity and a positive attitude towards counterfeits.

13.2.3. Susceptibility to Normative Influence (SNI)

Earlier research suggested that product evaluation is obtained by consulting with referent peers. Festinger [FES 54] claimed that an individual needs to compare himself or herself with other persons to prove his or her own beliefs. A normative group might have a high- or a low-opinion of a foreign product depending on the product category; for example, a German car, a French wine and Italian shoes might be highly acceptable, but an American car, a Spanish wine and Chinese shoes might not be [CHO 95]. Whether a consumer is highly influenced by a normative group might depend on his susceptibility to interpersonal influence [BEA 89]. Susceptibility to interpersonal influence is a general trait that varies between individuals and a person's relative susceptibility in one situation tends to have a significant positive relationship to his or her susceptibility in a range of other social situations [BEA 89]. Generally, susceptibility to normative influence has to do with the status that a consumer may perceive that he or she acquires among the consumer's reference group after acquiring a determined product. In particular, Slama and Singley [SLA 96] claim that value-expressive types of influence are very likely to be exerted by the group of reference or target audience of the consumer's self-presentation. Consistently, Escalas and Bettman [ESC 05] concluded that consumers report higher self-brand connections for brands with images that are consistent with the image of an in-group whereas consumers reject the social meanings of brands that arise from out-group brand usage. Therefore, the following hypotheses are posited:

H3: There is a positive relationship between "SNI" and "brand parity".
H4: There is a positive relationship between "SNI" and "value expressive".

13.2.4. *Value-expressive function*

The value-expressive function is related to the individual's desires to enhance his or her self-concept in the eyes of others [PAR 77]. Grewal, Metha and Kardes [GRE 04] found that consumers are reluctant to abandon the products that fulfill the value-expressive function. This results in longer inter-purchase intervals, in addition to greater liability for publicly-consumed rather than privately-consumed products. Moreover, status-conscious consumers have been found to be more likely to be affected by brand symbolic characteristics (high/low status) and by the degree of congruency between the brand user's self-image and the brand's image [OCA 02]. By extension, we assume that the more reluctant the consumers are, the more risks they are willing to take and the less they are influenced by the differences between the major brand and its alternatives. Therefore, the following hypotheses state:

H5: There is a positive relationship between "value expressive" and "risk perception".
H6: There is a negative relationship between "value expressive" and "brand parity".

13.2.5. *Conceptual model*

In an attempt to better understand the application of what is suggested in the literature, we propose a model that exhibits the relationship among the variables and the purchasing behavior for counterfeits in China; see Table 13.1.

Construct	X^2	X^2/df	p-level	RMSEA	GFI	AGFI	RMR	TLI
Price Consciousness	5.42	1.35	.246	.034	.992	.973	.020	.990
Risk Perception	21.13	2.34	.012	.078	.970	.91	.049	.980
Brand Parity	1.50	.754	.470	.034	.997	.987	.051	.999
SNI	.567	.28	.752	.000	.999	.995	.009	.999
Value Expressive	6.58	1.64	.159	.046	.991	.969	.023	.960

Table 13.1. *Results of single-construct measurement models*

13.3. Research design

Five existing scales shaped the instrument used in our study. The "risk perception" was measured using the three items of the risk factor developed by McQuarrie and Munson [MCQ 86]. "Brand parity" was assessed using five items of the Muncy [MUN 96] scale. The SNI was measured using a shorter version of four items of the SNI scale developed by Bearden, Netemeyer and Teel [BEA 89]. "Value expressive" was measured using a five-item factor developed by Park and Lessig [PAR 97]. To evaluate a "customer's attitude toward counterfeits", a single item was used. All the measures were assessed using a five-point Likert-type scale ranging from strongly disagree to strongly agree. Six additional items addressed demographics.

13.3.1. *Data collection*

Data were collected during the late fall of 2003 from adult consumers in Shanghai, China. Shanghai is China's most industrialized city and it is also the most populous with the country's highest population density. Nine graduate students from the School of Law and from the School of Art at the Fudan University in Shanghai were trained to conduct the survey. The interviewers were located in the Yangpu district of Shanghai in three main business places: (1) Qu Yang Rd, (2) E-Mart Supermarket and (3) Da Run Fa Supermarket. After an initial starting point, by a random process, every third person on the street was asked to participate. A total of 581 residents were approached and 302 agreed to participate for an effective response rate of 52%. The sample was 51% female, with an age range of 18 to 65 and an average-age range of 25–29.

13.4. Data analysis

13.4.1. *Assessment of the measurements*

First, in an attempt to assess the reliability and validity of the multi-item scales for the five model constructs of the attitudes toward counterfeits, a confirmatory factor analysis was conducted. The chi-square values were not significant at .10 level (Table 13.1), indicating a difference between the predicted and the actual matrices and demonstrating acceptable fits. Similarly, the fit indicators, such as the goodness-of-fit index (GFI), adjusted goodness-of-fit index (AGFI) and Tucker-Lewis index (TLI) indicated good fit for all the constructs. In addition, the root mean squared error of approximation (RMSEA) and the root mean residual (RMR) were both at a marginally acceptable level [HAI 98].

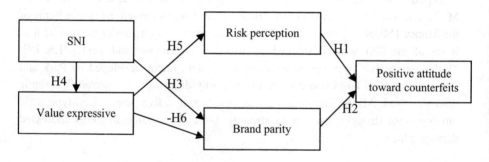

Figure 13.1. *Proposed model*

Additionally, Cronbach alphas confirmed internal consistency. All the individual scales were above .62, exceeding the minimum standards of .60 suggested for exploratory research by Nunnally [NUN 67]. The overall reliability was .68.

13.4.2. *Results*

13.4.2.1. *Model testing*

A structural equation model was used to test the model. The results indicated that the model fit significantly and the chi-square values were not significant at .10. Overall, the model demonstrates acceptable fits and low level of errors: chi-squared = 5.11, X^2 /df = 1.70, p = .163, GFI = .993, AGFI= .966, TLI = .954, RMSEA = .048. The model is shown in Figure 13.2.

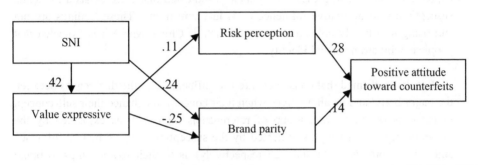

Figure 13.2. *Results*

13.4.2.2. *Hypotheses testing*

To test the hypotheses, we examined the regression weights in the model. As predicted, all hypotheses were supported. Low "risk perception" toward counterfeits was positively related to "positive attitude toward counterfeits" (.28) [H₁]. "Brand parity" was positively related to "positive attitude toward counterfeits" (.14) [H₂]. SNI was related to "value expressive" (.42) [H₄] and "brand parity" (.27) [H₃]. "Value expressive" positively affected "risk perception" (.11) [H₅] and negatively affected "brand parity" (-.25) [H₆].

13.5. Discussion

Our study analyzed variables affecting the positive attitude toward counterfeits in China. The conceptual and nested models were tested using structural equation modeling. The regression weights obtained provided support for the findings from previous studies. This revealed that low risk perception toward counterfeits, high brand parity, high susceptibility to normative influence and high value expressive positive attitudes toward counterfeits.

In low-income countries, the economic benefits of purchasing counterfeits might explain the popularity of the practice. However, our model indicated that in developing countries with growing income, like China, the strong impact of susceptibility to normative influence in both value expression and brand parity are better predictors of this widespread practice. The nested model revealed that there exists a strong susceptibility to normative influence (.42) reflected in the value-expressive function. Regression weights also indicated that there exists a moderate susceptibility to normative influence (.24) in brand parity. These findings are not surprising in a highly collectivist country such as China, where it is expected that people exhibit strong social identity.

Results confirmed that consumers are less influenced by the differences between the major brand and its alternatives when their concern to enhance their self-concept in the eyes of their target group of reference is high. This is explained by the moderate regression weights indicated by the susceptibility to normative influence and value-expressive (.24 and -.25 respectively) as to their relationships to brand parity. This might be an indication of a stronger consumer culture in this country.

The low risk perception accounts for a large percentage (.28) of the positive attitude toward counterfeits. Policy makers might be concerned about the communication of the economic damage derived from the preference of these products. Regression weights also indicated that following perceived low risk, brand parity (.14) would be the second best indicator of positive attitudes toward counterfeits. This finding might suggest that Chinese consumers are becoming more conscious of brand characteristics and might not be willing to compromise the status implied by their brand of choice.

Two limitations of the study were identified. First, the research was limited to one country, which questions the generalizability of the study to other countries. Future research could explore our proposed model in other lower-income Asian collectivist cultures with similar levels of counterfeit purchases. In addition, tests of the model in countries exhibiting a different system of values, such as Latin American countries, would also lead to more generalizable results. Secondly, the respondents in study did not represent the entire Chinese population; the data was collected in one district of Shanghai, which limits the generalization of the results among the Chinese consumers. In addition, although the sample was randomly selected, it did not assure the equivalence of the Chinese population. In fact, social classes were not represented since 57.2% of the respondents classified as low middle class.

Despite its limitations, this study provides valuable insights in the understanding of consumers' attitudes toward counterfeit products in China. Our study contributes through the provision of empirical evidence of attitudes toward counterfeiting in developing countries. In sum, results indicate that Chinese consumers exhibited positive attitudes toward counterfeits. Low perceived risk coupled with a very high social influence increases the likelihood of a consumer's consideration of acquisition of counterfeits. Our proposed model also contributes by helping policy makers to focus on the real factors supporting the consumption of counterfeits.

Future work could explore the effect of price consciousness on the likelihood that a consumer will purchase the authentic product. In addition, the consequences of attitudes toward counterfeit products, such as avoidance or negative attitudes toward particular brands, could also be explored. The importance of the research concerning attitudes lies in the possible mediating role they might play in influencing purchase intentions.

13.6. References

[ANG 01a] ANG, SH, PENG, SC, ELISON, AC (2001) "Spot the difference: consumer responses towards counterfeits", *Journal of Consumer Marketing*, no 18, pp 219–35

[BEA 82] BEARDEN, WO and ETZEL, MJ (1982) "Reference group influence on product and brand purchase decisions", *Journal of Consumer Research*, no 9, pp 183–94

[BEA 89] BEARDEN, WO, NETEMEYER, RG and TEEL, J (1989) "Measurement of consumer susceptibility to interpersonal influence", *Journal of Consumer Research*, 15, pp 473–81

[BLO 93] BLOCK, P, BUSH, RF and CAMPBELL, L (1993) "Consumer accomplices in product counterfeiting: a demand side investigation", *Journal of Consumer Marketing*, no 10, pp 27–36

[CHA 06] CHAPA, S, MICHAEL S, (2006), "Product category and origin effects on consumer responses to counterfeits: comparing Mexico and the US", *Journal of International Consumer Marketing*, vol. 18, no 4

[CHO 00] CHOW, DCK (2000) "Enforcement against counterfeiting in the People's Republic of China", *Northwestern Journal of International Law & Business*, vol 20, no 3, pp 447–74

[CLO 96] CLOW, K, TRIPP, CC and JAMES, K (1996) "The importance of service quality determinants in advertising a professional service: an exploratory study", *Journal of Services Marketing*, no 10, pp 52–72

[DEL 00] DELENER, N (2000) "International counterfeit marketing: success without risk", *Review of Business*, no 21, pp 16–20

[ESC 05] ESCALAS, JE and BETTMAN, JR (2005) "Self-construal, reference groups and brand meaning", *Journal of Consumer Research*, vol 32, no 3, pp 378–89

[GRE 02] GREEN, RT and SMITH, T (2002) "Executive insight: countering brand counterfeiters", *Journal of International Marketing*, no 10, pp 89–106

[GRE 03] GREWAL, R, CLINE, TW and DAVIES, A (2003) "Early-entrant advantage, word-of-mouth communication, brand similarity and the consumer decision-making process", *Journal of Consumer Psychology* 13(3), pp 187–97

[GRE 04] GREWAL, R, MEHTA, R and KARDES, F (2004) "The timing of repeat purchases of consumer durable goods: the role of functional bases of consumer attitudes", *Journal of Marketing Research* 41(1), pp 101–15

[GRO 88] GROSSMAN, G and SHAPIRO, C (1988) "Counterfeit-product trade", *The American Economic Review*, no 78, pp 59–77

[HAI 98] HAIR, J ANDERSON, R, TATHAM, R and BLACK, W (1998) *Multivariate Data Analysis* (5th edn), Upper Saddle River, NJ: Prentice Hall

[KAP 06] KAPLAN, E (2006) "The uneasy US-Chinese trade relationship", *Council on Foreign Relations*, http://www.cfr.org/publication/10482/uneasy_uschinese_trade_relationship.html

[LIC 93] LICHSTEIN, DR, RIDGWAY, N and NETEMEYER, RG (1993) "Price perception and consumer shopping behavior: a field study", *Journal of Marketing Research* 30, pp 234–45

[MCQ 86] MCQUARRIE, EF and MUNSON, JM (1986) "The Zaichkowsky personal involvement inventory: modification and extension", in Anderson, P and Wallendorf, M (eds), *Advances in Consumer Research*, vol 14, pp 36–40

[MOG 02] MOGA, T and RAITI, J (2002) "The TRIPS Agreements and China", *The China Business Review*, no 29, pp 12–18

[MUN 96] MUNCY, JA (1996) "Measuring perceived brand parity", in Corfman, K and Lynch, J (eds) *Advances in Consumer Research*, vol 23, Provo, UT: Association for Consumer Research, pp 411–17

[NIA 00] NIA, A and LYNEE, J (2000) "Do counterfeits devalue the ownership of luxury brands?", *Journal of Product and Brand Management*, no 9, pp 485–97

[NUN 67] NUNNALLY, J (1967) *Psychometric Theory* (1st edn), New York, NY: McGraw-Hill

[OCA 02] O'CASS, A and FROST, H (2002) "Status brands: examining the effects of non-product-related brand associations on status and conspicuous consumption", *Journal of Product and Brand Management*, vol 11, no 2/3, pp 67–86

[PAR 77] PARK, CW and LESSIG, VP (1977) "Students and housewives: differences in susceptibility of reference group influence", *Journal of Consumer Research* 4, pp 102–10

[SIL 05] SILCOX, CR and COLBURN, PH (2005) "Counterfeit products present additional business risks for distributors and contractors," *IAEI Magazine*, http://www.iaei.org/subscriber/ magazine/05_c/silcox.htm

[SIM 99] SIMONE, J (1999) "Countering counterfeiters", *The China Business Review*, no 26, pp 12–16

[SLA 96] SLAMA, ME and SINGLEY, RB (1996) "Self-monitoring and value-expressive vs utilitarian ad effectiveness: why the mixed findings?", *Journal of Current Issues & Research in Advertising* 18(2), pp 39–52

[STO 03] STOETTINGER, B, PENZ, E and SCHLEGELMILCH, BB (2003) "Why the real thing is sometimes less attractive: insights into the purchasing behavior for counterfeit goods", in *AIB Conference Proceedings*, Monterrey, California: Academy of International Business, Abstract 31

[TRO 02] TROCKI, V (2002) "Sales of counterfeit products to rise to 18% of world trade in two years", *PRWeb: The Free Wire Service,* http://www.prweb.com/releases/2002/5/ prweb39586.php

List of Authors

Atanu ADHIKARI
ICFAI
Hyderabad
India

Chantal AMMI
MINT, Institut National des Télécommunications
Evry
France

Rafika BEN GUIRAT
ESC Tunis
University of Manouba
Tunis

Sindy CHAPA
University of Texas
USA

Jadvyga CIBURIENE
Kaunas University of Technology
Kaunas
Lithuania

Hanna-Kaisa DESAVELLE
Tampere University of Technology
Tampere
Finland

U. DEVASENADHIPATHI
Pondicherry University
India

Partho GANGULY
Institute of Business Management and research
Bangalore
India

Monica D. HERNANDEZ
Kansas State University
USA

Kaouther JELASSI
MINT, Institut National des Télécommunications
Evry
France

Toufik KHARBECHE
MINT, Institut National des Télécommunications
Evry
France

Ana LISBOA
Instituto Politecnico de Leiria
Leiria
Portugal

Saku MAKINEN
Tampere University of Technology
Tampere
Finland

Anastasiya MARCHEVA
Tsenov Academy of Economics
Svishtov
Bulgaria

Tunc MEDENI
Japan Advanced Institute of Science and Technology
Tokyo
Japan

Velan NIRMALA
Pondicherry University
India

A.K. RAO
Indian Statistical Institute
Calcutta
India
California State University
San Diego
USA

Carla RUIZ MAFE
University of Valencia
Valencia
Spain

Silvia SANZ BLAS
University of Valencia
Valencia
Spain

Euler G.M. de SOUZA
Japan Advanced Institute of Science and Technology
Tokyo
Japan

Lei TANG,
MINT, Institut National des Télécommunications
Evry
France

Index